SLANDER

ANN COULTER

SLANDER

LIBERAL LIES ABOUT THE AMERICAN RIGHT

 CROWN PUBLISHERS NEW YORK

Published by Crown Publishers, New York, New York.
Member of the Crown Publishing Group, a division of Random House, Inc.
www.randomhouse.com

CROWN is a trademark and the Crown colophon is a registered trademark of Random House, Inc.

Printed in the United States of America

Library of Congress Cataloging-in-Publication Data
Coulter, Ann H.
    Slander : liberal lies about the American right / Ann Coulter.
    Includes index.
    1. Liberalism—United States.   2. Mass media—Political
aspects—United States. I. Title.
    JC574.2.U6 C68   2002
    320.52'0973—dc21   2002006049

ISBN 1-4000-4661-0

10 9 8 7 6 5

First Edition

FOR ROBERT JONES

ACKNOWLEDGMENTS

Thanks to my long-suffering friends who give me ideas and editing advice, which I habitually ignore. Among them are Hans Bader, Frank Bruni, Elli Burkett, Jim Downey, Miguel Estrada, Melanie Graham, David Limbaugh, Jay Mann, John Harrison, Gene Meyer, Jim Moody, Jeremy Rabkin, and Jon Tukel. In the event that any of them are nominated to confirmable positions or work for the *New York Times:* They are absolutely not responsible for what I write.

Also not responsible for what I write is my amazing, brilliant editor, Doug Pepper, proving that I don't dislike editors as a class, and my sainted agent, Joni Evans.

Novenas should be said to Brent Bozell and the Media Research Center, who have been on the case long before I was.

Thanks always and forever most of all to my two brothers, John and Jim, and my parents, Mother and Father.

Finally, with sincerest thanks to Pinch Sulzberger and the entire staff of the *New York Times,* without whom this book would have been impossible.

CONTENTS

SLANDER

ONE

LIBERALS UNHINGED

The natives are superficially agreeable, but they go in for cannibalism, headhunting, infanticide, incest, avoidance and joking relationships, and biting lice in half with their teeth.

MARGARET MEAD

Political "debate" in this country is insufferable. Whether conducted in Congress, on the political talk shows, or played out at dinners and cocktail parties, politics is a nasty sport. At the risk of giving away the ending: It's all liberals' fault.

As there is less to dispute, liberals have become more bitter and angry. The Soviet threat has been vaporized, women are not prevented from doing even things they should be, and the gravest danger facing most black Americans today is the risk of being patronized to death.

And yet still, somehow, Tom DeLay (Republican congressman from Texas) poses a monumental threat to democracy as we know it. The left expresses disagreement with DeLay's governing philosophy by calling him "the Meanest Man in Congress,"[1] "Dangerous,"[2] "the Hammer,"[3] "the Exterminator,"[4] and the "Torquemada of Texas."[5] For his evident belief in a Higher Being, DeLay is compared to savage murderers and genocidal lunatics on the pages of the *New York Times*. ("History teaches that when religion is injected into politics—the Crusades, Henry VIII, Salem, Father Coughlin, Hitler, Kosovo—disaster follows."[6])

Liberals dispute slight reductions in the marginal tax rates as if they are trying to prevent Charles Manson from slaughtering baby seals. Progress cannot be made on serious issues because one side is making arguments and the other side is throwing eggs—both figuratively and literally. Prevarication and denigration are the hallmarks of liberal argument. Logic is not their métier. Blind religious faith is.

The liberal catechism includes a hatred of Christians, guns, the profit motive, and political speech and an infatuation with abortion, the environment, and race discrimination (or in the favored parlance of liberals, "affirmative action"). Heresy on any of these subjects is, well, heresy. The most crazed religious fanatic argues in more calm and reasoned tones than liberals responding to statistics on concealed-carry permits.

Perhaps if conservatives had had total control over every major means of news dissemination for a quarter century, they would have forgotten how to debate, too, and would just call liberals stupid and mean. But that's an alternative universe. In this universe, the public square is wall-to-wall liberal propaganda.

Americans wake up in the morning to "America's Sweetheart," the *Today* show's Katie Couric, berating Arlen Specter about Anita Hill ten years after the hearings.[7] Or haranguing Charlton Heston on the need for gun control to stop school shootings.[8] Her co-host, Matt Lauer, wonders casually why the federal government has not passed a law on national vacation time.[9] The *New York Times* breathlessly announces "Communism Still Looms as Evil to Miami Cubans"[10] and *Time* magazine columnist Barbara Ehrenreich gives two thumbs up to "The Communist Manifesto" ("100 million massacred!").[11]

We read letters to the editor of the *New York Times* from pathetic little parakeet males and grim, quivering, angry women on the Upper West Side of Manhattan hoping to be chosen as that day's purveyor of hate. These letters are about one step above *Tiger Beat* magazine in intellectual engagement. They are never responsive, they never include clever ripostes or attacks; they merely restate the position of the *Times* with greater venom: *I was reminded by your editorial that Bush wasn't even your average politically aware Yalie; he was too busy branding freshmen at his fraternity house.*

In the evening, CBS anchor Dan Rather can be found falsely accusing Republicans of all manner of malfeasance[12] or remarking that a president who has been impeached, disbarred, and held in contempt for his lies is an "honest man." Diane Sawyer pronounces that "the American people" are yawning at the news that the president was engaging in sodomy with a cigar and oral-anal sex with a White House intern.[13]

Hollywood movies preach about kind-hearted abortionists, Nazi priests, rich preppie Republican bigots, and the dark night of fascism under Senator Joe McCarthy. Hollywood starlets giddily announce on late-night TV how much they'd like to give Bill Clinton a "certain type of sex" (as Paula Jones called it).

And then Americans wake up for another day of left-wing schlock, beginning their day with the CBS *Early Show*'s Bryant Gumbel somberly asking smut peddler Hugh Hefner for his views on a presidential campaign.[14]

We read national magazines that pretend to be reasonable while seething with the impotent violence of women. We wade through preposterous news stories on Enron, global warming, Tawana Brawley, "plastic guns," the melting North Pole, the meaning of the word "is"—until you can't keep up with the wave of lies. It's like being in an earthquake listening to all the gibberish.

When arguments are premised on lies, there is no foundation for debate. You end up conceding to half the lies simply to focus on the lies of Holocaust-denial proportions. Kind and well-meaning people find themselves afraid to talk about politics. Any sentient person has to be concerned that he might innocently make an argument or employ a turn of phrase that will be discerned by the liberal cult as a "code word" evincing a genocidal tendency. The only safe course is to be consciously, stultifyingly boring.

It isn't just public figures who have to be worried—though having millions of people listening to their spontaneous on-air remarks obviously raises the stakes a bit. But even a private conversation can be resurrected a decade later. Just a few years ago, a killer walked largely because a detective involved in the case had used the "N-word" almost ten years earlier. In a conversation with his then-girlfriend, Mark Fuhrman spun out imaginary dialogue for a movie script, and in so doing committed a hate crime. If the jurors in the O. J. Simpson case could have given Fuhrman the death penalty, he'd be sitting on death row right now. Cutting off your ex-wife's head is a lesser offense in America than using certain words.

Vast areas of public policy debate are treated as indistinguishable from using the N-word (aka: the worst offense against mankind). Thus, Representative Charles Rangel (D-N.Y.) took issue with the Republicans' proposed tax cuts, saying: "It's not 'spic' or 'nigger' anymore. They say, 'Let's cut taxes.'"

The spirit of the First Amendment has been effectively repealed for conservative speech by a censorious, accusatory mob. Truth cannot prevail because whole categories of thought are deemed thought crimes.

For a fleeting moment, after the September 11 attack on America, all partisan wrangling stopped dead. The country was infused with patriotism and amazingly unified. The attack on America was such a colossal jolt, liberals even abandoned their endless pursuit of producing *some* method of counting the ballots in Florida that would have made Al Gore president.

Liberal sneers about President Bush's intelligence suddenly abated—at first for reasons of decorum, but then because of the indisputable fact that Bush was a magnificent leader. In a moment of crisis, the truth overcame liberal naysaying. After having demeaned President Bush as a lightweight frat boy hopelessly ignorant of foreign policy, even Democrats were overcome with relief that Al Gore was not the president.

The bipartisan lovefest lasted precisely three weeks. That was all the *New York Times* could endure. Impatient with the national mood of patriotism, liberals returned to their infernal griping about George W. Bush—or "Half a Commander in Chief," as he was called in the headline of a lead *New York Times* editorial on November 5, 2001. From that moment on, the left's primary contribution to the war effort was to complain.

They complained about the detention of terror suspects, they complained we were going to lose the war, they complained about military tribunals for terrorists, they complained about the Bush administration's failure to solve the anthrax cases instantly, they complained about monitoring terrorists' jailhouse conversations, they complained about the war taking too long, they complained about a trial for John Walker, they complained about (nonexistent) ethnic profiling at airports, they complained about the treatment of prisoners at Guantanamo, and they complained about Bush's "axis of evil" speech.

And they complained about all the damn flag-wavers. The infernal flag-waving after 9/11 nearly drove liberals out of their gourds. For the left, "flag-waving" is an epithet. Liberals variously called the flag a "joke,"[15] "very, very dumb,"[16] and—most cutting—not "cosmopolitan."[17] New York University sociology professor Todd Gitlin agonized over the decision to fly the flag outside his apartment (located less than a mile from Ground Zero), explaining: "It's very complicated."[18]

It must have been galling that no one in America cared. Eventually, the

New York Times gave up harping about Bush's handling of the war and turned its full attention to attacking Enron.

Here the country had finally given liberals a war against fundamentalism and they didn't want to fight it. They would have, except it would put them on the same side as the United States. In the wake of an attack on America committed by crazed fundamentalist Muslims, Walter Cronkite denounced Jerry Falwell. Falwell, it seems, had remarked that gay marriage and abortion on demand may not have warmed the heart of the Almighty. Cronkite proclaimed such a statement "the most abominable thing I've ever heard." Showing his renowned dispassion and critical thinking, this Martha's Vineyard millionaire commented that Falwell was "worshipping the same God as the people who bombed the World Trade Center and the Pentagon" (the difference being liberals urged compassion and understanding toward the terrorists).

Indeed, an attack on America by fanatical Muslims had finally provided liberals with a religion they could respect. Heretofore liberals deemed voluntary student prayers at high school football games a direct assault on the Constitution. But it was of urgent importance that Islamic terrorists being held in Guantanamo be free to practice their religion. This despite the fact that we had been repeatedly instructed that the terrorists were not practicing "true Islam."

Less than three months after Islamic terrorists slaughtered thousands of Americans, ABC's *20/20* ran a major report titled "Abortion Clinics in U.S. Targeted by Religious Terrorists." As Jamie Floyd reported: "Since September eleventh the word 'terrorists' has come to mean someone who is radical, Islamic, and foreign. But many believe we have as much to fear from a homegrown group of anti-abortion crusaders."[19]

New York Times columnist Frank Rich demanded that Ashcroft stop monkeying around with Muslim terrorists and concentrate on anti-abortion extremists.[20] Rich claimed that only pure political malice could explain Attorney General Ashcroft's refusal to meet with Planned Parenthood while purporting to investigate "terrorism."[21]

Yale law professor Bruce Ackerman recommended dropping the war against global terrorism ("declare victory at the first decent opportunity"!) and instead concentrate on "home-grown extremists."[22] In lieu of a military response against terrorists abroad and security precautions at home, liberals wanted to get the whole thing over with and just throw conservatives in jail.

Rarely had the great divide in the country been so manifest. Liberals hate

America, they hate "flag-wavers," they hate abortion opponents, they hate all religions except Islam (post 9/11). Even Islamic terrorists don't hate America like liberals do. They don't have the energy. If they had that much energy, they'd have indoor plumbing by now.

L ong before the war, conservatives had a vague sense that liberals didn't much like them. Consider that a president whom liberals themselves called "indefensible, outrageous, unforgivable, [and] shameless" had staved off removal from office merely by calling his opponents "right-wing Republicans."[23] It was apparent then that we were dealing with a species of primitive religious hatred.

Clinton's lies under oath in a judicial proceeding were such a shock to the legal system that just weeks before every Senate Democrat would vote to keep him in office, the entire Supreme Court boycotted Clinton's State of the Union address—one of many historical firsts in the Clinton years. That stunning rebuke was meaningless. Liberals were impervious to any logic beyond Clinton's mantra that his opponents were "right-wing Republicans."

Professional Democrats have clintonized the entire party and they will destroy anyone who stands in their way. All that matters to them is power. They believe their moral superiority allows them to do things that would appall ordinary people.

In May 2001, former Clinton strategists James Carville and Paul Begala released a "Battle Plan for the Democrats" on the op-ed page of the *New York Times*. Their central piece of advice was for Democrats to start calling President George Bush names. "First," they said, liberals must "call a radical a radical." Other proposals included calling Bush dangerous and uncompassionate: "Mr. Bush's agenda is neither compassionate nor conservative; it's radical and it's dangerous and the Democrats should say so."[24]

That's it. That's the new plan. It's the same as the old plan. Call Republicans names.

In a comic spasm of sophistry, the Democrats' Big-Think men wrote: "We don't believe the spin that stopping Mr. Bush's assault on middle-class programs will hurt Democrats with voters." Evidently someone was retailing the yarn about an "assault" on the middle class being hugely popular. But Carville and Begala begged to differ. (Even the editor must have been overwhelmed by the spin on that one.) These must have been the guys who helped President Clinton formulate his thoughtful response to Newt Gingrich's "Contract with America." In his unifying, statesmanlike way, President Clinton referred to it as a murderous hit man's assignment, repeatedly calling it the "Contract on America." Go out right now and ask any liberal what was objectionable about the "Contract with America" and see if you get a more reasoned argument than that.

Meanwhile, the left's political Tourette's syndrome has gone completely unremarked upon. All parties to the debate carry on as if it's totally normal for two of the most famous Democratic consultants to be recommending name-calling as political strategy. Clinton seemed to be making a good argument against impeachment by perseverating about a "right-wing" conspiracy out to get him.

An annoying typical Republican response to liberal hate speech is to attack one's friends in order to appease one's enemies. Democrats still hate the Republican appeasers; they just hate them a little less. And when it comes time for the left to tear down the conciliators, these Republican "moderates" won't have many friends left willing to defend them. As Winston Churchill said, appeasement reflects the hope that the crocodile will eat you last. With some portion of (admittedly craven) Republicans casually acknowledging the liberal premise that conservatives are mean and hateful, the left is emboldened to carry on with ever greater insolence.

When Senator Jim Jeffords left the Republican Party, he explained his defection by saying he was against slavery, supported the Union side in the Civil War, and opposed McCarthyism. (He did concede that his decision to leave the Republican Party was perhaps of "smaller consequence.") But then he continued in the same ludicrous vein, saying he had joined the party believing it stood for "moderation" and "tolerance." Alas, he said, "Increasingly, I find myself in disagreement with my party."[25]

Back in the party's halcyon days—when Jeffords presumably did not find himself in disagreement—he opposed Reagan's tax cut, supported the elder Bush's tax hike, supported Clinton's tax hike, and opposed the younger Bush's tax cut. The Big Tent may accommodate a lot of kooks, but if the Republican Party doesn't stand for tax cuts, it is nothing but a random assemblage of people—tax-cutters, tax-gougers, whatever. Jeffords was a big fan of Hillary Clinton's socialist health care plan, which was such an unprecedented federal takeover of private industry that even the Democrats finally blanched. He voted against Clinton's impeachment and against Clarence Thomas's confirmation. Needless to say, he has always been pro-abortion.

So maybe the problem wasn't the Republicans' sudden lack of "tolerance" and "moderation," but Jeffords's slow realization that he had always been in disagreement with his party.

The only reason Northeastern liberals such as Jeffords call themselves Republicans in the first place is class snobbery. They disdain Democrats, whom they view as the dirty working class, and think being a Republican should entail nothing more than thrashing the servants.

Yet the left's hegemonic control of the media had once again cowed a nominal Republican into averring to the left's preposterous demonization of Republicans. It always follows the same script: First there is the outrageous accusation from the left, then the abject apology from some pathetic panty-waist on the right, and then—who's to say Republicans are not racist scum? The cycle of Dumb and Dumber bickering with each other continues without end in sight.

Instead of actual debate about ideas and issues with real consequences, the country is trapped in a political discourse that increasingly resembles professional wrestling. The "Compassionate Conservative" takes on the "Republicans Balancing the Budget on the Backs of the Poor." The impossibility of having any sort of productive dialogue about civic affairs has become an immovable reality.

Often short on details, the classic liberal response to a principled conservative argument is to accuse Republicans of planning a second Holocaust. No matter how inured one becomes to liberal hate speech, the regularity with which Republicans are compared to Nazis still astonishes. One would almost think fascist dictatorial regimes demanding governmental control of the major means of production were an immoderate extension of efforts to trim the income tax.

Weeks before the Starr Report was released, Keith Olbermann, host of *The Big Show* on MSNBC, said: "It finally dawned on me that the person Ken Starr has reminded me of facially all this time was Heinrich Himmler, including the glasses."[26]

In an upbeat message delivered on British TV on Christmas Day, 1994, Jesse Jackson compared conservatives in both the U.S. and Great Britain to Nazis: "In South Africa, the status quo was called racism. We rebelled against it. In Germany, it was called fascism. Now in Britain and the U.S., it is called conservatism."[27] The *New York Times* did not report the speech.[28]

Speaking to the Black and Puerto Rican Legislative Caucus forum at the capital, Representatives Charles Rangel (D-N.Y.) and Major Owens

(D-N.Y.) said the Republicans "Contract with America" was as bad as Hitler's Germany. "When I compare this to what happened in Germany," Rangel said, "I hope that you will see the similarities to what is happening to us." Owens was more explicit: "These are people who are practicing genocide with a smile; they're worse than Hitler."[29]

Representative and erstwhile Democratic presidential candidate Patricia Schroeder (D-Colo.) accused opponents to Henry Foster, Clinton's nominee for surgeon general, of "goose-stepping over women's rights,"[30] and informed the League of Women Voters that Rush Limbaugh's listeners "are the ones who are goose-stepping."[31]

When not secretly planning a second Holocaust, Republicans seem to busy themselves with ethnic cleansing, race baiting, and lynchings. Also plotting to bring back slavery. The liberal trope of associating Republicans with slavery is a daring smear inasmuch as the Republican Party was formed for the express purpose of opposing slavery. It was the Democratic Party that defended slavery. The Whigs—whence the Republican Party emerged—was "pro-choice" on the slavery issue.

Harvard law professor Alan Dershowitz described Florida's practice of not allowing convicted felons to vote as the secretary of state "ethnically cleansing the voting lists."[32] Representative Kweisi Mfume (D-Md.), said the Republicans' plan to cut funding for twenty-eight useless House caucuses constituted "ethnic and philosophical cleansing."[33]

Striking an especially high note in the 2000 presidential campaign, Vice President Al Gore aggressively implied that Bush's Supreme Court nominees would bring back slavery. Not only that, but Justices Antonin Scalia and Clarence Thomas were already hard at work on the Republicans' pro-slavery initiative. In numerous campaign speeches, Gore said Bush's pledge to appoint "strict constructionists" to the Court—such as Scalia and Thomas—reminded him of "the strictly constructionist meaning that was applied when the Constitution was written and how some people were considered three-fifths of a human being." If you were one of the swing voters waiting to see which of the candidates supported slavery, at least Gore had cleared up the confusion. The man was actually demagoguing slavery.

At the risk of seeming overly legalistic, Bush, Scalia, and Thomas do not subscribe to a legal philosophy that would bring back slavery. "Strict constructionism" means only that judges should interpret laws rather than write them. It has nothing to do with slavery. Moreover, Gore's implication that it would have been nicer if slaves had counted as full persons in the Constitution is the pro-slavery position. Since the three-fifths clause refers only to congressional apportionment, counting slaves as full persons would have given the slave-holding South *more* votes in Congress.

Toward the end of the campaign, Al Gore began regaling audiences with lurid reminders of the barbaric racist dragging death of James Byrd in Texas and accusing Bush of near complicity in the murder for failing to support a "hate crimes" law. With members of the Byrd family by his side, Gore asked in astonishment, "Why after the tragedy that befell James Byrd should [Bush] oppose a hate-crimes law?"[34] The only thing missing were clips from *Roots,* with Bush's face superimposed on the evil slaveowner's.

As is now well known, since Gore continued to lynch-bait Bush during the debates, Byrd's killers had already received two death sentences and one life imprisonment. Liberals oppose the death penalty, but in the case of Byrd's killers, death was not enough. They would not rest until the killers were also found guilty of "hate" and forced to attend anger-management classes. Byrd's daughter, Renee Mullins, narrated an NAACP television ad for Gore that showed film footage of chains dragging on a dirt road. Mullins's narrative lacked even Gore's subtlety in equating Bush's opposition to a "hate crimes" law to the murder itself: "When Governor Bush refused to support the hate-crimes bill, it was like my father was killed all over again."

One wonders what words liberals could ever deploy to identify a real bigot in our midst. In liberal-speak, the words for George Bush are indistinguishable from the words for David Duke.

A false argument should be refuted, not named. That's the basic idea behind freedom of speech. Arguments by demonization, rather than truth and light, can be presumed to be fraudulent. Real hate speech does not have to be flagged and labeled. It speaks for itself. If a person makes an argument that is, in fact, "racist" (anti-Semitic, sexist, looksist—whatever), that fact ought to be self-evident. Simply restating the argument would expose the wily bigot—if bigotry it is—without a big warning label screaming "Racist!" "Sexist!" "Homophobic!"

But ad hominem attack is the liberal's idea of political debate. They self-consciously hold themselves outside the argument and make snippy personal comments about anyone who is actually talking about something. The Republican's motives are analyzed, his intelligence critiqued, his personal life unearthed. If it were true that conservatives were racist, sexist, homophobic, fascist, stupid, inflexible, angry, and self-righteous, shouldn't their arguments be easy to deconstruct? Someone who is making a point out of anger, ideology, inflexibility, or resentment would presumably construct a flimsy argument. So why can't the argument itself be dismembered rather than the speaker's personal style or hidden motives? Why the evasions?

It ought to raise eyebrows that no one can ever seem to get a real live quote from a Republican demonstrating all this hate evident to *New York Times* editors. If conservatives actually were seething with such boundless hatreds, one might expect it to bubble over into their public discourse every once in a while. Like what Monica Lewinsky testified to, in her scintillating concluding statement to the grand jury: "I hate Linda Tripp." (Would that have been deemed cute if Tripp had said it?)

Or what columnist Rob Morse wrote in the *San Francisco Examiner:*

I'm trying to forget, but I'm not quite ready to forgive everybody yet.

Linda Tripp should be exiled to an island with no TV studios, book deals or interviewers, just an endless loop of her taped conversations with Monica played over loudspeakers.

Ken Starr should be sent to a Siberian gulag built in the general shape of colonial Salem.

Henry Hyde, Bob Barr and the other 11 House impeachment managers should be placed in a soundproof chamber for life with only bread, water and one microphone to fight over.[35]

Suppose Jerry Falwell had put together a list of those he was "ready to forgive." How do you imagine that would have played?

Noticeably absent from Morse's list of those he is "not quite ready to forgive" were: (1) Bill Clinton and (2) Monica Lewinsky—the only two people in the impeachment affair positively known to have lied and tried to fix a trial in order to deny an American citizen her rights under the law. What was Hyde's crime against God and man?

Gore campaign manager Donna Brazile called Colin Powell an "Uncle Tom." Seemingly unaware of her boss's race, she vowed that she would not "let the white boys win in this election." Brazile said Colin Powell and Republican Congressman J. C. Watts "have no love and no joy" and would "rather take pictures with black children than feed them." Democratic strategist Peter Fenn defended Brazile, saying she was trying "to be inclusive."[36] Colin Powell failed to appreciate the inclusiveness, saying he was "disappointed and offended" by Brazile's comments. J. C. Watts called her inclusive statements "racist."[37] Gore—striving for inclusiveness—refused to apologize to Powell or Watts.

Meanwhile, when he was still co-host of the *Today* show on NBC, Bryant Gumbel casually asked J. C. Watts whether it bothered him to be associated with "conservative extremists who are historically insensitive to minority concerns." This is in contrast to Democrats who are "inclusive."[38]

After Supreme Court Justice Clarence Thomas wrote an opinion contrary to the *clearly* expressed position of the *New York Times* editorial page, the *Times* responded with an editorial on Thomas titled "The Youngest, Cruelest Justice." That was actually the headline on a lead editorial in the Newspaper of Record. Thomas is not engaged on the substance of his judicial philosophy. He is called a "colored lawn jockey for conservative white interests," "race traitor," "black snake," "chicken-and-biscuit-eating Uncle Tom,"[39] "house Negro" and "handkerchief head," "Benedict Arnold"[40] and "Judas Iscariot."[41]

All this from the tireless opponents of intolerance. The "lawn jockey" name in particular was a huge hit with the inclusive crowd. *Emerge,* an African-American magazine, ran on its cover a caricature of Thomas as a grinning lawn jockey with the title "Uncle Thomas: Lawn Jockey of the Far Right." An illustration accompanying the article portrayed a grinning Thomas shining Justice Antonin Scalia's shoes. The late federal judge Leon Higginbotham said Thomas rendered "Uncle Tom Justice." Syndicated columnist Julianne Malveaux said she hoped Thomas's "wife feeds him lots of eggs and butter and he dies early, like many black men do, of heart disease."[42] And thus were exposed the logical flaws in Thomas's judicial philosophy!

If liberals have a principled argument against Justice Thomas, they're not telling. But they really don't like him. Thus they malign Thomas in terms that would constitute a hate crime if it came from anyone but a liberal.

What liberals mean by "goose-stepping" or "ethnic cleansing" is generally something along the lines of "eliminating taxpayer funding for the National Endowment for the Arts." But they can't say that, or people would realize they're crazy. So instead they accuse Republicans of speaking in "code words." This is one of the most enraging twists on the left's refusal to debate. Since authentically racist behavior would be apparent on its face, the concept of "code words" allows liberals to call anyone a racist. The basic idea is that the untrained masses cannot be expected to comprehend a confusing world on their own, so the liberal clergy will translate for them. In a 1994 *New York Times* editorial on Newt Gingrich, the Pious Gray Lady explained:

> Welcome to Speaker Gingrich's Retro-World. Mr. Gingrich . . . communicate[s] in the venerable code words of Barry Goldwater and George Wallace.
>
> The code words, of course, originally had much to do with race; Senator Goldwater and Governor Wallace bandied them, after all, in a battle for Deep South electoral votes. . . . But this race-based, anger-charged politics mutated in Mr. Gingrich and some others of his generation into a more generalized moral authoritarianism.[43]

New York magazine's Jacob Weisberg and the Reverend Jesse Jackson also noticed the amazing similarities between Gingrich and George Wallace. (Liberals don't even have original ideas when they call Republicans names.) If Gingrich's legislative plan had, in fact, included provisions to resegregate the schools, wouldn't someone have noticed? Instead liberals are left to make vague allegations about an apocryphal secret "code" calculated to inflame pogrom-oriented Americans.

One reporter on *Inside Washington* discerned the Republican desire to murder gays in the "air." (It's sort of complicated—but involves a "three-step process.") Discussing the murder of Matthew Shepard, the gay man brutally killed by two thugs in Wyoming, Deborah Mathis of Gannett News Service explained how conservative Republicans were responsible for Shepard's death.

> The Christian right per se and some particular members on Capitol Hill have helped inflame the air so that the air that these people breathed that night was filled, filled with the idea that somehow gays are different, and not only are they different in that difference, they're bad and not only are they bad, they are evil and therefore can be destroyed. The next step to that, it's a three-step process, and they certainly weren't part of any plan to do that, but again, what air are they breathing now? It's the air filled with that hate . . . I mentioned Trent Lott, Jesse Helms and Dick Armey particularly. The Christian Coalition, the Family Research Council and the Concerned Women for America.[44]

Mathis could remember the names of the destroyers with some precision, but the "three-step process" became rather vague between step one and step three. Without the second and third steps—the part where Republicans start hectoring the populace that gays "are evil and therefore can be destroyed"—the first "step" doesn't amount to much. Aren't gays "different"? Because if gays aren't different, then heterosexuals are different and Republicans have a lot more murders to answer for than Matthew Shepard's.

In another translation from the liberal rabbinate, a *Washington Post* columnist casually compared serious and substantial men like Shelby Steele and Clarence Thomas to a cringing, servile slave from the miniseries *Roots* on the basis of . . . a "metaphor." As the author readily conceded, only highly advanced intellects—such as her own—were capable of grasping this particular "metaphor."

> There is a scene [in *Roots*] where kidnapped African Kunte Kinte won't settle down in his chains. "Want me to give him a stripe or two, boss?" the old slave, Fiddler, asks his Master Reynolds.
>
> "Do as I say, Fiddler," Reynolds answers. "That's all I expect from any of my niggers."
>
> "Oh, I love you, Massa Reynolds," Fiddler tells him. And instantly, my mind draws political parallels. Ward Connerly, I think to myself. Armstrong Williams. Shelby Steele. Hyperbole, some might say. I say dead-on.
>
> "Clarence Thomas," I say to Cousin Kim. And she just stares at me. She may be a little tender yet for racial metaphors. I see them everywhere.[45]

If anyone talks in code, it is not the people who need the Internet and talk radio merely to communicate with one another. Only total hegemonic control of all major means of news dissemination in America could possibly give rise to the insane pig Latin patois of the left.

Conservatives can't even pin down liberals on the word "abortion." That's a "choice"—not school "choice" or pension plan "choice" or arts funding "choice." "Choice" refers to one lone medical procedure that will never cross the lips of a liberal: "abortion." This would be on the order of gun-rights activists refusing to use the word "gun." And if "abortion" is unspeakable, "baby" is actually punishable. Funnily, you never hear a pregnant woman say: "Put your ear to my stomach and listen to your little fetus sister," or "I felt the fetus move today!"

Race discrimination tends to attract the most preposterous Orwellian circumlocutions, such as "equal opportunity" and "affirmative action." Even if the race discrimination is designed to discriminate in favor of historic victims amply deserving of preferential treatment, it is still discrimination. But liberals would sooner say the Lord's Prayer in a public school than utter the words "race discrimination" to describe "race discrimination."

Also in the English-to-liberal dictionary, "liberal" is translated as "moderate" or "centrist"—and "conservative" is "far right wing" or "ultra-conservative." Adjectives like "moderate" and "far right wing" are a crucial part of the journalistic rewards system for politicians. It is how pompously boring newspapers and magazines hurl epithets at politicians they don't like and suck up to the ones they do. In the entire New York Times archives on LexisNexis, there are 109 items using the phrase "far right wing," but only 18 items that use "far left wing." There are 149 uses of "ultra-conservative," but only 59 uses of "ultra-liberal." Nineteen uses of "conservative extremist," but only eight uses of "liberal extremist." For purposes of comparison, other word pairs, such as "really hot"/"really cold" turn up in roughly equal numbers. Only when it comes to politicians are adjectives like "centrist" and "extremist" used to convey no factual information beyond "good dog!" and "bad dog!"

Consider the utter vacuousness of the phrase "moderate Republican." Moderate ought to mean right in the middle—not too liberal and not too conservative. So why not just say "Republican"? In the New York Times archives, "moderate Republican" has been used 168 times. (Good dog!) There have been only 11 sightings of a "liberal Republican." In a typical formulation, the Times reported that a compromise tax bill had been forged in the Senate by pulling together "moderate Republicans and conservative Democrats."[46] Why not "liberal Republicans" and "moderate Democrats"?

Most peculiarly, the Times explained in an editorial that President Bush planned to "eke out majorities by wooing conservative Democrats to his side, even if that might alienate some moderate Republicans."[47] When a "moderate Republican" is so liberal that he is less likely to support a Republican president than some Democrats, doesn't that finally make him a "liberal"? "Moderate Republican" is simply how the blabocracy flatters Republicans who vote with the Democrats. If it weren't so conspicuous, the

New York Times would start referring to "nice Republicans" and "mean Republicans."

The *Washington Post* describes Democratic Senator John Kerry of Massachusetts and Senator Chuck Robb of Virginia as "centrists."[48] On the basis of interest group ratings in 1999, Kerry and Robb's counterparts on the right are Trent Lott (R-Miss.), Bob Smith (R-N.H.), Connie Mack (R-Fla.), and Don Nickles (R-Okla.).[49] I can assure you, the word "centrist" will never be found near any of their names.

Liberals claim conservatives use "code words" and as proof they babble about vague ephemeral concepts—a "metaphor," "proxies," a "three-step process," indistinct feelings "in the air." Meanwhile, conservatives can produce a chart of word-to-word translations from liberal code: Moderate = liberal; far right wing = conservative; centrist = 95 ADA rating; choice = abortion; affirmative action = race discrimination. Even the phrase "code word" is a code word for liberals lying about Republicans. Liberals can't just come out and say that they want to take more of our money, kill babies, and discriminate on the basis of race. So instead they compare Republicans to George Wallace—a Democrat.

Had enough of the love? We're still not done because . . . Republicans are also dumb and ugly. If Republicans are so stupid (and poorly dressed!), it's hard to understand why Democrats haven't been able to get as much as 50 percent of the country to vote for them in any national election for the last twenty-five years.

On CNN's *Capital Gang* on July 24, 1999, Margaret Carlson analyzed a Republican's bill to cut taxes, saying: "I mean, the only thing that could explain this love of tax cuts is a lowered IQ."[50] Writing in the *Washington Post,* columnist Richard Cohen made one of his typically incisive points, explaining that the Republican Party is "dumb as a post." In case the nuance of Cohen's logic was lost, he continued, saying the Republican Party "is defined by a hostility toward minorities—all sorts of minorities—and by a craven cowardice on the part of its more moderate members. The truth of the matter is that the party is having a crackup. If it were a person, it would be medicated."[51]

Howell Raines, former editorial page editor of the *New York Times,* who covered the Reagan White House with the *Times*'s trademark objectivity, asserted that "Reagan couldn't tie his shoes if his life depended on it."[52] And still, somehow, he won the Cold War. Al Gore told Virginia voters at a campaign rally that they should re-elect Virginia Senator Chuck Robb because his opponent, Oliver North, was supported by "the extreme right wing—the extra-chromosome right wing."[53] (The presence of an "extra chromosome" is the birth defect that creates Down's syndrome.) The *Washington Post* famously reported as hard fact that the followers of Jerry Falwell and Pat Robertson "are largely poor, uneducated and easy to command."[54] Paula Jones was attacked by *Newsweek*'s Evan Thomas as "some sleazy woman with big hair coming out of the trailer parks." Aren't these the same people constantly demanding campus speech codes, an end to "intolerance," and "hate speech" laws—so that no one's feelings get hurt?

More than any of their other hate speech, the left's attacks on women for being ugly tell you everything. There is nothing so irredeemably cruel as an attack on a woman for her looks. Attacking a female for being ugly is a hideous thing, always inherently vicious. Unless it's a guy in a dress. That's always funny. Two unbending rules of the universe are: (1) It is horrendous to attack a woman for her looks and (2) A guy in a dress is hilarious. Everyone knows this.

So which women are constantly being called ugly? Is it Maxine Waters, Chelsea Clinton, Janet Reno, or Madeleine Albright? No, none of these. Only conservative women have their looks held up to ridicule because only liberals would be so malevolent. A blind man in America would think the ugliest women ever to darken the planet are Paula Jones, Linda Tripp, and Katherine Harris. This from the party of Bella Abzug.

Journalists have called Linda Tripp "Barracudaville," smelling of "gunpowder and garlic," "ugly and evil," and "Howard Stern in a fright wig,"[55] "a snitch, and an ugly one, at that."[56] Syndicated columnist Julianne Malveaux referred to the "ugly stick [Tripp's] been beaten with—there's something wrong with that woman, I'm serious."[57] Actress Rose McGowan (*Jawbreaker*) told the *Village Voice:* "One thing that gives me pleasure is how ugly [Tripp] is. That's a karmic point. She deserves to be ugly."[58] Another female (!) columnist, Heather Mallick, wrote: "Linda Tripp's the hulking dykey one and book agent Lucianne Goldberg's her ugly sister."[59] In the book *Monica's Story,* the author, Andrew Morton, also wrote of the "two ugly sisters, Linda Tripp and Lucianne Goldberg, [who] ensured that Monica never made it to the ball."[60] Liz Langley, a (female) opinion columnist, said Linda Tripp and Paula Jones were neither "attractive nor possessed of human DNA." They "look like a bloated carcass and whatever's pecking at it."[61]

This isn't John Goodman playing Linda Tripp in drag on *Saturday Night*

Live. It is *Newsweek,* the *Washington Post,* pundits and columnists launching these attacks. This isn't humor, it's hatred. They aren't trying to be funny, they're trying to make their victims hurt.

You will never appreciate the full savagery of the left until you get in their way. Wincing while others are attacked cannot compare. Imagine it is you, your wife, or your daughter they have set about to destroy. Then it won't matter if the authors of the hate speech are hideous, talentless wretches. You will hear the words calling you ugly and stupid and you will believe, if only fleetingly, that the whole world sees you that way. Tripp ended up getting two face-lifts and liposuction. Paula Jones got braces and a nose job.

In what ought to have been a case study of the Stockholm syndrome, both blamed themselves for the sadistic attacks on their looks. Linda Tripp later apologized to the country for her ugliness, telling *People* magazine: "I didn't realize how ugly I was," and "I was horrified as well as the rest of the nation, really."[62] Paula Jones also blamed herself for the malevolent attacks: "I can laugh at myself, you know. I mean, I looked, you know, that way. And I look different now."[63] Despite Jones's going under the knife to quell complaints about her looks, *Time* magazine would not be mollified. The magazine sniffed that Jones was getting a nose job because she "apparently felt her affection for the camera was not sufficiently requited." In response to Jones's explanation that she "was sick of being made fun of by cartoonists," *Time* sarcastically snipped: "This should really help."[64]

Even polished, wealthy, Harvard-educated, attractive women will be attacked for their looks if they get in the Democrats' way. When Florida Secretary of State Katherine Harris was suddenly cast into the limelight because Al Gore was a sore loser, liberals promptly launched sadistic attacks on Harris's looks. A *Boston Globe* columnist wrote that unless Harris "was planning to unwind at a drag bar after facing that phalanx of cameras Tuesday night, the grease paint she wore should be a federal offense."[65]

In the careful analysis in the *Washington Post,* reporter Robin Givhans wrote that Harris "seems to have applied her makeup with a trowel."[66] Givhans continued: "Her skin had been plastered and powdered to the texture of pre-war walls in need of a skim coat. And her eyes, rimmed in liner and frosted with blue shadow, bore the telltale homogenous spikes of false eyelashes. Caterpillars seemed to rise and fall with every bat of her eyelid." This major investigative report graced the front page of the *Post*'s Style section. The issue of Harris's mascara no-no's was framed as a matter of national urgency: "One wonders how this Republican woman, who can't even use restraint when she's wielding a mascara wand, will manage to use it and make sound decisions in this game of partisan one-upmanship." The public, it was said, "doesn't like falsehoods, and Harris is clearly presenting herself in a fake manner. . . . Why should anyone trust her?"[67]

Al Gore advisor Mark Fabiani later explained the Democrats' attacks on Harris, glibly telling the *New York Times*, "We needed an enemy." He said attacking Harris was "the right thing to do, and it worked."[68]

A central component of liberal hate speech is to make paranoid accusations based on their own neurotic impulses, such as calling Republicans angry, hate-filled, and mean. With no sense of self-irony, the left spitefully stereotypes Republicans as—among other loathsome characteristics—spiteful stereotypers. There is maybe just the tiniest element of projection and compulsion in all this.

New York Times columnist Bob Herbert wrote an entire column on the Republicans' "Mean Strategy." As Herbert wearily explained, "Back in 1998 I offered the Republican Party some unsolicited advice." It was: " 'Give up the politics of meanness,' I said. 'It's killing you.' " Alas, he concluded, "the G.O.P. never seems to learn."[69] Liberals have compared conservatives to Down's syndrome children, wished them dead of cholesterol-induced heart attacks, malevolently attacked women for their looks, called Clarence Thomas every racist name in the book, repeatedly stated they "hate" Republicans, and now—in addition—they say Republicans are "mean."

After a rape victim spoke to the Republican National Convention in 1996, NBC's Tom Brokaw interviewed the speaker, posing this conundrum to her: "[The Republican Party] is a party that is dominated by men and this convention is dominated by men . . . Do you think before tonight they thought very much [about] what happens in America with rape?"[70]

When Juanita Broaddrick went public with her claim that Bill Clinton had raped her, liberals wouldn't give her the time of day. Having flamboyantly accused Republicans of ignoring rape victims, liberals were later freed of the responsibility of having to pretend to care about rape themselves. In polls—considered determinative on most matters by Democrats—80 percent of respondents who heard Broaddrick's allegations thought they were true (62 percent) or possibly true (18 percent). Only 20 percent of respondents did not believe Broaddrick's assertion that a sitting United States president committed rape.[71] NBC had spent months investigating every aspect of Broaddrick's claims to rout any possible inconsistencies in her story. They found none. As is often the case with rape, no eyewitnesses were present for the actual rape, but as far as rape allegations ever go, Broaddrick was, at the very least, an extremely credible witness.

Still, out of pure political calculation, NBC refused to run Lisa Myers's interview with Broaddrick describing her rape at the hands of Bill Clinton until after the Senate had acquitted Clinton in his impeachment trial. Dan Rather did not mention Broaddrick's rape allegation once on the *CBS Evening News.* He later explained that he had refused to report a plausible charge that the president was a rapist out of respect for Clinton's "private sex life."[72] Every single Senate Democrat and all but five House Democrats voted against the impeachment or removal of a president whom they knew was, more likely than not, a rapist.

Those are cold, hard facts about how Democrats treated a credible rape charge. You can look them up. But according to the objective news reporting of Tom Brokaw, it's Republicans who don't care about rape.

Maybe a diligent LexisNexis search would turn up a few comparable quotes from the thousands of right-wing politicians and pundits. Maybe. Frankly, I doubt it. For one thing, even the more spirited remarks of conservatives tend to come from humorists and polemicists. Moreover, if a conservative calls you a drunk, it means you're a drunk. If a conservative calls you stupid, you are stupid. These are not simply ritualistic denunciations of any political opponent. Liberals lie even when they call people names.

At the risk of helping liberals formulate more persuasive arguments, there are a few pointers that might help them upgrade from the overheated demagogic rhetoric of fanatical cult members. A little variation in epithets would at least create the illusion of having an argument. "Nazi" can be used properly in a sentence, but it tends to lose its sting when you call every Republican a Nazi. "Stupid" is also a fine word, but not for twenty-five Republican presidential candidates in a row. Using the same words to describe school vouchers as to characterize the Holocaust tends to leave the impression that you forgot your point.

For the left, name-calling need bear no relationship to the facts: It is mere liturgy. There are many things Newt Gingrich could be called, for example, but "stupid" is not among them. However, the ritual imprecation must be uttered. Thus, the Tacoma, Washington, *News Tribune* advised Gingrich, "Stop blurting out dumb stuff."[73] *San Francisco Examiner* columnist Rob Morse sneered—there was Gingrich trying not to "say something stupid" again and rarely producing "one barely decent line." Newt's "landing gear," Morse said, "never is fully locked."[74] Using the popular Quote-Someone-Who-Agrees-with-Us technique, the *New York Times* repeated the remark of a California accountant who called Gingrich "an idiot—he's just an idiot who plays to the media."[75] (An overture the media deftly managed to resist.) Gingrich's "Contract with America"—the document that helped give Republicans control of Congress for the first time in half a century—was derided by one columnist as "politically stupid."[76]

Finally, when right-wingers rant, there's at least a point: There are substantive arguments contained in conservative name-calling. One of Newt Gingrich's more pithy turns of phrase, for example, was to call Bob Dole "tax collector for the welfare state." In addition to the welcome bipartisanship of attacking a member of his own party—and not from the left—Gingrich's attack conveys a meaningful concept. It succinctly degraded Dole's legislative function as consisting of nothing more than taking the taxpayer's money. Dole had failed to oppose behemoth government; he was a cog in the system that Democrats had created. All that in six words.

By contrast, what does it mean to say Republicans are making "war on the kids of this country"? It must mean something because Democrats say it a *lot*. President Clinton said of Republicans in 1995: "What they want to do is make war on the kids of this country."[77] As First Lady, Hillary Clinton said: "If the wrong side wins in this war on children, what will be lost is our notion of who we are as a people and what we stand for as a society."[78]

It's not just the felon and his bride who talk this way. Democratic Representative Patricia Schroeder said, "The first thing being thrown off the ship [by Republicans] are women and children."[79] Democratic Representative John Lewis said of Republicans: "They're coming for our children, they're coming for the poor, they're coming for the sick, elderly, and the disabled."[80]

Far be it from me to complain of colorful language, but these diatribes are utterly meaningless. They make no deeper point than "I hate you." The lack of specificity is the giveaway. Republicans could just as easily say the Democrats are making "war" on the kids of this country (by condemning them to fatherless welfare-supported families, a life of tax-gouging, a bankrupt social security fund, and huge federal deficits to repay). Republicans could call Democrats the "wrong people," too. But Republicans have an actual point to make, so they don't say that.

Republicans couldn't get away with political argument that sounds like Linda Blair in *The Exorcist* even if they wanted to. They don't own the mainstream media. As Freud observed, communal neuroses will always be much harder to detect because they define an entire group, not an individual distinct from the group. Perhaps if conservatives exercised hegemonic control over the media, they would be venom-spewing haters, too. But they don't, so they aren't. Any Republican impropriety will be endlessly held up to scorn in a series of *New York Times* editorials, then picked up by the networks and featured on *Good Morning America.* Everything feminists claim about working women having to be smarter, better, and tougher than their male counterparts really is true of conservative Republicans.

Usually the best that liberals can do in the way of Republican "hate speech" is to cite the funny jingles or hyperbole of talk radio hosts and explicit controversialists. Even here, the alleged "hate speech" is not likely to be honestly quoted. Rather it is paraphrased, unfairly excerpted, summarized, or—if the liberal is the *Washington Post*'s Howard Kurtz—invented out of whole cloth.

It's true that Rush Limbaugh has identified a particular breed of feminists as "feminazis." Not all feminists, just those who appear to prefer abortion ("choice") to childbirth. Limbaugh is also an openly opinionated talk radio host—not the president, the vice president, a United States senator, editor of the *New York Times,* or a putatively objective TV news anchor.

By contrast, hate is the coin of the realm for liberals at all levels of status, power, objectivity, and cache. There is no difference between the fanatical ravings of a foaming-at-the-mouth James Carville and the utterances of a United States senator. Champion desecrator of life Senator Teddy Kennedy said this about a respected federal judge on the Senate floor:

> Robert Bork's America is a land in which women would be forced into back alley abortions, blacks would sit at segregated lunch counters, rogue police could break down citizens' doors in midnight raids, schoolchildren could not be taught about evolution, writers and artists would be censored at the whim of government, and the doors of the federal courts would be shut on the fingers of millions of citizens for whom the

judiciary is often the only protector of the individual rights that are the heart of our democracy.

That's how the left expresses substantive disagreements with the legal philosophy of a sitting federal judge. Is it Hitler, or is it a former Yale professor? It can be categorically stated that no sitting Republican United States senator has ever accused an ideological opponent of anything along the lines of trying to bring back segregated lunch counters.

It can also be categorically stated that no network news anchor would describe a Democratic National Convention as a "craftily designed . . . broadcast image of tolerance and diversity that's starkly at odds with reality." That's how ABC's Jim Wooten casually reported on the "reality" of the Republican National Convention.

It can further be categorically stated that NBC's Matt Lauer would never have insinuatingly asked a Democrat to "look me in the eye" when answering Lauer's question. When interviewing President Bush, Lauer said: "So you can look me in the eye and say that you are a president committed to cleaning up the environment?"[81] Even when Hillary Clinton was retailing huge whoppers to Lauer in the famous "Vast Right-Wing Conspiracy" interview (affirming, for example, that what "the president has told the nation is the whole truth and nothing but the truth"[82]), Lauer never imperiously demanded that Hillary "look me in the eye" as she openly lied to him.

Scurrilous attack ads from the Democratic National Committee are gleefully replayed by the major networks and pointedly endorsed. After the 2000 election, the Democrats ran a commercial falsely suggesting that President Bush was befouling our pure drinking water by putting "more" arsenic in it. This was a lie. But the deceptive commercials were replayed by TV news programs along with testimonials to their accuracy.

The claim that Bush had effected a "rollback" of current policy was more misleading than some of Joe McCarthy's more outlandish assertions. Bush had merely delayed a prospective change to a sixty-year standard governing arsenic in drinking water. This was evidently a matter of such burning urgency that the former president of the United States, Bill Clinton, had done nothing about it during seven years and three hundred–odd days in office. It was not until three days before he left office that IMPOTUS lowered the arsenic standard from fifty parts per billion to ten parts per billion. Even Clinton's eleventh-hour alteration in the standard was not to take effect until the year 2006. The DNC's demagogic, hateful television commercial showed a little girl asking, "May I please have some more arsenic in my water, Mommy?" The narrator then intoned: "George W. Bush tried to roll back protections against arsenic in drinking water." Except there was no rollback.

CBS News reporter John Roberts played a clip of the inaccurate Democrat ad and then critically asked: "Democrats ask what happened to Mr. Bush's vaunted promise to change the tone in Washington and put an end to partisan sniping?"[83] NBC's Tim Russert followed his presentation of the outrageously misleading ad with the announcement "There's nothing inaccurate in that ad."[84]

Despite the neurotic compulsion to attribute all liberal stunts to "both sides," conservatives couldn't get away with nonsense like this even if they wanted to. It is a stunning reflection of the left's monopoly of the news that an opinionated, partisan talk radio host is more accurate than television news programs.

Assuming that in more than ten thousand hours of radio and television commentary Rush Limbaugh had made a similarly exaggerated claim, I searched LexisNexis for the indignant news reports on Rush's alleged distortions. There are plenty of denunciations of Rush for being inaccurate, but it turns out, liberals lie even when accusing conservatives of lying. "Fairness & Accuracy in Reporting" (FAIR)—hilariously dedicated to exposing the right-wing bias in media (and cold days in hell)—had compiled an allegedly "meticulously researched" anti-Rush report. The Rush distortion that was the left's major exposé, the contretemps to end all contretemps, the anti-Rush reporter's "favorite bit" from the "meticulously researched" FAIR report,[85] was Rush's claim that after a California woman had been mauled to death by a mountain lion, "a fund for her children had received about $9,000 and a fund for the orphaned lion cub (the lion was killed) set up by 'a bunch of animal rights activists' had received $21,000." According to the "meticulous" research of FAIR, it was triumphantly proclaimed, "There never was such a fund for the cub." The real story, one columnist proclaimed, had been "explained on ABC's *20/20.*"

It was a great *gotcha* moment, except that, as usual, once you go to the trouble to look up the facts, it was a lie. Rush was right. There was a cub fund and it had received more money than the orphaned children's fund. Indeed, every detail was exactly as Rush had said. Though Rush was among the first to report on the disparity in the funds for the lions versus the humans, eventually the story became the subject of dozens of news articles.

New York Times reporter Michelle Quinn wrote, for example, that "the cub had received $21,000, while the children's trust fund had raised only $9,000" (just as Rush had said). She even quoted an environmentalist wacko defending the wildly disproportionate donations to the lion cub versus the orphaned children, saying, "People have support systems and animals don't."[86] The children's fund did eventually gain some ground, but only thanks to Rush. As the *Times'* Quinn also reported: "Since the disparity between the funds was publicized—Rush Limbaugh devoted part of his radio show on Tuesday to the subject—the children's trust fund has received an additional $3,000 in checks and cash."

Even the famed *20/20* report did not contradict Rush's account. The only issue disputed on the *20/20* segment was a point no one had made or could conceivably care about. To wit: *20/20* reported on how many "unsolicited public donations" the cub had received (a mere $3,000). This would have really nailed Rush (and the *New York Times* as well as scores of other news outlets) if any of them had ever claimed the $21,000 in donations to the cub had come exclusively from "unsolicited public donations." The single largest donation had come from a nonprofit zoo group—or, as Rush had said, "a bunch of animal rights activists."

Locating some minor inaccuracy by Rush Limbaugh on the order of those corrected daily in the *New York Times* turned out to be more difficult than I had imagined. It hardly seems worth the trouble to pursue FAIR's less impressive finds. But on the off chance that anyone ever does locate some minor inaccuracy by Rush Limbaugh comparable to those regularly nurtured by the major media, the point is this: Rush Limbaugh is not the president, the vice president, or a Massachusetts senator. He's not the *New York Times.* He's not ABC, NBC, or CBS. Arguably, the satirical commentary of a noted polemicist should not be treated with the earnest indignation better reserved for the invasion of Poland.

The best liberals can do to try to even the score on venom-spewing is to define every random nutcase in the country as "right-wing." But no matter how many times liberals say it, Nazis and white supremacists (all six of them) are not "right-wing." The Ku Klux Klan is not merely a somewhat more exuberant version of the Republican Party.

A 1992 column in the *Chicago Tribune* casually reported that Illinois Republicans were "not worried" about David Duke causing trouble for President Bush. "The reason: Conservatives such as Phyllis Schlafly, Don Totten and Denis Healy are already signed up for Bush."[87] Phyllis Schlafly was torn but ultimately came out for Bush rather than David Duke. This is libel masquerading as analysis.

If, for some peculiar reason, one were itching to draw a correlation between "white supremacist" nuts and one of the two mainstream political parties, Democrats are manifestly the more obvious candidate for that distinction. With their infernal racial set-asides, racial quotas, and race norming, liberals share many of the Klan's premises. The Klan sees the world in terms of race and ethnicity. So do liberals! Indeed, liberals and white supremacists are the only people left in America who are neurotically obsessed with race. Conservatives champion a color-blind society. They don't even get to the first step with racists.

Of course, one big difference between the Klan and liberals is that liberals have a lot more power. Though endlessly celebrated in sensational news reports, the random "Nazi" or Klan member is rare and comically unthreatening. Nazism is simply not a burgeoning phenomenon in America just now. Klan marches bring out more protesters than Klan members.

But there are a lot of liberals. They are painfully self-righteous, they have fantastic hatreds, and they could not see the other fellow's position if you prodded them with white-hot pokers. They are United States senators, *New York Times* editors, news anchors, and TV personalities.

And they are completely unhinged.

TWO

THE GUCCI POSITION

ON DOMESTIC POLICY

Liberals thrive on the attractions of snobbery. Only when you appreciate the powerful driving force of snobbery in the liberals' worldview do all their preposterous counterintuitive arguments make sense. They promote immoral destructive behavior because they are snobs, they embrace criminals because they are snobs, they oppose tax cuts because they are snobs, they adore the environment because they are snobs. Every pernicious idea to come down the pike is instantly embraced by liberals to prove how powerful they are. Liberals hate society and want to bring it down to reinforce their sense of invincibility. Secure in the knowledge that their beachfront haciendas will still be standing when the smoke clears, they giddily fiddle with the little people's rules and morals.

While the rich are insulated by their wealth from the societal disintegration they promote, the rest of us are protected from these Dionysian revolutionaries and their pet intellectual disenchantment only by our abiding belief in God. That's why religious people drive liberals nuts. Bourgeois morality allows people to have happy lives without fantastic wealth.

In the sixties, affluent, pampered liberals capitulated to the groovy countercultural mores of their college-age children, embracing free love and rampant drug use. It was all harmless fun. They knew the kids would eventually come home and go to law school. Poor blacks moving up to northern cities to start their lives were not so secure.

Neurotically promoting the idea of women in the military, liberals lightly instruct soldiers to learn to repress their sexuality. That's a brilliant liberal idea for better living: Train men to stop looking at women sexually. The left's ideal world is G.I. Jane showering while she chats with her Navy SEAL commander who registers no response at the sight of a naked woman. Liberals seek to destroy sexual differentiation in order to destroy morality. *The Vagina Monologues* is the apotheosis of the left's desire to treat women's sexuality like some bovine utilitarian device, stripped of any mystery or eroticism.

Another way liberals think women should be like men is in the relentless pursuit of casual sex. Of all the fictional devices used by Hollywood, the rampant promiscuity of beautiful women is the most ludicrous. But apart from the History Channel and C-SPAN, pretty much all they're doing on the lowbrow channels is fornicating. Casts of entire shows ought to have the clap by now. The real-life consequences of Hollywood behavior rarely figure into the plot lines. There's a lot of meaningless sex—but not so many abortions, venereal diseases, and bitter divorces. There are, however, many happy stories of beautiful, wealthy women having children out of wedlock. Despite overwhelming evidence of the incredible destructiveness of illegitimacy on every possible axis—crime, poverty, social pathology, welfare dependency, education—liberals will not relent in their glamorization of single motherhood. From *Murphy Brown* to NBC's *Friends,* having children out of wedlock is absurdly portrayed as the considered choice of many sophisticated women. In real life, about the only accomplished attractive women who raise illegitimate children are Hollywood actresses. They can afford it. On the basis of liberal squawking about welfare-to-work requirements, apparently the only women who liberals think should be stay-at-home mothers are single women on the dole.

Another way liberals flaunt their omnipotence is by toying with murderous predators. If liberals expressed half as much self-righteous indignation about crime as they do about the random case of police brutality, one might be inclined to take them seriously. Criminals they like. It's the police they hate. In his book *The White Negro,* Norman Mailer wrote: "One is Hip or one is Square. One is a rebel or one conforms, one is a frontiersman in the Wild West of American night life, or else a Square cell, trapped in the totalitarian tissues of American society, doomed willy-nilly to conform if one is to succeed." They have reinvented the master race and it is their own hip selves.

Mailer and his fancy friends hailed the murderer Jack Henry Abbott as an "intellectual, a radical, a potential leader, a man obsessed with a vision of more elevated human relations in a better world that revolution could forge." Mailer helped Abbott get out of prison and championed his literary—and social—aspirations. Abbott was interviewed on *Good Morning America*, published in the *New York Review of Books*, and feted at chichi Manhattan cocktail parties. Two weeks after the beautiful people toasted the murderer at a Greenwich Village dinner party held in his honor, Abbott killed again. When waiter (and aspiring playwright) Richard Adan stepped out on the street to show Abbott where to go to the bathroom, Abbott stabbed him and left him to bleed to death. Mailer termed the incident "tragic."

Jerzy Kosinski, one of the fabulous people who had been at the dinner party, later said: "Had Abbott proposed the Nazi solution, we would not have embraced him. There is a tendency to believe violence on the left is somehow justifiable. Had Jack Abbott substituted for the phrase Marxist-Leninist, Hitlerian-Mussolinian, I do not think Mailer would have written the introduction to his book, I do not think we would have gone to toast his success."[1]

Noticeably, more fancy high-priced lawyers jumped at the chance to represent American traitor John Walker—free of charge—than would have touched Paula Jones's case with a ten-foot pole.

Predators are great fun for liberals. Criminals and poor people allow them to swell with a sense of their own incredible self-worth. That's the whole point of being a liberal: to feel superior to people with less money. They enjoy pitying unfortunate wretches and trifling with killers. Only the grasping acquisitive middle class, with their petty rules and morals, are a nascent threat to liberal pomposity.

Consider that the leading Democrat argument against Bush's 2001 tax cut was to demand to know how exactly it would help anyone. Scratching their heads and babbling about long-term economic goals and short-term economic goals, liberals exasperatedly asked how a tax cut was supposed to improve people's lives. To state the manifestly obvious: People would have more money. That's an improvement right there. Liberals are so blocked on the idea that people's money should be their own, they can't see the big fat reward: more money! It's some metaphysical thing with liberals. More money will give people more money. Isn't that the goal? What am I missing?

The *New York Times* has transformed into a caricature of the old reactionary WASP establishment, swatting down the social-climbing middle class with their polo mallets. They are annoyed at the thought of new money emerging from the perpetual dynamism of capitalist economy. Really vicious liberals are constantly bragging that they *love* paying taxes. They want their taxes to be raised even higher! The ostensible point of these boasts is to induce admiration for their deep patriotism or unbounded generosity toward the poor. But the real point is to announce that they do not share the working class's petty concern with taxes.

Thus, for example, during the battle over George Bush's proposed tax cut, billionaire music mogul David Geffen loudly bragged, "Speaking for myself, I don't need a tax cut." He loved paying taxes, he said, because it's "a privilege to be an American citizen."[2] This is pure braggadocio, intended to convey the information that Geffen has more money than God. "I want to pay more taxes" is a way of saying that, no matter how much the government takes, they will still have enough money to keep drinking Dom Perignon and making out in the hot tub.

Liberals obsess over the environment for the same reason they love crowing about how much they love to pay taxes: It is a way of separating themselves from the coupon-clippers. The environment is only the left's most transparent expression of their contempt for the middle class.

Instead of "helping the poor" by cutting checks to the IRS from their unfathomable fortunes, it would be nice if liberals would just stop blocking ordinary people from using the public beaches. In early 2002, David Geffen, Barbra Streisand, Steven Spielberg, and about one hundred other Malibu Marie Antoinettes erected chain-link fences to keep hoi polloi off the public beaches adjacent to their beachfront estates. The California Coastal Commission was forced to intervene to demand that the Hollywood left stop blocking access to the beach. Steve Hoye, former head of the Malibu Democratic Club, expressed shock at the arrogance of what he called "some of the best, most liberal people in Malibu."[3]

Liberals use the environment as a battering ram against the acquisitive middle class bumping up against the prerogatives of the fabulously wealthy. While California was experiencing rolling brownouts a few years ago, liberals steadfastly objected to building more power plants on the grounds that it would ruin the aesthetic of their hot tub lifestyles. Liberals want to prevent drilling in mudflats in Alaska, a place they would never visit, because they already have their Jacuzzis and can afford the electricity bills. Meanwhile working people need energy and could use the jobs. One cultural suggestion the Not-on-My-Beach movement might take from their beloved France is nuclear power. That would solve the alleged "greenhouse effect" immediately. But despite its acceptance by our lily-livered French friends, the left doesn't like nuclear power, either.

Nothing would make liberal environmentalists so happy as an entire country that looked like the Hamptons: beautiful rich people living in solar-powered homes staffed with a phalanx of obedient servants who can't afford SUVs. Liberals believe their fabulous wealth is a product of their unique brilliance, and the rest of us should live like aboriginals to preserve the view.

Republicans are simultaneously portrayed as the swine in third class and "the rich" (which, on the basis of Democrat tax proposals, evidently means "any guy with an alarm clock"). But for the incessant mind-numbing repetition of liberal propaganda, people would recognize this as a blinding contradiction. In fact—and contrary to another liberal myth—conservatives are aggressively anti-elitist. Reagan was so beloved by working-class Americans that a new demographic had to be created in his name—"Reagan Democrats." Still, leftists couldn't overcome their counterfactual stereotypes and continued to denounce Reagan as the champion of "the rich." Liberal cartoonist Jules Feiffer said Reagan was "making the world safe for white, male, heterosexual millionaires."[4]

Republicans may resent the fact that unions give so much money to Democrats, but they don't hate the worker. Who would be more likely to have a beer with a trucker: Tom DeLay or Barbara Boxer? Democrats actually hate working-class people.

The preposterous conceit that Democrats are the Party of the People and Republicans the Party of the Powerful has been repeated so often that by now it is incapable of disproof. In fact, all conceivable evidence supports the theory that liberalism is a whimsical luxury of the very rich—and the very poor, both of whom have little stake in society.

While the Democratic Party hauls in enormous donations from Hollywood celebrities and multimillionaire trial lawyers,[5] the average donation to the Republicans is about fifty dollars. For years, the Republican National Committee has proudly posted the size of its average donation and tauntingly asked the Democrats to release theirs. The Democrats have doggedly refused to do so. During the 2000 campaign, a Democratic spokesman justified this refusal, saying that an abstract number representing the average donation constituted "proprietary" information.[6]

The most fabulously wealthy senators are invariably Democrats. After the 2000 election, there were four senators worth $200 million or more—and all four were Democrats: Senator John Kerry (D-Mass., $620 million), Senator Jon Corzine (D-N.J., $400 million), Senator Herb Kohl (D-Wis., $300 million), and Senator Jay Rockefeller (D-W. Va., $200 million).[7] If "moderate Republican" Lincoln Chafee (R-R.I.) ever figures out that he is in the wrong party, nine out of the top eleven would be Democrats.[8] (Republican multimillionaires are also more likely to have earned their money than to have married it.[9])

The jet set is especially self-congratulatory about its notable empathy in comparison to the middle class, whom they call "the rich." Liberals' insistence that the rest of the world pay homage to their depth and compassion is even more irritating than their incorrigible elitism.

College dropout and working-class-phony Michael Moore produced a documentary, *Roger and Me,* that was wildly popular with rich liberals who enjoy jeering at workers from the land of pork rinds. As a caustic review in the *New Yorker* summarized the point of *Roger and Me:* "Members of the audience can laugh at ordinary working people and still feel that they are taking a politically correct position." The UAW denounced Moore for the film.[10] The left reveres Moore as an authentic blue-collar type.

Only people who are grounded in a sense of their own value and who do not think the good life consists of being able to sneer at other people as inferior can resist the lure of liberal snobbery. If liberals couldn't exercise their adolescent sneers through their control of the mass media, there would be no liberals at all.

It is important for liberals to demean the people they oppose to reinforce their sense of class superiority. Anyone can associate himself with the elite by adopting the left's snooty superiority and laughing at Republicans for being dumb hicks. Adopting the prejudices of the powerful interests is a way of saying you are with the "in" crowd. You are with the cool Hollywood types who hang out with Gwyneth Paltrow, Sean Penn, and David Geffen—not the working-class hillbillies who go to NASCAR races.

Liberal propaganda gives the individual "a set of prejudices and beliefs, as well as objective justifications." Anyone can be validated by saying what the cool, good-looking, rich people say. A "new idea will therefore be troublesome to his entire being. He will defend himself against it because it threatens to destroy his certainties."[11] It doesn't matter if you, personally, are a smelly white-trash idiot who doesn't have a college degree. It is simply a means of asserting one's relative refinement. It is axiomatic that every intelligent cultured person is a liberal. That is why there will always be a powerful lure to the left's false and destructive ideas. To be cool, all you have to do is call Republicans "stupid" or some similarly brilliant riposte; express greater empathy for a tree in the Brazilian Amazon than a human fetus; state your deep affection for government-sanctioned theft; and support drug legalization, sexual promiscuity, and child-molesting murderers on death row.

Liberalism's leverage is not that it has broad support but precisely that it doesn't. Who listens to NPR? Who, outside of New York City, reads the *New York Times*? Who claims to be "frightened" of George W. Bush? The answer: People who are desperately eager to associate themselves with "respectable opinion"—as opposed to actual, widespread, local opinion believed by the riffraff. Broad societal prejudices are nearly irresistible. They fill a psychic need by creating a "majority" opinion and eliminating the need to process new information. Propaganda "greatly simplifies [the individual's] life and gives him stability, much security, and a certain satisfaction."[12]

Liberals need not bother with logical persuasion as long as they can prey on people's sense of weakness. "Any statement whatever, no matter how stupid, any 'tall tale' will be believed once it enters into the passionate current of hatred."[13] They don't need arguments, they've got Gwyneth Paltrow.

If liberal propaganda didn't work, it would be impossible to comprehend bimbo starlets and uneducated slobs attacking the intelligence of the man who won the Cold War. On the occasion of Reagan's ninetieth birthday, for example, Michael Moore opined on ABC's *Politically Incorrect:* "Personally, the problem with Reagan, as I see it, is that he was the beginning of the depleting of the political gene pool, when Americans settled for somebody who really wasn't and shouldn't have been in that office, wasn't quite there all the time. . . . Here's what Reagan did: He gave weapons to the Ayatollah, so that he could raise money for the contras, which then helped bring a crack epidemic into the United States. That's what Ronald Reagan did and that's his legacy! That's his legacy!"

To point out that Moore is a college dropout is not to adopt the classism and snobbery of the left. A lot of people who went to Southwest Texas Junior College are shrewder than Yale graduates. But try flipping around that scenario. Imagine a no-account college dropout attacking Al Gore's intelligence on national TV. The audience wouldn't get that. It would be strange and confusing. Larry Flynt, who never finished grade school,[14] said of President Bush (who was graduated from Yale College and Harvard Business School): "He is the dumbest president we have ever had."[15] Actor Martin Sheen, who never went to college after flunking his college entrance exam—"intentionally," he claims[16]—said Bush is "a moron, if you'll pardon the expression." (Strictly speaking, "moron" is a word, not an expression.)

When Reagan was president, there wasn't a college campus in the country where the mere mention of his name failed to inspire cackles of hateful laughter. (Except probably Hillsdale College and Bob Jones University.) Now it's "Bush" that prompts the knowing giggles. At law schools "Rehnquist" inspires the canned laughter. It seems unremarkable that Hollywood zeros and college dropouts sneer about the intelligence of the guy who won the Cold War.

Liberals bully people with their veiled class bigotry. They are snobs even when championing a grade-school dropout like Flynt, whose self-described first sexual experience was with the egg sac of a chicken.[17] In an article in the *Cincinnati Enquirer*,[18] redneck pornographer Flynt is described as a cross between George Washington and Bill Gates. He is a "radical," a brainstorming "rebel," and a "shrewd businessman." Flynt has savoir faire and a devil-may-care attitude: "It's a little past 6 P.M. and Larry Flynt is already courting eternal damnation."

By contrast, the attorney who prosecuted Flynt for obscenity offenses— a former Marine, no less—is described as "dowdy" and a "moral crusader." Flynt's opponents "shout," while Larry "smiles and nods," "quips," and "argues." Negative depictions of Flynt are put in quotes—"dirty old man" and a "girlie" magazine. (The depiction of the prosecutor as a dowdy moral crusader does not take distancing quotes. Being a dowdy moral crusader is evidently a hard fact.) For not capitulating to the smut peddler and immediately turning itself into Sodom and Gomorrah, the local community is said to be engaging in a "crusade." But when Flynt doesn't capitulate either, he is "strong-willed."

Let's review who's on a crusade here. The original publicity poster for the Flynt hagiography, *The People vs. Larry Flynt*—a movie that bears no relationship to reality—portrayed the Flynt character as Jesus on the Cross, superimposed on a woman's bikini-clad crotch.[19] Not only that, but Flynt is histrionically touted as a martyr for the First Amendment. The "raunchy rebel" is matter-of-factly said to have "helped safeguard free speech for all Americans."[20] In point of fact, Jerry Falwell's suit against Flynt wasn't "the People" against Flynt, since it wasn't a criminal case. It wasn't even a libel case: It was a tort case—intentional infliction of emotional distress.

So a prosecutor who prosecutes Flynt is on a "crusade" and Flynt is a martyr. The martyr gets lots of fawning news coverage, but the tyrannical crusader is the subject of sneering attacks. (As a rule of thumb, it's extremely unlikely that you're a martyr if the media calls you a martyr.) Flynt pronounces President Bush "dumb." No one knows or cares what the ex-Marine with a law degree thinks.

Now decide, you Mr. Pedestrian Nobody: Do you laugh at how stupid Republicans are or don't you? Do you say you are a feminist, pro-choice environmentalist who is "afraid" of George W. Bush and laughs knowingly at Dan Quayle? Or are you one of those hicks who watches NASCAR races?

There is no more pristine example of the left's "in"-crowd snobbery than their treatment of conservative author and activist Phyllis Schlafly. Taking on the role of Disinformation Commissar for the now-dead Soviet Union, the national news media maintain a rigid radio silence on Phyllis Schlafly, while endlessly celebrating mediocre feminist shrews. Her very name prompts derisive hoots from Hollywood starlets who couldn't approach Schlafly's IQ if they were having brains instead of silicone injected. To listen to the cool people, you could be forgiven for thinking Schlafly is one step above a cretin. In fact, Schlafly is one of the most accomplished and influential people in America.

After working her way through college (forty-eight hours a week in an ammunition plant, test-firing machine guns) where she earned straight As and graduated (a year early) Phi Beta Kappa and Pi Sigma Alpha, Schlafly won a scholarship to Harvard graduate school.[21] Though Harvard Law School did not admit women at the time, Schlafly's professors were so bowled over by her intellect, they were prepared to make an exception for her.[22] Her constitutional law professor called her "brilliant" and gave her an A. Her undergraduate political science professor wrote that her "intellectual capacity is extraordinary and her analytical ability is distinctly remarkable . . . [Schlafly] is the most capable woman student we have had in this department in ten years."[23]

Schlafly has written ten books, most of them on military policy—one an eight-hundred-page vivisection of Henry Kissinger and his policy of detente. Her first book, *A Choice, Not an Echo,* sold three million copies. (The average nonfiction book sells about five thousand copies.) That book led to Barry Goldwater's nomination and created the movement that eventually led to Ronald Reagan's presidency. Her military work was a major factor in Reagan's decision to proceed with High Frontier technology.

Most astonishing was her single-handed defeat of the Equal Rights Amendment. When Schlafly decided to take on the ERA, it was supported by every living ex-president, 90 percent of the U.S. Congress, almost every governor, and every major newspaper, television network, and magazine in the nation, including thirty-six women's magazines with a combined circulation of sixty million readers. Support for the ERA was written into both the Democrat and Republican Party platforms.

On the other side was Phyllis Schlafly. But as George Gilder has remarked, that was enough.[24] She was composed, brilliant, and relentless. Refusing to be intimidated by conventional thinking, Schlafly repeatedly raised questions that polite people thought it bad taste to mention. Thus, for example, she questioned how ERA would affect the draft, family law, abortion, gays, adoption, widows' benefits—even locker rooms. Though the amendment's proponents sneered at Schlafly's claim that the ERA would end the draft exemption for women, law professors would soon be making the same point in the likes of the *Yale Law Journal*.

When champions of women's equality scoffed at Schlafly for being one of those "women with absolutely no legal training [who] stand there brandishing law books, telling people what ERA 'really' means"—as Senator Birch Bayh (D-Ind.) put it—she went to law school. In her fifties, with a radio show, a syndicated column, and her battle against the ERA, she graduated on time near the top of her class.[25] Winning her reputation as the greatest pamphleteer since Thomas Paine, Schlafly mobilized an army of women—all before the Internet. In the end, Schlafly's arguments trumped the political platforms of both parties, both Republican and Democratic presidents and their wives, and a slew of Hollywood celebrities including Alan Alda, Carol Burnett, Marlo Thomas, and Jean Stapleton.

Reviewing a history of the sexual revolution in the *New Yorker*, John Updike later wrote: "If the court's 1973 *Roe v. Wade* decision, legalizing abortion, was . . . 'the crowning achievement of the sexual revolution,' the defeat of the Equal Rights Amendment, which ran out of time in 1982, with only three more states needed for ratification, was the legal triumph of the counter-revolution, led in this instance by Phyllis Schlafly."[26] If anyone on the left did this, we'd never hear the end of it.

Schlafly could have rested on her laurels after writing *A Choice, Not an*

Echo. She could have rested on her laurels after defeating the ERA. (She could have rested after being named—as her biography cheerfully notes—"1992 Illinois Mother of the Year.") Indeed, Schlafly could have rested on her laurels on any number of occasions over the past half-century. But she kept going. There is no important political debate for nearly half a century in which Schlafly's influence has not been felt.

None of this is widely known because Schlafly doesn't brag about it. There is certainly not the remotest possibility that the mainstream media will ever breathe a word of her extraordinary accomplishments. Schlafly had derailed the left's precious sexual revolution. Consequently, she is demeaned and censored by the champions of women's advancement. There is a raw "1984" blackout quality to the media's ideological refusal to acknowledge Schlafly while posting endless tributes to worthless feminist nothings. The primary result of the feminist movement appears to be a slew of articles on LexisNexis hailing and praising feminism with unseemly gusto.

Schlafly's feminist counterpart and molecular opposite is Gloria Steinem. While Schlafly is a serious intellectual, Steinem is a deeply ridiculous figure who succeeded as a journalist only by becoming the news rather than reporting it. That leftists treat them in exactly the wrong way suggests that they are totally blinded to the facts by their ideology.

Steinem's influence was limited to a narrow sliver of liberal women living in big cities. It just happened to be the sliver that controls news and pop culture. Thus, for three decades, Gloria Steinem could not get her toenails painted without a major feature spread in a glossy magazine covering the event in laborious and hyperbolic detail. No matter how stunning her failures, a gaggle of media feminists would warmly compliment Steinem for her bravery and wisdom in choosing Hint of Pink over Musty Sunset.

But apart from the ephemeral achievement of winning the hearts and minds of liberal women who pen endless articles praising Steinem, it's hard to get a handle on any concrete accomplishments. Her biggest cause, the Equal Rights Amendment, failed, when it was rejected by American women who lined up behind Phyllis Schlafly. A string of follow-up half-measures, such as the Economic Equity Act, failed. Her magazine failed. Her winsome anti-male campaign, captured by her slogan "A Woman Without a Man Is Like a Fish Without a Bicycle," failed. The feminist movement failed.

In a 1989 article subtitled "Feminism Is Not Dead," even *Time* magazine had to acknowledge: "Ask a woman under the age of 30 if she is a feminist, and chances are she will shoot back a decisive, and perhaps even a derisive, no." (But, the magazine rushed to explain, "they are not feminists, or so they say, but they do take certain rights for granted."[27])

Indeed, Steinem's life would seem to be the opposite of a feminist success story, if feminists consider it desirable for women to be judged by their accomplishments and not their looks and the men they acquire. *Ms.* magazine—Steinem's great accomplishment, her project in lieu of marriage and children—was a spectacular flop. Eventually, just to keep *Ms.* afloat, she had to sleep with Mort Zuckerman, a rich liberal media mogul—whom Steinem later casually admitted she didn't love.[28] For achieving the spectacular feat of actually sleeping with a rich Democrat, Steinem was again heaped with praise. In a column *defending* Steinem, Liz Smith wrote: "Not only did Zuckerman lend *Ms.* $700,000, but he has check stubs that show $406,151 in gifts to the magazine and its foundation. . . . The publisher also sent one of his own top executives to spend two weeks trying to overhaul the magazine."[29]

The point was not to prove Steinem had succeeded on her own, but precisely the opposite: to prove that she had batted her eyes and inveigled a man to save her failing business enterprise. There's a great role model for American girls: Go out and fail, then find a rich man to prop you up.

While Schlafly was writing about military policy, getting presidential candidates nominated, drafting Republican platforms, and raising six children, Steinem was writing a book about self-esteem, *Revolution from Within: A Book of Self-Esteem.* Steinem never had children and now goes around prattling about how unhappy her life has been. As she told ABC's *PrimeTime Live*—a program that would never interview Schlafly—"I was unmothered or unparented. I was neglected."[30] Meanwhile, Schlafly is a senior statesman in the Republican Party. She has had a dominant influence on the Republican Party platform for at least two decades. Ask any United States senator, Republican or Democrat: Would you rather have your pet bill opposed by Gloria Steinem or Phyllis Schlafly?

Yet in the mainstream media the "hero" is the unaccomplished feminist harpy. Steinem is "in." The elites cannot cite her bravery often enough, as she endures endless hardships on the cocktail circuit from Aspen to Beverly Hills. In the special 1986 issue of *Time* magazine's "Almanac of Victories, Disasters, Heroes and Hurrahs" for the years 1936–1986, Gloria Steinem was the "Hero" of 1971, along with such individuals as Winston Churchill (Hero, 1941), Allied Supreme Commander Dwight D. Eisenhower (Hero, 1944), and Mother Teresa (Hero, 1979).[31]

Steinem's job—or "career" in feminist-speak—is simultaneously vague and pompous. (Men always had "jobs," women have "careers.") The articles celebrating her nothingness chirp that Steinem is "also attempting a career in screenwriting, getting involved with such projects as a caper movie, the screen translation of her book, and a new, noncartoon version of *Wonder Woman.*"

The media's undying devotion to this banal feminist has produced highly intellectual exchanges such as this with Jay Schadler of ABC News:[32]

SCHADLER: When a woman dresses in a sexy way, what is she trying to say?

Ms. STEINEM: Well, you know, men's—I don't want to embarrass you, but I was about to say that your pants are at least as tight as mine. You know, we enjoy looking at men's asses.

She is a hero! Much like Supreme Allied Commander Dwight Eisenhower.

In a 1999 ABC News special report titled "A Celebration: 100 Years of Great Women," Barbara Walters fawned over Steinem and her fellow termagants for changing the world: "Feminist. This may be one of the most misunderstood words of this century. . . . But without them, we would be living today in a very different world." (Schlafly was mentioned only as an obstructionist sidebar to these courageous women.)

Evidently, the way the feminists created a "very different world" related to how in 1960, as Walters explained, " 'Father knew best' TV told us that true fulfillment was a clean house." But *today* TV tells us that true fulfillment is abortion, lesbianism, and prostitution. You've come a long way, baby. Indeed, the entertainment industry is one of the few bailiwicks where feminism is still taken seriously. In the wonderful new world created by feminists, an actress's surest route to an Academy Award nomination is to play a prostitute. Among the actresses to have been nominated for Oscars for the devilishly challenging task of portraying a prostitute are Julia Roberts (*Pretty Woman*), Kim Basinger (*L.A. Confidential*), Jane Fonda (*Klute*), Jodie Foster (*Taxi Driver*), Elisabeth Shue (*Leaving Las Vegas*), Sharon Stone (*Casino*), and Mira Sorvino (*Mighty Aphrodite*).

Though feminism hasn't made much of a dent in America, it has taken the worlds of news and entertainment by storm. Female celebrities are no longer in the mold of Sophia Loren, Grace Kelly, Lauren Bacall, Carole Lombard, or Audrey Hepburn. In the bright new feminized Hollywood, the female divas are Britney Spears, Madonna, Pamela Anderson, Elizabeth Hurley, Sarah Jessica Parker, and Jenny McCarthy. Whatever feminism is alleged to have accomplished, it did not create a world in which women are admired for something other than playing or being sluts.

While there are nauseating prose poems to Steinem, the mainstream media ignore Schlafly when not deploying their trademark elitist snubs. Revealing true facts about Schlafly would inevitably result in unfavorable comparisons with inconsequential feminists. Not one of Schlafly's books has ever been reviewed in the *New York Times.* Schlafly is preposterously demeaned with articles reporting that she is trying to remain "relevant."[33] After two decades of smearing and slighting Schlafly, in 1995 the *New York Times* denounced Schlafly as part of an "attack machine."[34]

While the hard news outlets merely sneer at her, *People* magazine promotes grotesque Schlafly caricatures using, for example, "harridan" as a synonym for "Phyllis Schlafly."[35] One *People* magazine article[36] snickeringly described a Los Angeles mountainside home that featured "six fiberglass gargoyles depicting, among others, Richard Nixon and Phyllis Schlafly." In a profile of drag queen Sister Boom Boom, *People* gleefully noted that Sister Boom Boom had "mocked Phyllis Schlafly and Jerry Falwell."[37] *People* magazine also quoted young Ron Reagan Jr. "tartly" saying: "Getting flak from the likes of Phyllis Schlafly is an honor. I'd wear a T-shirt that says, 'I took flak from Phyllis Schlafly.' You'd get applause when you walked down the street."[38]

Phyllis Schlafly never comes up with a witty or tart reply. She "fumes" (*Newsweek*)[39] or "opens her mouth" (*New York Times*) or "snaps" (*Newsweek*).[40]

Time magazine sarcastically portrayed women attending a Phyllis Schlafly luncheon at the 1984 Republican National Convention for imagining that they were the "mainstream." A Texas delegate said: "It amazes me that people would think this is not a cross section of the American public." To demonstrate what a preposterous conceit this was, *Time* magazine noted that the woman had "waved an encompassing arm at the room full of overwhelmingly white, conservative, married women whose greatest mark of diversity was whether they wore silk or synthetic."[41] (As regular readers of the elite media know, "mainstream" means "homosexual drug addicts living in Manhattan.")

The party favor at the Schlafly luncheon was General Daniel Graham's book on the Star Wars defense system, *We Must Defend America.* At the

Democratic National Convention event attended by Steinem, the party favors were condoms.[42]

It is an absolute moral certainty that no conservative, certainly not an influential one like Schlafly, will ever be acknowledged by magazine glossies busily passing out "Woman of the Year" awards to mediocre left-wing harpies. In 1992, *Glamour* magazine made Hillary Clinton its "Woman of the Year" for "never apologizing for who she is"—as if it were an incredibly brave act to be a liberal in America today. Anita Hill had been *Glamour* magazine's "Woman of the Year" the previous year but she was given a special mention in Hillary's edition because, the magazine raved, Hill's influence had only "multiplied over time, inspiring others to take chances, to stand up and win." It turned out that one of the women who was inspired to stand up and win was Paula Jones. Strangely, though, Jones was never honored as a *Glamour* magazine "Woman of the Year."

Other brave feminists honored by *Glamour* in 1992 included Carol Mosely Braun, Lieutenant Paula Coughlin (who brought sexual harassment charges against the Navy), Katie Couric ("for boosting ratings and feminism at the same time," as we have come to expect from TV personalities), feminist author Susan Faludi, and Whoopi Goldberg. Does it ever occur to anyone at *Glamour* that their "Woman of the Year" lists never include anyone who might possibly have voted for Ronald Reagan? Ever? Reagan was quite popular with Americans, even if he was not with the editors of *Glamour* magazine.

This is what it means to be part of the cool crowd in America. Liberal snobbery is no more rational or factually based than the "in" crowd in junior high school. The "in" crowd even posts lists in mainstream magazines announcing who is "in" and who is "out." Steinem is always "in" and Schlafly is always "out." Indeed, conservatives are always out, yesterday's news, fighting irrelevance, fading from the limelight. This is odd since if any conservatives were ever "in," they neglected to tell us. Matt Drudge has been "out" three times in *Vanity Fair,* but he's never been "in."

Rush Limbaugh—along with Schlafly—was said to be taking "a back seat" in 1993: He was "on the outs; 1993 is not the time to be Far Right in America."[43] The *Washington Post* pegged Limbaugh as out in 1996, giddily quoting a "Rush Room" proprietor who averred that "Limbaugh 'is fading right now' in popularity."[44] The *Phi Delta Kappan* magazine gave Limbaugh a snooty "Least Credible Article" prize for a 1995 column in *Family Circle*.[45] In 1997, the Bergen County *Record* noticed that "Rush Limbaugh's conservative star may be fading."[46] When it became clear that no amount of sneering would turn Rush into Jim Jeffords, the media ignored him. (Except Lewis H. Lapham, editor of *Harper's Magazine,* who is absolutely obsessed with Limbaugh, mentioning him in snotty asides in seventeen *Harper's* editorials since March 1993.[47])

It's not clear if it is possible for liberals ever to be "out," and if they are, what it means. But if you are a conservative and the mainstream media says you're out, buy beachfront property now! You know you're in when they say you're out.

The corollary is: You can always tell a rotten organization by the *New York Times'* predilection to call it "much admired" or "highly respected." This is how reporters convert their purely subjective feelings into hard news. When ABC was considering scrapping Ted Koppel's *Nightline* in early 2002 because of its low ratings, the most common reaction was "Is that still on?" At the *Times,* they were inconsolable. In a series of lengthy elegies, the program was factually described as "quality news," and an "admired news program."[48] Admired by whom precisely? Rush Limbaugh wasn't losing any of his audience, but the *Times* never calls his program "admired."

Truly pompous liberals have achieved such a refined level of snobbery, sometimes you wonder if they realize people are listening. During the 2000 presidential campaign the press was in a high dudgeon about Bush having traveled abroad only three times—in addition to his many trips to Mexico. But "beyond those trips," as the *New York Times* put it, Bush had traveled "only" to China, Gambia, Italy, Egypt, and Israel.[49] How many Americans consider that laughable?

Yet *Newsweek's* Jonathan Alter, among others, was nearly obsessed with Bush's petty provincialism for having traveled abroad so little. In the October 2, 2000, *Newsweek,* Alter wrote: "Despite his father's foreign-affairs background, which offered Dubya great opportunities to grow intellectually, Bush has traveled overseas only three times in his 54 years. Mexico is the only foreign country he has visited often and knows well."[50] On the October 11 *Today* show on NBC, Alter again raised the embarrassing fact: "This is a candidate who's only traveled overseas three times in his life."[51] Just three days later, Alter was still babbling on the Saturday *Today* show about Bush having "only traveled overseas three times in his entire life, and he's gotten educated on it some in recent months, but even he would not claim to be any kind of foreign policy expert."[52] And he still hadn't exhausted the subject. In the October 23 *Newsweek,* Alter breathlessly reported: "Until recently, Mexico was the only country outside the United States that seemed to engage [Bush's] interest; he has visited the Middle East once, in 1998 (one of only three trips he has taken overseas in his life)."[53]

Media sages were not so impressed with foreign travel when Bush's father was running against Bill Clinton. The senior Bush had been a Navy pilot in the Pacific in World War II, ambassador to the United Nations, ambassador to China, and director of the Central Intelligence Agency. Clinton's wide travel consisted primarily of his joining antiwar protestors across Europe and in Moscow during the Vietnam War.[54]

The public never would have known about Clinton's travels as a peacenik if the Bush campaign hadn't had the gaucherie to mention it. In response, the media did not lament Clinton's sparse (and somewhat unusual) foreign travels but attacked Bush for being so vulgar as to have raised the issue. The "admired, quality news" program *Nightline* titled its story on Bush's tactless questions "A Low Blow on Clinton's Russia Trip?"[55]

It is hardly surprising that liberals are terrified of campaign finance laws that allow ordinary people to participate in public political debate by contributing to political campaigns. Relaxed campaign finance laws are dangerous because they allow hoi polloi to get their two cents in. Noticeably, the news organizations frantically hawking the "money in politics" stories continuously neglect to mention that the media is wholly exempt from the campaign finance laws they adore.

There's no time to mention the media exemption when there are important stories to be run on courageous politicians like Senator John McCain, who champion the media's utterly self-interested demand for campaign finance restrictions. Carrying water for the media is known as "fighting powerful interests"—powerful interests that are not quite powerful enough to prevent the entire media from erupting in joy at the mere mention of McCain's name. The sinister, powerful interests McCain confronted were little old ladies sending $20 checks to the Christian Coalition. Even if the little old lady is Imelda Marcos, in politics power is information, and no special interest group in the history of the universe has wielded the power of the modern media in America.

Despite all the hysterical news accounts of money corrupting politics, what liberals really believe is that the power to influence elections by persuading voters should reside exclusively with the media. Thus, complaining of the campaign fundraising by Rudy Giuliani and Hillary Clinton in early 2000, Neal Rosenstein of the New York Public Interest Research Group told the *Washington Post:* "Hillary and Rudy are already in the paper every day."[56] The media should be the sole purveyors of information about political campaigns.

In the left's doomsday scenario, the campaign finance laws would permit political speech by people who worry about taxes and crime, don't have $200 million or a position with the elite media, or—God help us—have traveled overseas only three times. Liberals malign such people as "the rich." Only the mind-boggling resources of the left could persuade so many people that these elitist snobs speak for the little guy.

THREE

How to Go from Being a "Jut-Jawed Maverick" to a "Clueless Neanderthal" in One Easy Step

Excerpt from a deposition of a staffer in Senator Bob Packwood's office, 1975–1976:

> [I] entered his office. . . .
>
> Senator Packwood was alone, and he immediately closed the door and did not say anything to me, but grabbed me and had me pinned backwards with my back to the wall. And before I could say anything—I was very shocked—he stuck his tongue in my mouth and was French kissing me, without ever asking me or saying anything, without any warning.
>
> He grabbed and embraced me and kissed me against my will. And I could not remove him from me for quite a while. . . .[1]

Senator Bob Packwood had been madly chasing, groping, and slobber-kissing female staff and lobbyists since at least 1969.[2] By his own heavy-breathing account, there were "22 staff members I've made love to and probably 75 others I've had a passionate relationship with."[3]

All this was well known to Packwood's feminist supporters for decades, but he was never exposed. Packwood was "good on women's issues," which consisted primarily of his enthusiasm for killing off anything that might result from one of his successful sexual conquests.[4] But things changed dramatically when feminists didn't need him anymore.

Back when the National Abortion and Reproductive Rights Action League wanted Packwood's pro-abortion vote, the establishment media could not produce enough luminous adjectives about the man. Invoking the blabocracy's favorite words for utterly typecast tax-and-spend liberals, Packwood was called a "maverick" or a "gadfly." He had "courage" and "political savvy." There are literally hundreds of news items using these words in connection with Bob Packwood.

With the searing insight and novelty of expression that makes the *New York Times* a giant among giants, that paper dubbed Packwood a "jut-jawed iconoclast." Indeed, the *Times* blew through the whole arsenal of fawning adjectives on Packwood: "Audacity, individualism and political savvy have become Packwood trademarks."[5] In fact his trademark was: Voting the editorial position of the *New York Times.* In the watchdog media's typical take-no-prisoners style, only Packwood's friends would be quoted in articles about him. (Articles about disfavored Republicans quote only adversaries.) Thus, Representative Les AuCoin (D-Ore.) called Bob "one of the shrewdest political thinkers I've ever met."[6] Another audacious individualist, far-left former Republican Senator Lowell Weicker of Connecticut—a "maverick" as the *Times* put it—said he admired Packwood's "candor, courage and political common sense."[7]

Packwood's canny individualism was revealed to the media by his capacity to recite, nearly verbatim, the liberal catechism on abortion. Flush with favorable press on "choice," Packwood added to his growing popularity with the adversary press by periodically denouncing Ronald Reagan.

Liberal Republicans attacking conservative Republicans invariably produces widespread acclaim in the usual church circulars. Packwood spouted anti-Reagan clichés, and the *New York Times* instantly sprang to action praising Packwood as a "skilled legislative tactician" and a "canny political organizer."[8]

Inebriated on the favorable press, Packwood made the astonishing charge that Reagan was clinging to an "idealized concept of America" that left women behind. Republicans believed, he alleged, "women shouldn't be working."[9] Packwood, by contrast, wanted them right there in the office within groping distance. He also revealed to a gullible press that Reagan got confused in private meetings.[10]

The media were in a swoon. Packwood could have been the Boston Strangler, for all the adversary press cared. As long as he supported a woman's right to "choose" and engaged in delusional one-sided debates with Reagan, Packwood was protected. And not merely protected. Packwood was hailed in hallucinatory press notices ceaselessly citing his "courage."[11]

What was the evidence of this much-vaunted courage? The *New York Times* explained that Packwood had "emerged as a leading defender of abortion" and yet "does not scare easily." This is on the order of saying "the president rides in a bullet-proof car, and yet does not fear snipers." The press was glorious precisely because he was a "leading defender of abortion."

Though the threshold for liberal "courage" is rather low, the media impose an inordinately high threshold for sexual harassment charges against liberals. As long as Packwood was a "leading defender of abortion," the media would studiously ignore his legendary ham-handed groping.

The fairy tale affair between Packwood and the media, however, came to a tragic end the second feminists didn't need him anymore. In January 1993, feminists got themselves a president who was at least as committed to abortion as Packwood (and for pretty much the same predatory reasons). There was no possibility that President Bill Clinton would appoint a Supreme Court Justice who would vote to overrule *Roe v. Wade*. There was no possibility that he would sign into law even the most innocuous restriction on abortion. In fact, abortion may be the only issue on which Clinton did not flip, repeatedly vetoing a series of partial-birth abortion bans passed by large majorities in both the House and Senate.

Ironically, the very Republican administrations that Packwood had taken such glee in maligning for twelve years had indirectly been his salvation. Only after the 1992 election that put abortion's truest friend in the White House (and returned Packwood to the Senate with the vigorous support of the National Abortion Rights Action League) would Packwood's half-century of lechery finally see the light of day.

Florence Graves, the reporter who exposed the blow-dried predator, first learned of Packwood's serially lewd behavior in April 1992. As Graves remarked, it was, of course, "very likely" that loads of Washington journalists had known about Packwood for years. Despite her interest in pursuing the matter, "several news organizations" informed Graves they "were not interested in financing the story." She was able to scare up "no institutional support." A deal with *Vanity Fair* fell through.[12] Consider that this was in 1992—after Anita Hill had saved America by raising the critical issue of sexual harassment. Though Packwood had been molesting dozens upon dozens of female staffers and lobbyists for decades, they evidently weren't much interested in pursuing the matter, either. Luckily, he tended to be surrounded by women who shared his well-known devotion to abortion.

In one typical molestation story from the mid-seventies, Packwood grabbed and kissed Mary Heffernan, founder of the Oregon chapter of NARAL. Explaining her years of silence on the episode, Heffernan said: "For me, abortion rights were on the line. What would be the outcome if I called him on the carpet?"[13] In another almost insignificant incident, an eager abortion rights advocate on Packwood's staff described sitting in the senator's private office watching an abortion-rights video while he chatted up the staff in the office suite. He returned as the video was ending and proceeded to read a series of sexually explicit jokes to her.[14]

Only after Clinton was elected president would Packwood be cut loose from the protective adjectives of a pro-abortion press. Regurgitating *New York Times* editorials as his personal philosophy would not save him now. The moment Packwood's abortion-rights armor dropped, not only was his reprehensible personal behavior revealed, but everything else about him changed as well. His background, his intelligence, his personality, his looks, the state of his marriage—indeed his whole life story—were suddenly completely different. Once a "jut-jawed iconoclast," Packwood soon became a "graceless clod." Overnight, he went from being a "voracious reader" to being "clueless." Instead of being an audacious senator with "candor, courage and political common sense," he was a self-absorbed "baby." He had "no self-awareness, no sense of a world beyond his own little fiefdom, no comprehension of how others might view him."[15] Packwood finally found out what it was like to be a real Republican. It's not so much fun when the press doesn't like you.

Even granting that Packwood's abuse of women cast a different light on him, he was still the same man. But in the press accounts, all the shiny laudatory details about Packwood's career, family, wife, office, and home were summarily washed down the memory hole.

What happened to Packwood is a stunning example of the media's power both to destroy and to protect. It's absurd enough when the media describes Teddy Kennedy as a man of principle and Jesse Helms as a pandering bigot. In the case of Packwood, the media's good dog/bad dog descriptions were applied to the exact same human being.

When they needed him . . . Packwood was destined for "political stardom," according to the *New York Times.* He was called "a successful lawyer and bright young man."[16]

As soon as he became dispensable . . . Packwood was a man who "might have been successful selling insurance or probating wills back in Oregon."[17]

When they needed him . . . He was the grandson of "a member of the 1857 Oregon Constitutional Convention."[18]

As soon as he became dispensable . . . He was the "nerdy son of a timber lobbyist in the state legislature."[19]

When they needed him . . . His "partner throughout has been his wife, Georgie, 51, who met Packwood while working on his first campaign."[20] (Where, evidently, he meets all his girlfriends.)

As soon as he became dispensable . . . He was a pathetic divorcé, "estranged" from his children and "nearly broke." His Oregon "residence" was a trailer.[21]

When they needed him . . . A "voracious reader," his office was lined with books on British history and biographies of Disraeli and Oliver Cromwell.[22]

As soon as he became dispensable . . . His diaries were "pitiful for their lack of self-awareness."[23]

When they needed him . . . People magazine chirped: "Packwood's Senate staff currently has only three men, a source of considerable amusement to the 16 women."[24]

As soon as he became dispensable . . . His "staff seems set up as a personal sorority of cheerleaders for the captain of the football team to dip into," stated a column in the *Baltimore Sun.*[25]

In the final coup de grâce, making absolutely clear that he had been cut loose, the *New York Times* called Packwood "Nixonian."[26]

It kind of makes you wonder: Was Packwood ever all that canny, shrewd, and courageous, really? There is no intellectual honesty whatsoever in media descriptions of politicians. Journalism is war by other means.

The *New York Times* fumed and huffed about Packwood, snippily demanding that Senate Majority Leader Bob Dole throw Packwood out of the Senate: "If Mr. Dole has already forgotten why Mr. Packwood was forced to resign, the rest of America has not. . . . Mr. Packwood repeatedly tried to take sexual advantage of women dependent on him for jobs, altered evidence he thought might be 'very incriminating.' " A few years later, that same editorial page would be viciously denouncing the House of Representatives for impeaching President Clinton. Compare that to Pat Buchanan, who was one of the first to call on Packwood to resign, saying he had engaged in "egregious behavior . . . and an abuse of power by a United States senator."[27] By calling on Packwood to resign, Buchanan was parting company from politicians such as Republican Senator Bob Dole.

Being a "moderate" Republican satisfies the beast only as long as they still need you for pro-abortion votes and demeaning quotes about your "fellow" Republicans. But no matter how much the press seems to idolize this or that "moderate Republican," the moment the feisty independent maverick is unnecessary, he will transform, overnight, into Joey Buttafuoco.

The media may have a crush on liberal Republicans, but don't expect them to respect you in the morning.

As the Packwood case illustrates, politicians with something to hide— say, wild promiscuity, stupidity, Chappaquiddick, or a former membership in the Ku Klux Klan—had best be liberals. There may be other reasons to be a liberal—generalized hatred of America, for example—but one very good reason is that you need the media's protection. Only politicians with nothing to hide dare risk displeasing the New York Times editorial page.

There is no possibility, for example, that Jesse Helms could have remained in the United States Senate if he had killed a girl at Chappaquiddick like Democratic Senator Teddy Kennedy; if he had been a former Ku Klux Klanner like Democratic Senator Robert Byrd; if he had molested staffers like pro-choice liberal Republican Bob Packwood; or if he were a half-wit like pro-choice liberal Republican Jim Jeffords. Any conservative Republican who did any of these things would soon cease being a politician—or would cease being a conservative. Republicans cannot survive disgrace. Not even a "moderate Republican." But Republicans liked by liberals have something to hide—most often, craven stupidity.

All Republicans sense deep in their beings that they can stave off the bitter enmity of the media by being liberals. Especially by being stalwart defenders of abortion. The media's reward system is extremely effective with half-brights. Most politicians would rather face down the Viet Cong than be ridiculed by Katie Couric. It's one thing to be hung upside down and have bamboo shoots stuck under your fingernails. But for the media to accuse you of being against "progress and enlightenment"[28] (*New York Times* on Jesse Helms) or to call you an "airhead" (Katie Couric on Ronald Reagan)— well, that makes strong men tremble and weak men liberals.

It is baffling, therefore, that Republican activists often praise Republican politicians for being "respected" by the press. That's supposed to be the selling point: *The media seems to like him!* There is no surer proof of a Republican mediocrity than the media's respect. Remember: The media liked Jack Kemp once, too. As a rule of thumb, liberals are not the best source of information on the Republicans' strongest candidate.

Still, the media insists on straight-facedly reporting that Democrats are "scared of" running against birdbrains like Christie Todd Whitman, while claiming to "hope" Republicans would be foolish enough to nominate a sure loser like Ronald Reagan.

Consequently, it is highly instructive to note which Republicans the media dub "courageous," a "maverick," or "flinty." (The establishment press's admiring use of the adjective "flinty" in reference to sell-out Northeastern Republicans is as inevitable as the tabloids' use of "luscious" to describe Hollywood starlets.) Flinty Senator Jim Jeffords was showered with fulsome praise when he (officially) left the Republican Party. Having never in his life voted with the Republicans on any half-important issue, Jeffords's defection was about as newsworthy as Elton John coming out of the closet.

Yet the media described Jeffords's break with the Republican Party as if it were the greatest patriotic act since the Army Rangers scaled the cliffs at Pointe du Hoc. The *Los Angeles Times* wrote of the momentous event: "Sen. Jim Jeffords now walks in the footsteps of Winston Churchill, Ronald Reagan and Abraham Lincoln." ABC's Peter Jennings said: "It's political earthquake time in Washington." The *Times* cheered Jeffords's defection as an act of heroism. He was called a "maverick" who "has always played against type." The *New York Times* unleashed all the celebratory adjectives, calling Jeffords a "maverick," with degrees from Yale and Harvard. Yet still somehow he was "more down-home casual than East Coast polished." The *Times* also quoted a political science professor confirming that Jeffords was "a man of tremendous sincerity, and that came across today."[29]

Compare that to the *Times*'s editorial on Senator Richard Shelby's switch from the Democratic to Republican Party a few years earlier, subtly titled "Profiles in Opportunism."[30] The *Times* sniffed that Shelby's "desertion to the victorious Republicans this week was hardly a huge surprise." This was in contradistinction to Jeffords's defection, which was earth shattering.

While the media treats George W. Bush's Yale education like some sort of scam, Jim Jeffords's degree from Yale cannot be cited often enough. (And consider that Jeffords got into Yale long before the terrorizing reign of the SATs, back when admission to the Ivy Leagues turned on social class rather than standardized tests.) But the vigilant reader will find only the most sublimated references in the establishment press to the blinding fact that Jeffords is a little D-U-M-M. It is often noted, for example, that Jeffords "dislikes cameras and speeches." But this aversion is reported as if it were part of Jeffords's sturdy Yankee rectitude (flinty, you might say) rather than a genetic necessity.

Jeffords avoids live television interviews for reasons that will become obvious. In one of his rare (pretaped) interviews he explained why he was voting to acquit in President Clinton's impeachment trial. Forget that his point was moronic; just note the sentence structure:

> This has been a difficult process to make up ones minds in these issues. But, in my mind, the most critical issue with the numbers going to be that they he will not be convicted no matter what I will do has been to make sure that we handle this appropriately so that we do not establish bad precedents for future presidents. To me, that is the most important aspect of the process right now is to ensure that we do not set a bar so low that any future president will be liable for impeachment for just about anything.[31]

That is a direct, verbatim transcription of a United States senator's remarks on national TV about the most important Senate vote of his life. If Jeffords were not accorded the respect due all politicians who adopt ADA-approved positions, late-night comics might have finally discovered a dumb liberal.

There is no Republican alive who does not instinctively understand the protective coloration that being "pro-choice" affords. Support for abortion is the last refuge of Republicans who cannot rely on native intelligence or good living to avoid being destroyed by the media. The issue doesn't have to be abortion, of course, though it's hard to think of a position that provides such a bullet-proof shield for idiots and lechers. Try to think of a pro-abortion politician—Republican or Democrat—who is dumb. Simply as a matter of statistics, there must be boatloads of them. The fact that none leap to mind shows how well the media's protection racket works.

Indeed, there is only one prominent pro-choice Republican who has ever demonstrated that he does have the guts and IQ to stand up to media attacks: Rudolph Giuliani. As mayor of New York, Giuliani refused to yield to the left on a slew of other hot-button issues, aggressively opposing affirmative action administrators, pornographic artists, Legal Aid lawyers, useless government employees, and other key Democratic constituencies.

A nother profile in liberal courage is former New Jersey governor Christie Todd Whitman, appointed by President Bush to run the Environmental Protection Agency. The first giveaway that Whitman is "pro-choice" is how media gush over her. Referring to her amazing "popularity" as potentially a "national phenomenon," the *New York Times* quoted experts saying they could "understand why other politicians want to be like Whitman, because it means they want to be liked by the public."[32] The equation is rarely stated with such clarity.

The *Times* declared Whitman "the G.O.P.'s . . . New Idol." (It's always so touching when a newspaper that hasn't endorsed a Republican presidential candidate since Eisenhower informs Republicans who their "New Idol" is.) Whitman's groundbreaking "philosophy" was "sophisticated," "prosperous," "moderate," and "tolerant." But the thing is, the woman is a dimwit. (Are you beginning to see the pattern?) While accompanying state troopers on patrol in Camden in 1996, Whitman frisked a young black man—for a photo-op. Her human prop was a citizen who happened to be a genuine suspect. He had already been subjected to a real frisk, but was forced to endure a second phony "pat-down" by Whitman, while she grinned madly for the cameras, as if she were squeezing pumpkins at a state fair. In the ensuing hoopla about Whitman's rank insensitivity, a Republican campaign consultant remarked that Whitman was "caught in a political no-man's-land, without support from the left or the right."[33]

When Whitman was asked whether Bush should have an abortion litmus test for the Supreme Court, she boasted that as governor of New Jersey she had abjured litmus tests for her judicial nominees. "I'll tell you something," she began auspiciously. "I have now appointed five of our seven Supreme Court justices in New Jersey, and I never asked a one of them what they thought about a woman's right to choose."

As she explained: "It would have been inappropriate." It also would have been moronic inasmuch as state judges have absolutely nothing to say about the country's abortion policy. Presumably she didn't ask judicial nominees about their positions on getting more visitors to the Grand Canyon, either. You really wonder if she knows that *Roe v. Wade* is a decision by the Supreme Court of the *United States,* which can be neither repealed nor upheld by state supreme courts.

In any event, asking Whitman about judicial nominees would be like asking Bill Clinton for marital advice. Governor Whitman singlehandedly turned the New Jersey Supreme Court into the most ridiculous court in the nation, easily overtaking the once-infamous California Supreme Court and even beating back stiff competition from the Florida Supreme Court.[34] If Whitman had chosen judicial nominees by randomly pointing to names in a telephone book, New Jersey would have been better served. Obviously, the nation cried out for Whitman's expertise in choosing judicial nominees.

Like other "moderate Republicans," Whitman is at least smart enough to realize that she cannot rely on her genetic capacities to avoid being called stupid. Luckily for her, actual intelligence has nothing to do with being called smart by the media. Whitman's avid and outspoken support for abortion assured her status as a Republican "idol"—idolized exclusively by the media that decide who will and will not be called a Republican "idol."

This is precisely why abortion makes such an excellent litmus test for Republicans. Not because abortion is the most crucial moral issue facing the country today or because it is a winning issue electorally—both of which it is, incidentally. The reason it makes such a handy litmus test is that the media detests abortion opponents. Any politician who is pro-life has proved that he needs no camouflage, and can get by just fine without the media's phony "respect," thank you.

The media prattle on about money in politics, corruption, and influence-peddling on the basis of flimsy little "voter guides" distributed by the Christian Coalition. But whatever vast and insidious influence the Christian Coalition voter guides have, they sure couldn't have kept Bob Packwood in office throughout two decades of egregious sexual harassment. Only the media can own a politician.

If God himself emerged and told Teddy Kennedy to oppose abortion, he couldn't do it—at least not if he wanted to keep his job, which is dependent on the media forgetting about Chappaquiddick. Anyone with a skeleton in his closet has got to jump when the media says jump, or get out of politics.

Pimping for his masters, former Klanner and current Democratic Senator Bob Byrd voted against removing Clinton from office despite his conclusion that the president had committed "high crimes and misdemeanors." ("No doubt about it in my mind," Byrd told Cokie Roberts on ABC's *This Week.*)[35]

If the media's puppets ever diverge from the party line or otherwise become dispensable, people will start to notice little things like Byrd's former membership in the Klan, Jim Jeffords failing, on several tries, to put one single coherent sentence together, and Christie Todd Whitman not knowing what her own state supreme court does. They might even remember Chappaquiddick.

The media will tolerate any disreputable behavior in order to win. Principle is nothing to liberals. Winning is everything.

FOUR

CREATING THE
PSYCHOLOGICAL CLIMATE

Man must be penetrated in order to shape such tendencies. He must be made to live in a certain psychological climate.

JACQUES ELLUL, *Propaganda: The Formation of Men's Attitudes*

Generally, it is difficult to make sweeping statements about the political views of an entire industry—but it's surprisingly easy in the case of the media.

In the 1992 presidential election, a mere 43 percent of Americans voted for Bill Clinton. That same year, 89 percent of Washington bureau chiefs and reporters voted for Clinton. Only 7 percent voted for George Bush.[1] (It should be noted that, despite their adoration, even Bill Clinton has referred to the media as "the knee-jerk liberal press."[2]) Indeed, the media elites covering national politics would be indistinguishable from the Democratic Party except the Democratic Party isn't liberal enough. A higher percentage of the Washington press corps voted for Clinton in 1992 than did this demographic category: "Registered Democrats."

CNN's Peter Arnett said of the survey: "Howard Fineman [of *Newsweek*] probably voted for Clinton. I voted for Clinton, but, you know, when it gets to the vote, you do it, and then you go on with your journalism.

56

I don't think the two are really related." Clinton's press secretary Michael McCurry feigned shock, saying, "If these guys actually voted for Clinton, why don't they actually be nicer to him in print?"[3]

One of the rare voices of sanity was Wolf Blitzer, who said that if the survey was accurate, "It would suggest that there is a problem."[4]

The wildly disproportionate percentage of liberals in the media is not an insignificant point. The media determine how the news will be served up, how the players are characterized, what news to report, and what news not to report. The same clichés, biases, and outright lies are constantly reinforced through the media sound chamber.

One of the blabocracy's favorite lies is that the media is not liberal. They *love* this one, hauling it out at the slightest provocation, polishing absurd "studies" proving the media is—if anything—conservative, and running stories on "The Myth of the Liberal Media"[5] and "the so-called liberal press."[6]

A "study" analyzing the *New York Times*'s coverage of the 2000 presidential race conclusively proved that "this 'liberal bastion' published 50 percent more anti-Gore articles than anti-Bush, and nearly twice as many pro-Bush articles as pro-Gore."[7] Claims of "conservative bias" in the media at large are amusing oddities. But a claim that the *New York Times* has a conservative bias can be explained only by the sheer joy liberals take in telling lies. This is how liberals flaunt their massive control over news in America. The fact that everyone knows they are lying is part of the fun. They take insolent pleasure in saying absurd things, like college radicals giving revolutionary speeches at their parents' dinner table: *We will raid their wine cellars and have their women!*

The *Times* hasn't endorsed a Republican for president for half a century. Though the *Times* generally issues endorsements as if it is the Oracle of Delphi, in 1972 the *Times* endorsed George McGovern early and enthusiastically, and he carried one state. When vast majorities of Americans voted for Ronald Reagan and George Bush, the *New York Times* was endorsing Jimmy Carter, Walter Mondale, and Michael Dukakis. Even the last winning Democrat the paper endorsed—Bill Clinton—never got as much as half the country to vote for him. (Indeed, through its tried and true method of mechanically endorsing every Democrat, the *Times* hasn't endorsed a presidential candidate who got as much as 50 percent of the vote for over a quarter of a century.)

So, maybe the *Times* is "pro-Republican" compared to the *Berkeley Student Union.* But there is no possible calculus under which the *Times* could be called pro-Republican compared to "Americans"—arguably a more relevant control group.

It ought to tell you something that the "conservative bias" claim is too preposterous even for the *New York Times* to level. The *Times* regularly interprets standard Republican positions as fanatical, religiously based racist hate crimes. But even it can't screw up the nerve to say the media have a conservative bias. Instead, self-respecting journalists, like those at the *Times,* create a smokescreen for the liberal monolith by viciously attacking any mention of a "liberal media." The very idea is treated as a wacky theory hatched by troglodyte right-wingers. With some leftists babbling about "conservative bias," the position of the reasonable middle is simply to deny that there is any slant whatsoever.

Peter Jennings declared: "CNN is mainstream media, . . . ABC, CBS, NBC are mainstream media. And I think it's just essentially to make the point that we are largely in the center without particular axes to grind, without ideologies which are represented in our daily coverage, at least certainly not on purpose."[8]

Time magazine's Jack White denounced the suggestion of liberal bias in the media as "a lot of hokum." Indeed, if anything, the press is right-wing: "There is no liberal bias in the press on the whole. In fact, if there is a bias, it's on the other side. It's hard to find a person really, truly, of the liberal persuasion who is making any important decisions in any important media institutions in this country now. I've looked for them, I consider myself one, I have very few birds of a like feather around."[9]

It is a peevish liberal trope to claim, as liberal pundit Lawrence O'Donnell, former aide to Democrat Daniel Patrick Moynihan, does, to get "mail and viewer reaction that says I'm just one of those awful Republicans, and then I get mail that says I'm just one of those awful Democrats."[10] I'd like to see one of those letters accusing O'Donnell of being a Republican. I'd file them away with the ones telling Larry Flynt he's not filthy enough.

Some people say the media is liberal, some say it's conservative. In the end, who's to say? Some people accuse Dan Rather of being too conservative, some say he's too liberal. As Rather describes his role as a take-no-prisoners reporter: "I try to blow out lights on both sides of the street."[11]

NBC News correspondent Joe Johns argued that "it's very hard to draw a very clear picture about what the media are. For every liberal-leaning newspaper, there's the *Washington Times.*"[12] And for every person who is not struck by lightning, there's one who is. Liberal fairness is: They get all major means of news dissemination in America, and conservatives get the *Washington Times,* the editorial page of the *Wall Street Journal,* and now Fox News Channel.

In 1996, a longtime veteran of CBS News, Bernard Goldberg, wrote an article for the *Wall Street Journal* asserting that "the networks and other media elites have a liberal bias."[13] In response to Goldberg's statement of the blindingly obvious, Bob Schieffer, a CBS colleague, responded: "People are just stunned. It's such a wacky charge . . . I don't know what Bernie was driving at. It just sounds bizarre."[14] Dan Rather criticized Goldberg for writing his column for a "conservative" newspaper like the *Wall Street Journal.* Rather wrote this in a column published in the *New York Times*—which he hailed as an example of a "middle of the road" newspaper.[15] Norman Pearlstine, editor in chief of Time-Warner magazines, responded to Goldberg's bemused citation of Dan Rather referring to the *New York Times* as "middle of the road" by earnestly repeating that "The *New York Times* is middle of the road." And not only that, but "to call the *New York Times* left-wing is absurd," Pearlstine said.[16]

Evidently, to call any publication left-wing is absurd. Not one of them is—not one—not even the newspapers like the *New York Times* and the *Washington Post* that endorsed Walter Mondale for president the year voters in forty-nine states chose Ronald Reagan. As Pearlstine explained: "There is no active, aggressive, important publication of the left in America."[17] Either he means left-wing compared to *Pravda* or he was accusing the *New York Times,* the *Washington Post,* the *Detroit Free Press,* and the *Philadelphia Inquirer* (among many, many others) of being slothful, passive, and unimportant publications.

When Goldberg expanded upon his thesis in his number one best-selling book, *Bias,* Tom Shales, the *Washington Post* TV reporter, accused Goldberg of "haul[ing] out the old canard about the media being 'liberal.' " In addition, Shales made the point that the Emmy Award–winning Goldberg was a "full-time addlepated windbag," "a no-talent hack," "laughably inept," "not a bright shining star," "disheveled and bleary-eyed on the air," and "a flop as a network correspondent." If any of that were true, then the real scandal is that CBS News kept the inept windbag on air for thirty years. Shales also noted that Goldberg was "a lousy writer." Good writing is this, also from Shales's piece: "And we all know how unbiased those [*Wall Street*] *Journal* editorials are. Gosh it is soooo hard to figure out where they're coming from."[18]

To obscure the overwhelming liberal dominance of the media, the few designated media "conservatives" are cited tirelessly in testimonies to the ideological diversity in the nation's newsrooms. Democrats in the media are editors, national correspondents, news anchors, and reporters. Republicans in the media are "from the right" polemicists grudgingly tolerated within the liberal behemoth. Republican views must be accompanied by a conspicuous warning: "Partisan Conservative Opinion Coming!" Neutral news slots are reserved for Democrats exclusively. "Balance" is created by having a liberal host a debate between a liberal and a moderate Republican.

Thus, in a typical formulation, a Gannett newspaper article on the "revolving door" between politics and the media mentions Tim Russert, NBC's Washington bureau chief and *Meet the Press* host, and Strobe Talbott, former *Time* magazine reporter, in the same breath with three Republicans who have each held the novelty "conservative" seat on CNN's *Crossfire*—Mary Matalin, John Sununu, and Pat Buchanan.

Outside of *Fox News*, the "from the right" seat on *Crossfire* is one of the rare paid positions available for conservatives on TV. The distinction between opinion journalism and objective news coverage is seemingly impossible for liberals to grasp.[19] In addition to Buchanan, the media's other approved Republicans include William Safire and George Will. (Noticeably, even to win a position as the designated conservative "opinion" journalist requires an IQ approximately three standard deviations above Dan Rather's.)

Safire, the *New York Times*'s House Republican, voted for Clinton in 1992. He endorsed Clinton in a column (on the now hilarious grounds that Bush was "stonewalling" on a potential scandal within his administration).[20] It is thus quite possible that not one writer or editor at the *Times* voted for Bush in 1992, when his opponent got only 43 percent of the nation's vote. In any event, Buchanan, Safire, and Will's counterparts are not Tim Russert or Strobe Talbott. Their true counterparts are other polemicists, like Bill Press and Juan Williams. What conservatives object to is not liberal opinion commentary, but rather ostensibly objective news coated with smears.

Even conservative pundits must be branded as such, while liberals take no ideological label. On CNN, host Aaron Brown introduced his guests as "conservative Shelby Steele of the Hoover Institution" and "Richard Cohen of the *Washington Post.*" This prompted Steele to ask, "Is Richard Cohen a liberal?" Brown checked with Cohen, who replied: "On this issue." That's one for the philosophers: On what issue is Richard Cohen not a liberal? He's not a polygamist? He's troubled by forced abortions?[21]

The *New York Times* described George Will as being able to "turn in the blink of a commercial from the cultured interviewer into the committed (or commitable) right winger."[22] Even as a clearly labeled conservative, Will must be further maligned as "commitable."

The more liberals thrash about trying to prove that there are an equal number of conservatives as liberals delivering the news, the more glaring the inequity becomes. A nut website purporting to expose "conservative bias" in the media—titled "Liberal Media? Yeah, Right!"—contrasts such "center-right" journalists as Margaret Carlson and Al Hunt with the conservatives overrunning the media. The website identifies, in total, forty conservatives in the media. Almost every one is an opinion columnist. Two—William F. Buckley and R. Emmett Tyrrell—had to start their own magazines to be heard.[23]

In yet another specious comparison, one syndicated columnist proclaimed: "Just as many people get their 'news' from Rush Limbaugh as Dan Rather." Apart from the elusive objective/subjective distinction, it's interesting to note that Limbaugh wasn't hired and foisted upon an unsuspecting public by a media oligarchy. To the contrary, Limbaugh's media bosses thought he wouldn't sell and repeatedly fired him. It is American people—twenty million of them—who keep Limbaugh on the air. The fact that Limbaugh is simply allowed to exist is deemed the equivalent of every major network doggedly hiring and promoting only liberals to deliver and analyze the news.

At ABC News, "conservative" means the most conservative member of the Clinton administration. Throughout the 2000 presidential campaign, political commentary was provided by dueling analysts George Stephanopoulos and David Gergen—both of whom worked for Clinton. Gergen has, admittedly, also worked for Republican administrations. How about Gergen and Buchanan rounding out the left and right? No. That would be unthinkable. But it seems perfectly normal for the political spectrum at ABC News to stretch all the way from Clinton staffer to Clinton staffer.

Between the two former Clinton administration staffers, only the one who never worked for any Republican administration is the one who landed a permanent position at ABC News. But not to worry, ABC's Diane Sawyer grilled Stephanopoulos on his partisanship, saying: "You are so much about passion for politics, and it doesn't matter to you, I mean—I really mean this. You've been completely nonpartisan in covering the news."[24]

ABC chose as a "legal analyst" Jeffrey Toobin, a political hack duly celebrated for making things up,[25] engaging in unethical behavior, and sliming other liberal journalists for a want of alacrity in bending over for Bill Clinton. Sued by his former boss Independent Counsel Lawrence Walsh for violating confidentiality agreements Toobin signed with the office, a Kennedy-appointed federal appeals court judge found he had engaged in "conduct which manipulates procedure" and harshly denounced his "dubious behavior."[26]

After *Newsweek* reporter Michael Isikoff turned down Toobin's request to coauthor a book on Clinton, Toobin wrote his own book, which denounced Isikoff's solo project as "tawdry voyeurism"—without mentioning that he had tried to get in on Isikoff's voyeurism but was rejected. The *New York Times* book reviewer Michiko Kakutani called Toobin's book "highly partisan" and "willfully subjective," full of "dubious assertion[s]," "petty meanness," "contradictions and perplexing assertions."[27] The guy who was too partisan for the *New York Times* and too unethical for Lawrence Walsh was a perfect fit as ABC's "legal analyst."

Merely for having authentic conservatives debate liberals (authentic meaning "did not work for the Clinton administration"), Fox News Channel is known as the "conservative" network. Until a few years ago when Fox News Channel got Brit Hume, there has been only one host of his own television show who might possibly have voted for Ronald Reagan: John McLaughlin, of his namesake *The McLaughlin Group*. Ostentatiously conservative and opinionated, McLaughlin does not purport to be neutral. His show is balanced with two liberals and two conservatives.

Fox News personality Bill O'Reilly is denounced as a "conservative" by people who believe the nation's newsrooms accurately reflect the political spectrum. O'Reilly is anti–death penalty and pro–gun control, believes in "global warming," and thought Elian Gonzalez should go back to Cuba—not positions generally associated with the Republican Party. Indeed, O'Reilly's only manifest conservative credential is that he strongly disapproves of hucksters and liars.

Democrat pundit Lawrence O'Donnell captures the chummy, clubby relationship between the Democratic Party and the media when he explains that scholars with the conservative Heritage Foundation have an "advantage" in getting television bookings "when they're deliberately trying to book pro-and-con arguments." Affiliation with the liberal Brookings Institution, he said, makes television bookings trickier "because we don't know what you're going to say."[28]

I know what they're going to say! The tax cut is too big, military spending is too much, and we need an international treaty on the environment. Hearing media people describe liberals is like listening to a fish characterize water: *Water? What water?*

Clinton's national economic advisor Gene Sperling went to the Brookings Institution. Clinton's Federal Reserve Vice Chairman Alice Rivlin went to the Brookings Institution. Clinton's Secretary of the Treasury Lawrence H. Summers went to the Brookings Institution. (And don't forget: Nixon broke into the Brookings Institution.) About the only Clinton administration employees who didn't end up at the Brookings Institution are the ones delivering news at ABC.

Further distracting from the massive liberal hegemony of the media, any accidental Republicans who wander, Elmer Fudd–like, into hard news reporting are endlessly showcased to support the claim that "both sides"—Republicans as well as Democrats—pass through the "revolving door" between politics and journalism. But somehow only a Republican's passage through the "revolving door" ever provokes frenzies of media introspection and self-criticism.

Consequently, small children can recite in their sleep that Diane Sawyer once worked for Richard Nixon. But you have to do research to find out that Brian Williams, Lesley Stahl, Jane Pauley, Jeff Greenfield, Tim Russert, Ken Bode, Bill Moyers, Rick Inderfurth, Pierre Salinger—to name a few TV news personalities—all worked for Democrats.

In another generation, no one will remember George Stephanopoulos got his big break into network news on the staff of a Democratic president. And not just any Democratic president, but one who was impeached, held in contempt by a federal judge, and disbarred by the Supreme Court. Hiring Stephanopoulos would be the equivalent of a major network hiring Chuck Colson immediately after Watergate. Interestingly, though, none of President Nixon's henchmen made the jump to network news.

More contemporaneously, Tony Blankley's television career has not been so illustrious or remunerative as Stephanopoulous's. This is despite the fact that Blankley is telegenic, bright, politically astute, and—a bonus!—did not work for a felon. Rather, Blankley worked for one of the most consequential politicians in the last century—Newt Gingrich. Clinton's aide is a rising star in television news. Gingrich's will never be an "objective" political analyst anyplace. Instead Blankley is relegated to one of television's conservative novelty seats. Even Gingrich himself could be hired by only one network—Fox News.

Only Republican politics is deemed "partisan." Moving back and forth between left-wing politics and a media career is like moving from the *Washington Post* to *Newsweek*.

After a heavily criticized tenure as President Clinton's press secretary, Dee Dee Myers jumped to lucrative positions on cable news and with *Vanity Fair* magazine. She was hired at CNBC by Roger Ailes (the man now touted as the evil genius behind Fox News's conservative bias). *Vanity Fair* created the post exclusively for Myers.[29] She was scheduled to appear on the *Tonight Show with Jay Leno* soon after leaving the White House, but ended up canceling on account of a drunk driving charge.[30]

James Carville has served as guest host on CNN's *Larry King Live*.[31] It is impossible to imagine CNN choosing a guest host from among Carville's opposites, assuming such exist. Evidently there is no Republican in the entire universe capable of leaving his subjectivity at the door the way Carville can.

When Mark Green lost the New York mayoral election in 2001, the *New York Times* casually reported that among his likely next moves—a topic of interest to precisely no one, including Mrs. Green—was his serving "as a host on a serious television talk show."[32] A spot on television seemed a logical next step for a Democrat so liberal that even New York City had rejected him.

It's not easy to locate journalists who began their careers on the staff of a Democrat, since working for a Democrat isn't considered a political job. Only "Republican" constitutes a political affiliation. Working for a liberal politician is deemed good solid training for an independent, mainstream journalist. It is second only to being on Nixon's apocryphal "enemies list" as a nice shiny feather in your cap. Still, with the caveat that this is not a complete list, here are a few former Democratic staffers on television:

NBC's **Tim Russert** worked for New York Governor Mario Cuomo (D) and Senator Daniel Patrick Moynihan (D-N.Y.).

CNN's **Jeff Greenfield** was a speechwriter for Senator Bobby Kennedy (D-Mass.) and ultra-liberal New York Mayor John Lindsay.

CNBC's **Chris Matthews** was a speechwriter for Jimmy Carter and press secretary for House Speaker Thomas P. (Tip) O'Neill.

NBC News chief political correspondent **Ken Bode** was an aide to Representative Morris K. Udall (D-Ariz.) in his 1976 presidential campaign.

PBS's **Bill Moyers** was President Lyndon B. Johnson's press secretary.

NBC's **Brian Williams** worked in the Carter White House.

Rick Inderfurth spent a decade as an ABC News correspondent, sandwiched between working for Senate Democrats and the Carter administration[33] and becoming Clinton's assistant secretary of state for South Asian affairs.

Elizabeth Brackett of the *NewsHour with Jim Lehrer* worked on the mayoral campaign of Democrat Bill Singer in Chicago and was herself a candidate for some smaller Democratic positions.[34]

NBC's **Jane Pauley** was administrative assistant to the Indiana Democratic State Central Committee.

Pierre Salinger worked for the Kennedy administration and was briefly a Democratic senator from California (an appointed position the voters ousted him from two months later) before accepting a position with ABC News.

Democrat journalists not only far outnumber their Republican counterparts, but outflank them on the ideological spectrum. A surprising number of establishment journalists worked for far-left liberals whose closest counterpart on the right would be the John Birch Society.

Graduate for graduate, the office of Mayor John Lindsay seems to have launched more big-name media stars than the Columbia School of Journalism. Though at the beginning of his political career Lindsay called himself a Republican, even the *New York Times* wasn't fooled, describing his reign as a mélange of "failed liberal experiments ... unwieldy government super-agencies and a mistaken belief that the city could tax itself out of financial troubles."[35] Among the media careers that began on Mayor Lindsay's political staff are Lesley Stahl (CBS), Jeff Greenfield (CNN), Ken Auletta (*New Yorker*), Jeffrey Katzenberg (Disney and Dreamworks), and Steven Brill (muckraking liberal journalist at large).

As the poll of Washington political reporters suggests, print journalists also represent an ideological span from Democrat to far-left Democrat. Some of the former Democratic staffers who now write the news are the following:

David Shipley went straight from the Clinton White House, where he was speechwriter for both Bill and Hillary, to being a writer and editor at the *New York Times*[36]—where his wife, who worked for Gore, was fawningly profiled without mention of her husband's job.[37]

Ken Auletta, who writes about politics and the media for the *New Yorker,* embarked on his career in journalism by working for a series of liberal Democrats. Auletta served in the Johnson administration as special assistant to the undersecretary of commerce; worked on Senator Robert F. Kennedy's presidential campaign; managed both of Democratic Howard J. Samuels's campaigns for governor of New York; and was the executive director of the New York City Off Track Betting Corporation under Mayor John Lindsay. (A LexisNexis search turns up no documents that mention Auletta worked for Johnson, Kennedy, or Lindsay.)

Leslie Gelb was a national security columnist and deputy editorial page editor for the *New York Times* amid stints on the staff of Senator Jacob Javits, President Lyndon Johnson, and President Jimmy Carter.[38]

James Fallows, who was President Jimmy Carter's chief speechwriter, has been the Washington editor of the *Atlantic Monthly,* a writer for the *New York Times Magazine,* the *Industry Standard,* the *New Yorker,* and the *American Prospect.*

Tom Johnson, former publisher of the *Los Angeles Times* and former CNN chairman and chief executive, was an aide to Lyndon Johnson.

Walter Pincus writes about national security for the *Washington Post* and has been a consultant for both CBS and NBC News.[39] He "twice took sabbaticals" from journalism, as he put it, "to run investigations for the Senate Foreign Relations Committee when its chairman was J. W. Fulbright (D-Ark.)." His wife was a political appointee in the Clinton administration.

Jack Rosenthal was a Washington correspondent for the *New York Times* and served for many years as the editorial page editor. Rosenthal served in both the Kennedy and Johnson administrations, including as executive assistant to undersecretary of state in the Johnson administration.

John Seigenthaler was an assistant to Attorney General Robert F. Kennedy and also an assistant to President Kennedy's liaison to Governor George Wallace. He went on to become the editor and publisher of the *Nashville Tennessean,* editorial director of *USA Today,* president of the American Society of Newspaper Editors, and president of the Freedom Forum First Amendment Center at Vanderbilt University.

The number of former Democrat staffers in prominent media positions is especially impressive when you consider that the last Democratic administration for which there is complete data was Jimmy Carter. It's still too early to know where all the Clinton administration flacks will land. But we do know where a lot of them came from.

Sidney Blumenthal, a correspondent for the *New Yorker* and former reporter for the *Washington Post,* was Clinton's political advisor.

Donald Baer, assistant managing editor of *U.S. News & World Report,* became the director of White House speechwriting.

Carolyn Curiel, a *Nightline* producer and former *New York Times* editor, was a speechwriter.

Thomas Ross, senior vice president of NBC News, was special assistant to the president under Clinton and senior director of public affairs at the National Security Council.

Tara Sonenshine, a *Nightline* producer, worked for Clinton's National Security Council.

Strobe Talbott, *Time* magazine's Washington bureau chief in the late 1980s, who penned fawning paeans about candidate Clinton for *Time* during the campaign, promptly became Clinton's U.S. ambassador at large to the former Soviet Union and was soon promoted to deputy secretary of state.

Talbott's tributes to Bill Clinton for *Time* magazine during the campaign created no incensed outcries from the media watchdogs. Indeed, the *Washington Post* treated Talbott's unregulated campaign donations to Clinton as a recommendation for the job, rather than an outrageous ethical lapse. The *Post* nonjudgmentally noted simply that Talbott "brings with him not only a major policy brief—the former Soviet Union—but also a closeness to President Clinton."[40]

Hailing from a family of Democratic politicians also appears to be an excellent springboard for a career in journalism. Though liberals treated the discovery of a Bush cousin at Fox News like a latter-day Kim Philby scandal, working for the media is fairly common in Democrat families. In the Relatives of Politicians category of on-air television personalities alone, there are:

Chris Cuomo, ABC correspondent and son of former Democrat governor of New York.

Eleanor Mondale, *E!* correspondent and daughter of Democratic presidential candidate Walter Mondale.

Cokie Roberts, co-host of ABC's *This Week,* both of whose parents were Democratic congressmen; her father was Representative Hale Boggs, House majority leader.

Maria Shriver, NBC correspondent and niece of Teddy Kennedy.

Evan Thomas, the *Newsweek* Washington bureau chief and frequent CNBC guest who, when Bob Kerrey was considering a run for president, helped kill the *Newsweek* story on Kerrey killing civilians in Vietnam, is the son of Norman Thomas, a four-time Socialist candidate for president.

Even being the candidate yourself is a good precursor to a career in journalism provided you are a Democrat. After fluffing the pillows for John and Robert Kennedy from 1961 to 1968, Pierre Salinger was appointed a United States senator from California when the incumbent died. (He was beaten by a conservative Republican the moment Californians were consulted on the matter.) Upon losing his appointed Senate seat, Salinger went to work for ABC News. Since Salinger pledged to leave the country if Bush were elected, we may finally be free of him.

Running for president in the Democratic primaries was Jesse Jackson's stepping stone to his own show on CNN, unironically titled *Both Sides*. Jackson's show wasn't even a Mutt and Jeff routine, with a conservative analyst to provide balance. Jackson was the sole host. Jackson had already run for president twice and was contemplating a third run when CNN gave him his own show.[41] This would have been like CNN making Patrick Buchanan the sole host of *Crossfire* between his runs for president, except that Buchanan was a lot more popular with the American electorate than Jackson was. Indeed, Jackson isn't just a Democrat. He's the man who stood on Cuban soil and chanted, "Long Live Fidel Castro, Long Live Che Guevara!"[42]

An entertainment column in the *Los Angeles Times* took note of CNN's giving Jackson his own show and praised the network for broadening the ideological spectrum on TV. Jackson, it seems, would be the first "openly partisan liberal host of a public affairs talk or interview series." This was "important" because "the range of political opinion in public affairs shows usually ranges from moderate to conservative, almost totally excluding the left."[43]

We will raid their wine cellars and have their women!

Jackson's son also got his own television show—while actually serving in Congress. A CBS-owned Chicago television station, WBBM-Channel 2, gave the Democratic congressman his own talk show, *Chicago Focus with Congressman Jesse Jackson Jr.*[44]

There is nothing inherently wrong with partisan public service as a precursor to a career in journalism: It is not manifestly obvious why people without political experience would make superior journalists or be any less objective than *New York Times* editor Pinch Sulzberger or CBS's Dan Rather. But it would be nice if more than one party were permitted to make the transition through the infamous "revolving door." Being a liberal Democrat is simply not considered partisan, certainly nothing meriting comment. Only Republicans within the media club cry out for denunciatory editorials in the *New York Times*.

In the midst of this flowering of ideological diversity in the news business, CBS hired former Congresswoman Susan Molinari in 1997 to co-anchor a new Saturday morning show. Molinari's job was to cover cooking, fitness, and movies.[45]

Judging by the media reaction, you could be forgiven for thinking CBS had turned over its entire news division to the Republican National Committee. The *New York Times* editorialized on this offense to objective news reporting in a huffy piece titled "The GOP News from CBS." At the press conference announcing Molinari's hiring, the first question from the watchdog press was "How can you make Susan Molinari a quote-unquote CBS anchorperson when she's put no time in the news business and is an absolute amateur?" A CBS executive quickly justified the hiring, promising that Molinari would be limited to analysis, not commentary.[46] Or was it commentary but not analysis? In an example of how professional journalists nail down details like that—in contradistinction to "quote-unquote" journalists like Molinari—columnist Sandy Grady said Molinari was limited to "commentary, not analysis." But the *New York Times* reported she was restricted to "analysis" but not "commentary."[47] In any event, Molinari would be on a tight leash.

Anonymous Molinari critics were cited in the *New York Times* questioning "whether she can be neutral in reporting and interviewing, given her partisan Republican background."[48] Nonanonymous National Public Radio's Nina Totenberg showed how serious journalists work, remarking of Molinari's CBS gig, "Well, this really makes me want to puke. You know, at least CBS had the decency, when they hired Diane Sawyer from the Nixon White House, to make her go out and stand in the rain for a year or so, to earn her position.... [I]t really, it just makes me want to throw up."[49]

At the time of Totenberg's hard-hitting analysis, NPR's president was Delano Lewis, who had been chief fund-raiser for Washington Mayor Marion Barry. He had joined NPR when the former president Douglas Bennet, a Carter administration refuge, left to join the Clinton administration. Bennet had replaced Frank Mankiewicz, who had worked for George McGovern's 1972 presidential campaign.

But the press was seized with anxiety about Molinari's job giving cooking and sewing tips on a morning TV show. As the *New York Times* put it, there was concern about the "potentially awkward transition from being one of the nation's best-known advocates of Republican ideology to becoming a CBS News anchor."

More than one hundred newspaper articles were published on the threat to honest journalism posed by CBS's hiring of Molinari (moderate, pro-abortion Republican Molinari). The headlines barely convey the hysteria: "CBS Adds Molinari, Loses Credibility,"[50] "Hiring Susan Molinari, a Ratings-Hungry CBS Gave TV Journalism a Setback,"[51] "Molinari Move to CBS Blurs Journalistic, Political Lines,"[52] "Government-Media Revolving Door a Threat to Press,"[53] "Is It News, or Is It Propaganda?"[54] "The Faces Are New, the Biases Aren't,"[55] "Susan Molinari's Signing with CBS News Causing Quite a Stir."[56] The most detatched editorial title was from the *Hartford Courant*: "Susan Molinari Is Not Walter Cronkite."[57] Yes, Walter Cronkite was a pious left-wing blowhard. Molinari may have been a pro-choice "moderate Republican," but at least she was not Walter Cronkite.

Media liberals not only personally know no conservatives, but they frequently appear to be completely unaware that conservatives exist. They must still be puzzling over Reagan's landslides.

As impish fate would have it, at about the same time CBS hired Molinari, it was also hiring another former member of Congress: Democratic Senator and future presidential candidate Bill Bradley. Bradley was not restricted to decorating tips, but was hired to deliver serious news pieces on *CBS Evening News*. There wouldn't have been a peep about CBS hiring Bradley, who also had no experience in journalism, but for the hapless fluke of being so close in time to the Molinari emergency. As it was, Bradley's hiring was mentioned only as a sidebar to articles furiously condemning CBS for hiring Molinari. A LexisNexis search for 1997 turns up fifty news items that mention Molinari in the same sentence as "revolving door." Only twelve of those articles include so much as a reference to Bradley. Meanwhile every single news item that uses the term "revolving door" in a sentence with Bradley—all seventeen of them—also mentions Molinari.[58]

Having purged Susan Molinari from the media after a mercifully short ten months on air, only two Republican interlopers remain: Pete Williams and the "revolving door" champion Diane Sawyer.

After serving as Pentagon spokesman under Bush (41), Pete Williams became a correspondent for NBC News. Williams's move to NBC was marked by the calm, measured response one has come to expect from the pulpits of elite opinion. In a lengthy screed in the *Washington Post* criticizing NBC's hiring of Williams, a college professor proclaimed it "especially troubling" since Williams was "the antithesis of the qualities NBC and other news organizations should be looking for in reporters."[59] With the left's typical Vincent Pealean sanctimony, a writer for *Newsday* said Williams's move to NBC should be a "wake-up call for journalism" and accused Williams of having "consistently misled not only the media but the public on the reality of events" surrounding Pentagon business.[60] It seems that Williams did not promptly provide the U.S. press corps with information that would help the press demoralize American troops.

One columnist compared Williams to a reporter for the *News Tribune* who was demoted to the copy desk after she ran a campaign for a gay rights law and publicly joined the Freedom Socialist party.[61] (This was done in evident violation of her employer's prohibition on outside political activities.) The existential fact of being a Republican is equivalent to a liberal journalist leading a political campaign in violation of her newspaper's policy.

Media "experts," such as Everette E. Dennis of Columbia University's media center (technically, the more verbose Freedom Forum Media Studies Center) proclaimed Williams's job with NBC a "conflict of interest, I mean pure and simple." Marvin Kalb, then director of the similarly verbose Shorenstein Center on the Press, Politics and Public Policy at the Kennedy School of Government at Harvard, expressed concern that the Williams hire would further "blur the lines" between politics and journalism. (In a sublime famous-last-words moment, Kalb proposed the media adopt guidelines modeled on the Clinton administration's ethics rules.[62])

When Williams left the Pentagon, the Clinton administration replaced him with Kathleen deLaski . . . a correspondent for ABC News.[63] DeLaski's turn through the revolving door took her from ABC to the Clinton administration, and then back to journalism, on AOL's political website. She managed the transition without a whisper of protest and very few mentions of the "revolving door."

Only Republicans interrupting the left's lock on the media are subjected to bitter reproach. Every incident of a Republican sneaking into the news apparatus becomes an instant scandal. It is criminal to be a conservative, and conservatives must be hunted! There were forty-two news items on Pete Williams and the "revolving door" and eight news items on Kathleen deLaski and the "revolving door"—four of which also raised the troubling issue of Pete Williams.

The most famous alleged "Republican" in the mainstream media is Diane "Milhous" Sawyer. Sawyer's youthful indiscretion of working for Richard Nixon is persistently cited to support the proposition that the "revolving door" includes both Republicans and Democrats. Let's examine that.

In her early twenties, Sawyer got a low-level job in the Nixon White House through her father's connections. Sawyer has explained that she was simply looking for any job in politics and said, "If someone like George McGovern had offered me a job, I'd almost certainly have taken it."[64] Her only involvement in politics prior to becoming an assistant in Nixon's press office was to march in a campaign protest against mandatory Bible class at Wellesley College.[65]

While working at the White House, Sawyer ran into Nixon precisely once.[66] Indeed, Sawyer's job in Nixon's White House was so ministerial that when a dying rabbi and Nixon confidant claimed she was *Deep Throat*, Bob Woodward laughed out loud, noting Sawyer's "subsidiary role in the Nixon White House."[67]

As with Molinari and Williams, Sawyer's hiring at CBS News in 1978 became an instant scandal. CBS big feet Dan Rather and Robert Pierpoint were beside themselves with righteous indignation. Pierpoint informed a CBS vice president: "I don't like hiring people into news who have been involved in party politics."[68] Rather complained that Sawyer "had no credibility" and had "been discredited" by her work for Nixon.[69] Sawyer herself recalls that "conversations would stop as I entered the room."[70]

She later rectified things by giving Nixon a hostile interview, winning plaudits from the establishment press. In response to some unexceptional remarks Nixon made about female reporters treating first ladies unfairly because "women reporters think they have to be tougher" than men,[71] Sawyer reacted "like a wounded tigress" and snapped, "How do you know that women of the press are such carnivores?"[72] *Newsweek* called it Sawyer's "finest hour."[73]

Diane Sawyer's connection to Richard Nixon, youthful indiscretion though it was, is the stuff of media legend. But there is a virtual blackout on the information that Sawyer's CBS colleague Lesley Stahl was—in her thirties, as an emancipated adult—a speechwriter for left-wing John Lindsay.[74] In broad LexisNexis searches for news items mentioning "John Lindsay and Lesley Stahl," only eight items turn up. Searches for "Diane Sawyer and Richard Nixon" retrieved over seven hundred news items.[75]

Unlike Sawyer, Stahl was never required to distance herself from her left-wing political activism. Nor does she. When two thirds of Americans were telling pollsters they didn't believe Anita Hill, Stahl found Hill completely credible, saying she "brings out what every woman has always known and doesn't even talk about. . . . Like Anita Hill, most women don't stop a guy."[76]

Still and all, Diane "I would have worked for McGovern" Sawyer is a perennial fixture as the "Republican" in stories on the "revolving door" between politics and media. And she worked for a Republican only by accident, stumbling into a White House job in a Republican administration three decades ago. If we're going to have to keep hearing about the "revolving door" on the basis of a single news personality, Republicans at least ought to have the option of choosing someone other than Sawyer.

Bitterly complaining about a George Bush cousin working behind the camera at *Fox News* on election night, *Salon*'s Eric Boehlert proclaimed that "hiring George Bush's cousin to run a crucial part of its election coverage, the right-wing Fox Network hits a new low in conflict of interest. Why didn't the Fox News Channel hire George Will to man its Election Night Decision Desk? Or Peggy Noonan or William Safire? Hell, why not just go right to the source and hire George W. Bush himself?"[77]

Mainstream publications like the *Los Angeles Times* were still waving the bloody shirt a month into the Bush presidency. New York University professor Todd Gitlin wrote on the op-ed page that if a Gore cousin had been employed at one of the networks, "Can anyone reasonably doubt that the pundits would be working themselves into a nonstop lather charging 'the liberal media' as accessories to grand larceny?"[78]

How about this: Suppose that half a dozen relatives of Republican politicians were scattered throughout network news as well as major national publications, along with another dozen veterans of Republican politics—not as opinion journalists, but as objective news and political analysts. Suppose the only slots available to Democrats were liberal commentary positions— "From the left, Lesley Stahl." Pat Buchanan and Pat Robertson would be the dueling political commentators on *ABC News* (which would at least have the virtue of being a lively debate). George Will would be the host of *Meet the Press.* Peggy Noonan and Tony Blankley would provide objective political analysis.

That is the news media in America, except they're all liberal Democrats. The occasional heretics from the liberal orthodoxy are regularly trotted out for the ritualistic Orwellian "two minutes of hate." The one TV station that is not an ocean of liberal Democrats punctuated by the occasional "from the right!" opinion commentator is Fox News Channel. Liberals have responded to this one breach in the Wall of Sound by directing a vicious stream of invective toward *Fox News.*

FIVE

ADVANCE AS IF UNDER

THREAT OF ATTACK:

FOX NEWS CHANNEL

AND THE ELECTION

Liberals explicitly view the dissemination of news in America as a vehicle for left-wing indoctrination. Within the ruling oligarchy's control of television and national newspapers and magazines, there have long been only modest outlets for alternative political opinions, to wit: the *Washington Times* and the editorial page of the *Wall Street Journal.* But after years of abuse, the left has gotten used to the *Journal* and tries to ignore the *Times.*

Fox News drives them nuts.

A cable news station unbeholden to the left-wing orthodoxy presents a new marginalization challenge for liberals. Americans love TV. It's like the voice of God. The left's singular hatred for Fox News proves even they never believed their own fundamentally sophistical equation of the network news anchors with Rush Limbaugh. Still, even in pursuit of the liberal technique of always advancing as if under threat of attack, complaining of "conservative bias" on Fox News is amazingly brazen.

"Fairness & Accuracy in Reporting" (FAIR), comically dedicated to exposing conservative media bias from its headquarters in the Manhattan heartland, has been especially rigorous in ferreting out Fox News's slant.

In a shocking report released in July 2001, FAIR revealed that during the first few months of the George W. Bush administration—when the White House was Republican, the Senate was Republican, the House was Republican, and the new administration's appointees were all Republican—Brit Hume's news report interviewed almost entirely . . . Republicans! FAIR termed this discovery "breathtaking" and accused Fox News of "mislabeling a conservative news product as fair and balanced."[1]

Joan Konner, professor and dean emerita at the Columbia University Graduate School of Journalism, casually describes Fox News as "a blatantly biased, conservative news service that is challenging the longtime supremacy of the more balanced news networks."[2] Fox News may modulate slightly to the right, but the idea that its anchors betray their political predilections more than Peter Jennings or Dan Rather do is absurd.

As part of its insidious attempt at mind control, Fox News invited a protester against "conservative bias" on Fox News, Cheryl Guttman, to make her case on Fox's polluted airwaves. Her argument is quoted at length only in the interest of comedy.

> *Hannity & Colmes*'s liberal co-host, ALAN COLMES: I'd like to understand from you what your beef is.
>
> CHERYL GUTTMAN, democracymarch.org: Well, what our beef is, is that we feel that the media is really biased in a conservative fashion, even though people have been told it's biased in a liberal fashion. There were twice as many stories criticizing Gore in the election, for instance. Since . . .
>
> COLMES: All right. Go ahead. But why are you—but why are you protesting—that's all right. You're allowed to speak. But why are you protesting us? Why are you picking on Fox?
>
> GUTTMAN: Well, we feel Fox is the most egregious because they say they're fair and balanced, but studies have shown that they're more conservative.
>
> COLMES: Well, that's very interesting. Now you were saying before we got on the air here that you've never seen this show.
>
> GUTTMAN: Yes, but studies have shown. . . .
>
> *(Laughter)*

COLMES: Well, wait a minute. Wait a minute—you are putting yourself on the line. You're going out there in that street. That's today out there in front of *Fox News,* and you're protesting something that you've never even seen!

GUTTMAN: There's something else, too.

COLMES: You've never even seen the show!

GUTTMAN: No, but there's something else, too. Fox hired John Ellis, and John Ellis, who is obviously biased, called the election for Bush.

COLMES: Yeah. You know what you're doing, Cheryl? Look, I'm a liberal, and I've been attacked by liberals for being on the Fox News Channel, and liberals have been meaner to me than conservatives have because of what I do here every night. I may have to join the vast right-wing conspiracy.

Look, John Ellis—do you know that—now maybe you're dealing from talking points or things you've read since you apparently don't watch the Fox News Channel. Are you aware of the fact that John Ellis worked for NBC for about ten years prior to coming to Fox? Did you complain that NBC was conservative because John Ellis worked there?

GUTTMAN: Well, as I understand it, he quit because of a conflict of interest. So why did Fox hire him? And he was instrumental in calling the election for Bush, even though it was too close to call.

COLMES: He quit the *Boston Globe.* He didn't quit NBC.

GUTTMAN: Okay. I'm sorry.

COLMES: You ought to get your facts straight. If you're going to protest, you really ought to, first of all, watch the programming you're protesting, know what's on the channel you're protesting, and understand the facts.

GUTTMAN: I'm not—I'm not an expert. I'm an organizer, okay?

COLMES: But if you're organizing a protest and you've agreed to appear on this show to give your point of view, the fact of the matter is that John Ellis worked for the *Boston Globe.* He quit that. Prior to that, he spent ten years with NBC, and nobody complained. Why is it only when he worked for Fox News is there an uproar about it?

GUTTMAN: Because he called the election for Bush and, psychologically, people felt that means Bush won.[3]

T he Fox News protesters were not isolated nuts. They were nuts, just not isolated. The John Ellis myth quickly developed into a typical phony media scandal.

It is true that Ellis is George Bush's cousin, was employed at Fox News on election night 2000, and had talked to the candidate that night. After that, everything—everything, from the small facts to the larger implications—is demonstrably false.

Reveling in their childlike fascination with the law, journalists began tossing off phrases such as "conflict of interest" and "proprietary information" in the same breath with Ellis's name. No one ever stops to analyze liberals' legal babble to see that it is a series of incoherent factual gibes adding up to a totally contradictory account. They just keep moving fast and shouting out catchphrases to win the battle of the narrative.

In fact, the networks' open partisanship on behalf of Al Gore on election night was far more egregious than anything they impute to John Ellis in their neurotic legalistic fantasies. By prematurely and incorrectly calling Florida for Gore, the networks actually cost Bush votes. Whatever John Ellis did, he didn't do that.

If one Republican at Fox News can trump the propagandistic effect of ABC, NBC, CBS, CNN, MSNBC, and CNBC combined and swing a presidential election, the Democrats may as well give up right now.

Yet Ellis's position on the Fox News decision team became part of an all-out media witch hunt. Noticeably, the nation's editorial pulpits expressed absolutely no interest in the networks' incorrect projections for Gore. It was only the correct call for Bush that led to blinding outrage.

As the *Boston Globe* put it: "In the wake of the networks' election-night exit-poll fiasco, no one has generated more scrutiny than John Ellis, the man who heads the Fox News team responsible for figuring out the election night predictions."[4]

CNN's Judy Woodruff proclaimed: "[I]t's a conflict of interest to have someone related to the candidate in that position."[5] *Salon*'s Eric Boehlert discerned a "vast right-wing conspiracy" in Fox's hiring of "a partisan Bush cousin," claiming that "his flawed call of Florida" had created "the false impression that Bush had won the election."[6] More than six months after the election, CNN's Bill Press was still berating Ellis for the appalling act of making an accurate election-night projection.[7]

Howard Kurtz, ombudsman apologist for liberal media bias, ran a full exposé in the *Washington Post* on the Bush cousin fracas.[8] In an article headlined "Bush Cousin Made Florida Vote Call for Fox News," Kurtz said "media circles were buzzing" over the "question of why Fox had installed a Bush relative in such a sensitive post." He uttered the full mantra, saying the projection "turned out to be wrong" (it didn't) and "created the impression that Bush had 'won' the White House." (He did win, and, in any event, presidential elections aren't decided by "impressions.") At least Kurtz limited his insanity to claiming Fox News's 2:16 A.M. projection was merely "crucial." This was in contradistinction to the incorrect call for Gore while the polls were still open and that actually affected the voting. That was sharp reporting. Only the correct call for Bush cried out for its own Oliver Stone movie.

Kurtz quoted Tom Rosenstiel, identified as "Vice Chairman of the Committee of Concerned Journalists," hyperventilating that the correct call for Bush was "wrong, unnecessary, misguided, foolish, unthinkable"! (An earlier concern of the Concerned Journalist was that Roger Ailes had forced Bill Clinton to make "his speeches more malicious than they would otherwise be"—citing Paul Begala as his source.[9]) Rosenstiel also feverishly claimed that Ellis was "actually deciding" the election result. Soon Rosenstiel will be attacking weathermen who predict rain, thus "actually deciding" the weather. Indeed, Ellis would have had more capacity to effect the vote had he been a weatherman. Then at least he could have predicted rain and suppressed the Democratic vote.

And Ellis's influence would have been astronomically greater if he were a television personality like Matt Lauer propagandizing daily on NBC's *Today* show, as when he gushed to Al Gore about his phony convention kiss—"After watching that kiss I know how you survived thirty years, Mr. Vice President. Way to go!" Or if he had been ABC's Terry Moran, who asked Gore if, given his vast experience and knowledge, he was "frustrated" during the presidential debates to "look across the stage" and see George Bush.[10] Leading a team that projects election results leaves somewhat less room for forthright political propaganda.

The Minneapolis *Star Tribune* recycled the psychological advantage theory, accusing Fox News of instigating "a chain of events that led to the preliminary impression that Bush was the winner."[11] Representative Henry Waxman (D-Cal.) denounced the call for creating a "presumption that George Bush won the election."[12]

Even the left's pop culture scrub team was promoting the ludicrous psychological boost theory. Movie reviewer Roger Ebert took a break from scribbling tributes to *Booty Call* to denounce the Republicans for having "establish[ed] effective 'memes'; in the minds of the public and the pundits" persuading them that Bush had won. A "meme," he explained, "is like a gene, except that instead of advancing through organisms, it moves through minds."[13]

Of course, one other factor that simply cannot be discounted as a factor in helping create the "impression" that Bush won is that he won. He won the original count in Florida. He won three recounts, including two exclusively in Democrat bastions (in violation of the Constitution's Equal Protection Clause, according to seven Justices of the U.S. Supreme Court). He won the count of the absentee ballots. He won the watchdog media's interminable recounts conducted for one full year after the election. He even won on the *New York Times*'s unique vote-counting method that involved throwing out military ballots.[14] So that's something to consider.

Marvin Kalb of Harvard's Shorenstein press center criticized Fox News for creating the "wrong impression" by hiring Ellis. While this quote appeared in a Howard Kurtz *Washington Post* column (high degree of skepticism necessary), Kalb's remarks were consistent with the tenor of the general media caterwauling. Having a cousin of Bush's in the news business was wrong, Kalb said, because Ellis would "seem to be the one making the call."

Without performing any in-depth investigation—such as asking Paul Begala—I believe one possible explanation for why Ellis might "seem" to be the one making the call is that everyone in the press kept saying Ellis was the one making the call.

Whenever liberals' lies are about to be exposed, they blame the target of their lies for having created the circumstances that allowed liberals to lie about them. This is often known as creating "an appearance of impropriety." It was Fox News's fault for hiring Ellis, because by hiring Ellis, Fox opened the door for liberals to falsely accuse Ellis of throwing the election to Bush.

Ellis was also incongruously blamed for embroidering his role. Amid a litany of his treacheries detailed in the *Washington Post,* Fox News staffers were described as "angry at what they see as Ellis exaggerating his role."[15] This was in an article titled "Bush Cousin Made Florida Vote Call for Fox News." Wait—so did Ellis have a big role in making the Florida call or was it a small role that he was exaggerating?

There are advantages to controlling the media: Eventually the head of Fox News was required to defend its employment of Ellis in a congressional hearing.

Fox News's 2:16 A.M. call for Bush violated no ethical standards nor—as we now know—was it inaccurate. The most that could be said about it is that it gave Bush some amorphous "psychological" advantage.

Any statement about an election after the polls are closed can have absolutely no effect on the vote total. Nor did liberals ever claim otherwise. Rather they blathered incoherently about the supernatural "psychological" influence of mystical "memes." By contrast, calling Florida for Gore while Florida polls were still open had a substantive effect on the outcome. Not only did the networks erroneously announce that Gore had won Florida, but they repeatedly declared that the polls were closed in Florida when they were not. CBS News alone announced eighteen times that the polls were closed in Florida during the last hour the polls were still open.[16]

Three separate studies have confirmed the blinding obvious fact that by calling Florida for Gore beginning at 7:49 P.M. the networks suppressed thousands of votes in the heavily Republican Florida Panhandle and cost Bush votes.

Looking at Republican and Democratic voting patterns across Florida in every presidential election since 1976, economist John Lott compared the vote in the Panhandle to that in the rest of the state in the 2000 election. He found "an unusual drop-off in Republican voting rates in Florida's 10 western Panhandle counties in 2000."[17] The drop-off was evident relative to both the prior presidential elections and the rest of the state. Lott estimated that the erroneous projection for Gore cost Bush between 10,000 to 37,000 votes.[18]

A poll of Panhandle voters conducted by John McLaughlin & Associates also concluded that the early projection for Gore cost Bush about ten thousand votes. Evidently, many Republican Panhandle voters went home after hearing confident assertions that their votes were irrelevant, anyway— or even that the polls had closed. (As Dan Rather had assured CBS viewers on election night: "If we say somebody's carried the state, you can take that to the bank.")

Even a study commissioned by Democrat strategist Bob Beckel found that Bush suffered a net loss of eight thousand votes in the western Panhandle because of the premature, inaccurate call for Gore.[19] (Beckel later made news when he tried to persuade Bush electors to switch their votes to Gore.)

The networks were dramatically, viciously wrong about their phony projection for Gore, and have never apologized for dragging the nation through an election crisis of their own creation. To the contrary, the big question for the media was whether a cousin of George Bush's tricked Fox News into (correctly) calling Florida for Bush fifty-five seconds before the next stations to call it, long after the polls had closed, long after most people had gone to bed, and thereby gave Bush a "psychological" advantage, helping "create the suggestion" that he had won.

Like most liberal propaganda, the accusation against John Ellis started with a wee little wisp of truth and immediately dovetailed into an ocean of lies.

First, and most painfully obvious, network decision teams don't sit around drinking piña coladas all day and shout out winners when the mood strikes them. Calling elections is a number-crunching process involving scores of analysts both inside and outside the network. One lone analyst could not single-handedly decide any election-night projections. There are literally hundreds, maybe thousands of people involved in the process of gathering and analyzing election-night data.

The now-notorious Voter News Service, used by all the networks, assembles sample precinct data and raw vote totals from every state and county in America. That data gets plugged into computer analyses continuously throughout election day to produce statistical estimates of probable outcomes all over the country. Four people on the Fox News decision team were methodically analyzing the VNS data and—this being the media—the other three were Democrats.

Fox News had been the third network to project a Gore win in Florida earlier in the evening. Was that erroneous call a clever ruse to throw everyone off the scent before Ellis sneakily threw the election for Bush at 2:16 A.M.?

In a major report on how the networks had blundered into making a correct call for Bush at two in the morning, the *Los Angeles Times* suggestively reported that the networks were "following the lead of Fox News—where Bush's first cousin John Ellis worked as an analyst." The theory that John Ellis was single-handedly responsible for Fox News's projection is fatuous enough. The idea that he was responsible for the projections of all the other networks requires something of a conspiratorial mind-set. But as explained by Concerned Propagandist Rosenstiel, after Fox called the election for Bush, the other networks were "pressured by Fox's decision" to call the state for Bush, too. That "collective error helped create the suggestion of a race won by Bush."[20]

It was a "suggestion" made all the more insidious by virtue of being true.

It is, after all, an incontrovertible fact that Fox News was right: Bush won. At no point from the moment Fox News called Florida for Bush—even after endless media-sponsored recounts continuing one year into the Bush administration—did Gore ever surpass Bush's lead.

But moreover, not only would all the other "decision desk" analysts at Fox have had to be part of the malevolent Ellis conspiracy, but VNS would have had to be in on it, too. When Fox News called Florida for Bush, the VNS numbers indicated—accurately, as it turns out—that it would be impossible for Gore to overcome Bush's lead. By 1:30 A.M., with 95 percent of Florida's precincts counted, VNS had Bush winning with about a sixty thousand–vote lead.[21] At 2:00 A.M. Gore would have needed to win 64 percent of the remaining 5 percent of votes to surpass Bush's lead.

Under normal circumstances, the decision desks at every network would have called Florida for Bush as soon as Gore's incoming votes began to fall below 64 percent. As the few remaining precincts were reported, Gore was only getting 60 percent and his numbers continued to shrink. Florida should have been called for Bush.[22] But, oddly enough, though all the networks were looking at the same VNS data, something was preventing them from calling the state for Bush. It was not until Fox News broke the logjam and projected Florida for Bush that the other networks followed—and with some alacrity.

If Gore had been the one in the lead with the same numbers, Fox News would not have had to be the first to give Florida to Bush. We know that because when Gore had a less impressive lead earlier in the evening, all the networks did give Florida to Gore.

The left's conspiracy theory holds that the rapid calls for Bush by the other networks were all part of John Ellis's devilish plan. Somehow Fox's projection forced—forced—the other networks to call Florida for Bush. ABC, NBC, and CBS announced that Bush had won only because Fox had, and pay no attention to the VNS numbers showing Bush had won. But the fly in the Xanax is, there was evidently no such competitive pressure earlier in the evening with the (incorrect) projection for Gore. Florida was a do-or-die state. If Bush lost in Florida, short of divine intervention, he would have lost the election. NBC was the first to incorrectly project a Gore win in Florida at 7:49. CNN waited six minutes to incorrectly project Gore—an eternity in election projections. ABC waited an interminable thirteen minutes to make the incorrect call.[23]

So it is telling that—unlike the early evening projection for Gore—when Fox called Florida for Bush at 2:16:46 A.M., it opened the floodgates.

Within three minutes and forty-one seconds, every other network had made the same call. NBC and CBS had the Bush victory up within sixty seconds of Fox News.[24] Executives from the other networks uniformly denied being influenced by Fox's projection.[25] They may have other reasons for saying so, but it has to be admitted, a case can be made that it was not Fox, but the fact that Bush had won Florida, that persuaded the networks to project that Bush had won Florida. The networks had ponied up millions of dollars for the VNS service. It's not insane to think they were using it.

The only serious question was how all the networks had managed to project Gore the winner of Florida earlier in the evening, incorrectly, leading directly to a national crisis that nearly upset a two-centuries-old orderly transfer of power.

Naturally, therefore, the watchdog media concentrated like a laser beam on . . . John Ellis, for his sinister role in helping Fox News accurately project Bush the winner of Florida.

The accusation against Ellis is a pristine example of left-wing scandal-mongering. The allegation is meaningless, even if true. But the truth of the charge doesn't matter once it has ricocheted through the media sound chamber. All that anyone can remember is that some Republican had to extricate himself from a morass of allegations portraying him as some sort of legal malefactor. This is propaganda by the book: The incessant, mind-numbing repetition "exceeds the individual's capacities for attention or adaptation and thus his capabilities of resistance."[26]

Every conservative public figure would need a full-time investigative and legal staff to refute the endless stream of defamatory attacks. By the time the insinuations are exposed as baseless nonsense, it's old news, yesterday's story; the media has "moved on." Meanwhile it takes DNA evidence that the president lied under oath to get the media to take note of malfeasance by a fellow liberal.

It didn't take long for the opinion cartel to begin improving upon the story of John Ellis, Evil Malefactor. Their feigned outrage about a Bush cousin working at Fox News was too preposterous for anyone but Howard Kurtz to believe. Thus, in short order, Ellis was also accused of engaging in unethical conduct for having talked to his cousin George W. Bush on election night.

Far from unethical, Bush was a fabulous contact. Political sources provide information VNS numbers can't. Bush would be gathering his own intelligence directly from governors about voting trends, precinct analyses, recent electoral shifts, and so on.[27] All network decision teams would be trying to gather the exact same information—including the ones who later allowed Ellis to be slandered for having a better contact than they did.

The only thing Ellis couldn't do was give proprietary VNS data to Bush—or anyone outside of Fox News. This is a well-known prohibition, certainly well known to someone like Ellis, who had covered three presidential elections at NBC News from 1978 to 1989. That Ellis talked to Bush is not evidence that he violated the VNS agreement any more than walking into a bank is evidence that you robbed it. But the irrelevant fact that Ellis talked to Bush quickly transmogrified into the baseless claim that Ellis had, in fact, given Bush proprietary VNS information.

The lead paragraph in one of the *New York Times*'s election articles was this: "Senior executives for the Fox News Channel acknowledged last night that John Ellis, an executive who played a central role in the first decision on election night to project that George W. Bush had won the presidency, and who is a first cousin of Mr. Bush, spent much of the night in communication with the candidate."[28]

Days later, *Times* columnist Paul Krugman elevated the insinuation from the *Times*'s "Hysterical Jeremiad Election Series" to hard fact: "John Ellis, the political analyst now notorious for his inappropriate role at Fox News . . . gave Mr. Bush confidential poll information."[29]

This was a pure smear—completely unsubstantiated and utterly implausible. Ellis's professionalism and integrity had never before been questioned. He expressly denied violating the VNS agreement in a detailed account of the evening. No evidence was ever produced contradicting him.

The accusation exhibited all the earmarks of paranoid liberal reasoning. Even if this "proprietary information" yarn were true—and it wasn't—it still wouldn't have altered the fact that Bush won. (Unless Bush has supernatural powers to change county vote totals, in which case we are *so* lucky to have him as our president!) Liberals might as well have accused Ellis of padding his Fox News expense account and thereby somehow throwing the election to his cousin.

The beauty of a calumny like that against Ellis is that it's too boring and complicated for the average citizen to listen to for more than ten seconds. The purported infraction always has the aroma of criminality, but the precise details of the indictment are too tedious for anyone to follow. Only liberals could use ennui as a weapon. Using conspiratorial, but actually meaningless, language, liberals blacken the opposition with the very irrelevancy of their charges. They toss out vague unproved allegations, claim the accused "acknowledged" or "did not disavow" some noncontroversial point, and by their indignant tone of voice besmirch a person's reputation. In paranoid liberal fantasies, this is pretty much how McCarthyism worked.

C lassic propaganda "can approve today what it condemned yesterday."[30] Modern liberals have gotten it down to a matter of hours. On election night, they condemned at 2 A.M. what they had approved at 7 P.M. The incorrect 7 P.M. projection actually altered the vote tally in a presidential election. It was made before the polls had closed. It was wrong. It violated a 1985 agreement with Congress not to announce a state's results before the polls had closed in that state.[31] It was based on data from less than 2 percent of Florida precincts.

Media propagandists called the incorrect projection for Gore merely "a technical problem," but said the correct call for Bush later in the evening "really humiliated" the networks."[32] No one knows the name of anyone involved in election projections at 7 P.M. There have been well over four hundred news items about the contemptible John Ellis. This is despite the fact that the early call for Gore should have raised red flags all over the media. When ABC called Florida for Gore, three ABC analysts were warning against it.[33]

The Associated Press called Florida for Gore even though its own internal numbers had Bush winning—but it refused to call Florida for Bush later in the evening when both its internal numbers and the VNS numbers showed Bush the winner.[34] Evidently, the AP was suddenly seized with doubts about VNS's methodology only when it showed Bush the winner. For doggedly resisting calling Florida for Bush, the AP was praised in the *Los Angeles Times.*[35] The fact that AP projected a Gore win in Florida when its own internal numbers had Bush in the lead went unremarked upon.

One rara avis that mentioned the pro-Gore bias in election projections referred to "media-conspiracy theorists" *on both sides:* "One side complained that the networks skewed coverage to help Gore. Others blasted Fox News Channel for tapping a George W. Bush cousin to run its election-night 'decision desk.' "[36] Some say the media is liberal, some say it's conservative, so who's to say? Indeed, it's not easy to remember which network first made the incorrect call for Gore. All the networks are blamed jointly for the incorrect Gore projection.

Liberals are so obsessed with the psychological effect of their own loud-mouthed propaganda that it never occurred to them that Fox News might have called Florida for Bush because Bush had won. The networks announce election projections tactically, as political strategy. Naturally, they assumed Fox News had to be doing the same. We would never have known this, but for their vicious attack on John Ellis.

This is what happened on election night 2000: Throughout the evening, Gore's wins were posted rapidly, but all of Bush's wins consistently demanded further study. This intriguing phenomenon might have been written off as a coincidence if liberals hadn't revealed their own modus operandi by declaring war on John Ellis at Fox News.

Gore won Maine by 5 percentage points and was declared the winner within 10 minutes of the polls closing. Bush won Colorado by 9 points; it took CNN 2 hours and 41 minutes to make that call. Even Bush's 15-point margin of victory in Alabama took CNN 25 minutes to project. Bush won North Carolina by 13 points; CNN waited 39 minutes to announce a winner. Bush won Georgia by 12 points; CNN waited 59 minutes.

These were not anomalies.

Arizona, Bush . . . . 7 points (51–44)—2 hours, 51 minutes
Michigan, Gore . . . . 4 points (51–47)—1 hour, 24 minutes

Arkansas, Bush . . . . 6 points (51–45)—3 hours, 42 minutes
Pennsylvania, Gore   . . . . 4 points (51–47)—1 hour, 24 minutes

Tennessee, Bush   . . . . 3 points (51–48)—3 hours, 3 minutes
Minnesota, Gore . . . . 2 points (48–46)—1 hour, 25 minutes

West Virginia, Bush   . . . . 6 points (52–46)—3 hours, 16 minutes
Washington, Gore   . . . . . 5 points (50–45)—1 hour, 8 minutes[37]

No matter how the projections are compared, there was a consistent rush to declare states for Gore throughout the night. Some states were called immediately upon the polls closing; among those, Gore's average margin of victory was 18 points. Bush's average was 26 points. Indeed, it took the networks more time to give Bush states he won by 12, 9, or 7 points than to give Gore a state he lost (Florida: 52 minutes).[38]

If you were trying to conceive of an experiment to test whether the networks' rapid-fire calls for Gore and languid election projections for Bush were a meaningless fluke or steely-eyed political strategy, you couldn't do better than being the first to announce Bush had won at two in the morning, and waiting to see if liberals accused you of a political dirty trick. Their intricate analysis of how calling Florida for Bush at 2:16 A.M. created an unstoppable Zeitgeist, a psychological boost, an impression that began the steamroller for Bush, exposed their own motives behind the quick projections for Gore.

Liberals conceive of news reporting as political propaganda and assume, therefore, that everyone else does, too. Their entire election-night coverage was an aggressive partisan campaign on behalf of Gore.

The left's tendentious naming process is pure political strategy. They think words can alter reality. This was evident in the highly edifying explanations of Florida law during the election mess that liberals had created.

Contrary to anything reported in the mainstream media at the time, Florida law explicitly required Katherine Harris, the Florida Secretary of State, to certify the vote on November 14, seven days after the election. The law states, for example: "If the county returns are not received by the Department of State by 5 P.M. of the seventh day following an election, all missing counties *shall be ignored* and the results shown by the returns on file shall be certified" (Section 102.111).

And again it provides: "Deadline [note helpful title] returns *must* be filed by 5 P.M. on the 7th day following the ... general election." (Section 102.112).

Another section granted Harris discretion to refuse late returns. The discretion resided solely with the secretary of state, not to be confused with "the Florida Supreme Court," "the U.S. Supreme Court," "CBS News," or "the Gore campaign": "If the returns are not received by the Department [of State] by the time specified, such returns may be ignored and the results on file at that time may be certified by the department."

There are a lot of murky, complex issues in the law. This wasn't one of them. The *New York Times* referred to these blindingly clear statutory provisions as "the Republicans *contention* that state law allowed no leeway in the deadline." Unambiguous statements of the law are known as Republican "contentions."

In accordance with the law, Harris certified the election returns on November 14. But seven days was not enough time for Gore to steal the election. Though he had lost the election, lost the recount within seven days, and also lost the third manual recount to the point permitted by law, two weeks after the election Gore was asking the Florida Supreme Court

(SCOFLA) to give him yet a fourth time at bat. And they did. SCOFLA simply "interpreted" the words "seven days" in the statute to mean "seventeen days." That actually happened.

Liberals believe hard statutory deadlines are valid only when the Democrat wins. But if the Democrat loses, deadlines are merely helpful suggestions. Gore had lost under the law, so the opinion cartel set about defining the unambiguous seven-day deadline imposed by Florida law as optional. Just a suggestion. Nonbinding thoughts tossed out by the legislature.

Since the media behemoth was now describing a straightforward statement of the law as a Republican "contention," Harris had no choice but to submit to SCOFLA's illegitimate, unlawful, not to say risible extension of the clear statutory deadline. This was despite Harris's insistent protestations that she believed her original certification made seven days after the election—in accordance with the law—was the legally binding one. But Gore still lost.

Thus it was even more stunning that when Gore lost the illegitimate fourth ballot count—unlawfully ordered by SCOFLA and cheered on by the media—the left's own invented deadline suddenly became the personal beliefs of the secretary of state. In the inestimable reporting of CBS News anchor Dan Rather, the second certification was all Harris's idea:

> The reason we're on the air right across the board nationally right now is because Florida's secretary of state, who—Republican, as we mentioned before, campaigned actively for George Bush, well connected to the—governor—Bush's governor brother, Jeb Bush in Florida, . . . she will certify, as she sees it, who gets Florida's 25 electoral votes. . . . Vice President Al Gore leads in the national popular vote. He leads in the Electoral College vote. . . . What's happening here is that the certification, as the Florida secretary of state sees it . . . it will be, in at least the opinion of the secretary of state, that the results will be final. The secretary of state, as she has restated here, in effect, believes that the election certification that she gives should stand. . . . This is the secretary of state and others certifying the statewide outcome, as they view it.[39]

Rather didn't wait even a decent few hours to issue contradictory propaganda. In the midst of the "her view" miasma, Rather admitted that Harris "has said the certification she wanted to give on November 14th should stand." So whose idea was the November 24 certification, anyway?

A month after the left's attempted election grab had been thwarted,

Diane Sawyer was still bitter. In an interview, Sawyer even-handedly intro-duced Harris thus: "From Day One she seemed completely inflexible, insist-ing on the narrow letter of the law. She enforced strict deadlines even when one county asked for just two hours more, and she tried to block the hand recount of those punched but disputed ballots. The Bush team was thrilled, the Gore team was outraged."[40]

Fortunately the Supreme Court was outraged, too—not by Harris fol-lowing the law, but by SCOFLA's utter disregard for clear statutory dead-lines. Without institutional boundaries to curtail endless navel-gazing, the left would rule by force. The law imposes rules precisely so that liberals can-not endlessly jawbone hypothetical possibilities until they have their way. The Supreme Court, normally revered by the left for its capacity to bypass democracy, had thwarted the will of a determined liberal press.

But the press would have its revenge. The court's rather unexceptional ruling was widely derided in the media as a "coup d'etat,"[41] an "injustice,"[42] the "Dred Scott of the 21st century," and a "de-legitimation of the authority of the court."[43] It was evidence of "political partisanship where there was sup-posed to be none."[44] The Supreme Court itself was said to be "historically scarred."[45] It was widely claimed that the "right-wing majority cared more about its own retirement schedule than about the institution itself."[46] A Bush presidency had been "rammed down our throats by Antonin Scalia."[47] The blabocracy angrily vowed that the ruling would be "the subject of contro-versy for years to come."[48] All this from the people who think the court cov-ered itself in honor with a lawless and divided ruling in *Roe v. Wade.*

Liberals have used their control of the media to force one U.S. president to resign and to prevent another president from being removed—despite the far more scandalous conduct of Bill Clinton compared to Richard Nixon. A vicious media campaign kept Judge Robert Bork off the Supreme Court and has kept many other conservative judges off the lower courts. The left's hys-terical news coverage curtailed any tinkering with the Leviathan attempted by Newt Gingrich and a Republican Congress. But the 2000 election marked the first time the left had used its hegemony over the media to try to trump the electoral college. When the coup failed, the press blamed John Ellis and right-wing bias in the media.

SIX

SAMIZDAT MEDIA

Liberals don't try to win arguments, they seek to destroy their opponents and silence dissident opinions. The monopoly media of television, newspapers, and magazines can inflict liberals on the public without paying a price. Noticeably, however, liberals fail in any media realm where there is competition. In the three media where success is determined on the free market—radio, books, and the Internet—conservatives rule. A competitive marketplace in speech has the ominous effect of producing Rush Limbaugh. Only a monopoly could produce Dan Rather.

It is a source of never-ending irritation to liberals that Americans like to hear conservatives. Liberals are like the dog food company president who furiously demands to know why their dog food isn't selling. "We've got the snappiest jingles," he rails, "the best agronomists, the slickest advertising campaign, the best billboards, and the flashiest labels! Why aren't people buying our dog food?" Finally, an employee meekly explains: "The dogs don't like it."

Having denied liberal bias in the media by parading Rush Limbaugh as the equivalent of Tom Brokaw, Peter Jennings, Dan Rather, Katie Couric, Matt Lauer, Bryant Gumbel, *Time, Newsweek,* the *New York Times,* the *Washington Post,* and so on, liberals then undermine their own specious equation by training a torrent of abuse on Rush Limbaugh and other popular conservative voices. Thus, Rush Limbaugh has been blamed for the Oklahoma City bombing. The editorial page of the *Wall Street Journal* was accused of driving Vince Foster to suicide. Fox News is charged with plotting to steal a national election. Matt Drudge is evidently accused of extracting semen from Bill Clinton and placing it on Monica Lewinsky's dress. That is what liberals believe psychologically: They simply feel that Drudge's scoop on Clinton's "essence" should have been false, just like the Tawana Brawley hoax should have been true.

Katie Couric has blamed conservative speech for the vicious murders of James Byrd Jr. in Texas and Matthew Shepard in Wyoming.[1] Painting conservative speech as a source of imminent danger helps lay the groundwork for the left's larger point that conservative speech is not "speech." But despite the fact that liberals strongly disapprove of conservative speech—and I mean strongly—wherever there is consumer choice, the public keeps choosing conservatives.

Liberals try to extend their monopoly over the elite media to the competitive media with nauseating cross-promotions of any and all liberals. There is absolutely no dreary leftist to come down the pike who will not instantly be acclaimed as a poet. Even the vicious smearing of conservatives is not as insufferable as the suck-up profiles and interviews of liberals: *How can you be so honest?*[2] There are fabulous sycophantic write-ups in the *New York Times*, gushing interviews on the *Today* show, celebrity-status profiles in *Time, Newsweek,* and *Vanity Fair.* If the antitrust laws were applied to the endless cross-promotions of leftists in the media, *Vanity Fair*—to say nothing of the *New York Times Book Review*—would be shut down.

Finally, the self-appointed champions of free speech come to the realization that hectoring alone will not shut down the Samizdat press. It must be regulated. The First Amendment protects taxpayer-funded photos of bullwhips up men's anuses. It says nothing about Matt Drudge. University of Chicago law professor Cass Sunstein argues in his book *Republic.com* that by allowing people to choose "what they want to read, see, and hear," the Internet is a threat to "a well-functioning system of democratic deliberation."[3] It's never *Debbie Does Dallas* or the publication of classified Pentagon documents that provoke such urgent re-examinations of the First Amendment. When liberals warn that free speech imperils "the capacity of citizens to govern themselves," you know conservatives must be opening their yaps again.

When impeached former president Bill Clinton identified Rush Limbaugh as the cause of the Oklahoma City bombing, he unleashed all the typical liberal curse words for conservatives. He blamed "loud and angry voices" heard "over the airwaves in America" that were making people "paranoid" and spreading "hate."[4] Clinton couldn't have been more specific if he had fingered "that guy Al Franken called a big fat idiot."

It was perfectly clear, for example, to Dan Rather, who said, "President Clinton named no names, but made it clear who's talking that talk."[5] It was also clear to Bryant Gumbel, who made the very same point the next day on the *Today* show. Lacking Clinton's nuance, Gumbel said: "The bombing in Oklahoma City has focused renewed attention on the rhetoric that's been coming from the right. . . . Right-wing talk-show hosts like Rush Limbaugh, Bob Grant, Oliver North, G. Gordon Liddy, Michael Reagan, and others take to the air every day with basically the same format: detail a problem, blame the government or a group, and invite invective from like-minded people. Never do most of the radio hosts encourage outright violence, but the extent to which their attitudes may embolden and encourage some extremists has clearly become an issue."[6] A philosophy professor at Hollins College, Peter S. Fosl, ponderously compared "Rush Limbaugh, Newt Gingrich and other conservative media personalities" to "the Hutu broadcasters who urged on Rwandan militias in their deadly business."[7]

When conservative talk show hosts did not instantly admit complicity in the bombing, but instead objected to the president's gratuitous attack, it became a generalized catfight between liberals and conservatives. Ombudsman of the Liberal Consensus Howard Kurtz commented on the president's ridiculous accusation by criticizing both sides in "this partisan blame game."[8]

Paradoxically, about the time President Bill Clinton was denouncing conservative talk radio hosts as "promoters of paranoia" whose "loud and angry voices" led like night into day to the Oklahoma City bombing,[9] practically every big-name liberal was clamoring for the opportunity to become the next Rush Limbaugh. The very week the president was blaming talk radio for the Oklahoma City bombing, Harvard professor Alan Dershowitz was promoting his own talk radio show. Reminiscing about liberals' favorite mythological event, Dershowitz began fulminating about attacks on speech "in the McCarthy era."[10] He was not referring to the president who had just launched a direct attack on the free speech of talk radio hosts—but to the talk radio hosts. (Always advance as if under threat of attack.) It seems the talk show hosts were guilty of "hypocrisy." When in doubt, accuse conservatives of hypocrisy. Conservatives may give lip service to "free speech and civil liberties," Dershowitz explained, but in fact they were hypocrites. They were hypocrites not because of anything the talk show hosts had ever said or done, but because, according to Dershowitz, conservatives "would" be "trying to stop the left from speaking" if it were the McCarthy era.

In a classic cross-promotion, *Vanity Fair* included Dershowitz in its 1996 "radio stars" of "Hall of Fame."[11] Dershowitz's show was canceled less than a year later. Liberals had tried to extend their monopoly of the elite media to the competitive radio media, but the dogs didn't like it.

That same year, both Gary Hart and former Connecticut Governor Lowell Weicker got their own radio shows. Both were billed as a "response to Rush Limbaugh." As the silver-tongued Weicker put it, they planned to "respond to the unanswered BS that is all over the country."[12] Hart and Weicker were rhapsodically feted in the establishment media. Finally, the public would be able to hear what liberals think! To mark the occasion, CNN repeatedly ran a Judy Woodruff interview with the intrepid pioneers.[13] A few months later, both radio shows had fizzled.

Another Great White Hope for liberal talk radio was Mario Cuomo, former Democratic governor of New York. Cuomo was given a giddy send-off on *CBS This Morning*. In the "adversarial press" tradition, Cuomo was hit with a tough question by CBS host Harry Smith: "Will you continue to use this passion, will you continue to use this eloquence?"[14] Clinton flack Paul Begala explained Cuomo's irresistible appeal: "If you were to construct on paper what our side needs, the computer would spit out Mario Cuomo." Cuomo had it all: "He's brilliant, he's articulate, he's funny, he's feisty."[15] Naturally, he was touted as the "counterbalance to Rush Limbaugh."

Cuomo was a bigger flop even than all the other Limbaugh wannabes. Cuomo's show—"the liberals' answer to Rush," as it was promoted—consistently ranked at the bottom of the quarterly Arbitron ratings. The show was canceled just over a year after it began.[16]

Perhaps the most heavily promoted Alternative-to-Limbaugh was Jim Hightower, the former Texas agriculture commissioner. Hightower was regularly compared to Rush Limbaugh and Michael Reagan in the mainstream media (except not a jerk like them!). Thus, *The Nation* avidly hawked Hightower as the "long-awaited relief from Rush-polluted airwaves," and pleaded with its readers to please tune in![17]

What put Hightower in the tradition of these "fellow radio stars," as one newspaper flattered Hightower, was that he had a book. The difference was, of course, that Hightower's book had "wit and wisdom—as opposed to

Limbaugh's canned recitations of corporate mantras and Reagan's tortured attempts to forge a print relationship with his father."[18] The other difference, based on hard fact rather than liberal sneering, was that Limbaugh's and Reagan's books were runaway best-sellers. Limbaugh's was number one on the *New York Times* best-seller list for over a year. The only "best-seller" list Hightower ever made anywhere was at a single bookstore in Albany. He made that prestigious list for one week.

An article in *Mother Jones* magazine attributed Hightower's unpopularity with radio listeners to an invisible force that kept him "locked out of major urban areas." The same article said Limbaugh's success was due to his "pandering" to listeners.[19] Liberals have thus accused Limbaugh both of being manipulated by his audience and of manipulating them—to blow up buildings, for example.

The "pandering" accusation was interesting. It raised the intriguing possibility that the mysterious force holding Hightower back was his unpopularity with listeners. Could the invisible force be the hidden hand of the market? After Hightower was finally canceled, both *Mother Jones* and Hightower were still relentlessly pursuing the riddle of the free market. A *Mother Jones* interviewer asked Hightower, "Do you think it's possible for a show like yours to actually attract advertisers?" Hightower responded, "We're exploring that right now."[20]

Until his show was canceled, Hightower recognized that consumer choice determines success on radio, extolling radio as a "very democratic little box."[21] But when Hightower was canceled through lack of audience interest, he blamed "program directors and general managers," who think, "Hey, Rush Limbaugh seems to be working, I need a Limbaugh, too."[22] That is a pretty good working definition of how capitalism produces goods and services that people want.

Meanwhile, all of Limbaugh's conservative rivals have skyrocketed while taking none of his audience. Of the "top ten" radio shows in ratings—and there are actually twenty-seven on account of ties—nine are political shows. Eight of the nine are conservative. This includes, of course, Rush Limbaugh, consistently ranked as the most-listened-to radio show, followed by G. Gordon Liddy, Mike Siegel, Neal Boortz, Mike Gallagher, Michael Savage, Matt Drudge, and Michael Reagan.[23]

In July 1995, Cuomo and Gary Hart were laboring along on one lonely radio station apiece. Former Virginia Governor Douglas Wilder was stuck at eight stations. Jerry Brown was the liberal talk radio champion with forty-two stations. That same year, Pat Buchanan was on 170 stations, Oliver North on 122, and Rush Limbaugh was heard on well over 600 stations.[24]

It's curious how difficult it is to obtain information on LexisNexis about the failure of liberal talk radio hosts. It is easy to track every single radio station that has ever canceled a conservative talk show host because those cancellations will be played up as evidence of a national trend. When one tiny little station with one hundred listeners in Ohio cancels Rush Limbaugh, there are breathless headlines—"Station is not amused, pulls plug on Limbaugh."[25] But liberal market failures are immediately washed down the memory hole. Consequently, though the dates are murky, among the liberal talk radio hosts who have been canceled are Jerry Brown, Ed Koch, Mario Cuomo, Lowell Weicker, Alan Dershowitz, Gary Hart, Jim Hightower, and Douglas Wilder.

The one ceaseless liberal presence in this sea of consumer choice is National Public Radio—which is largely sheltered from market forces by the government. NPR stations are subsidized by the government, and most beneficially, they do not have to compete in any meaningful sense for their FCC licenses. Evidently, ABC, CBS, NBC, and every major newspaper and magazine in the nation is not a sufficiently powerful propaganda machine.

Even long after the crazed, cost-cutting, Grinch Republicans took a hatchet to "public" funding of liberal radio, the Corporation for Public Broadcasting was receiving hundreds of millions of dollars in taxpayer money, with more coming.[26] "Public" broadcasting typically receives more than 36 percent of its funding from forced taxpayer "support."[27] If you can't beat them, pay yourself with tax revenues.

Radio may not be the beautiful dog-eat-dog capitalism of the Internet, but consumers have more choices than ABC, NBC, and CBS. Even with the increasing consolidation of radio stations into a few big corporate hands, there are more than a thousand talk radio stations. *New York Times* columnist Thomas L. Friedman has expounded upon the democracy-promoting properties of the radio. The "real information revolution," he said, is in radio. Give them radio and the people "will do the rest."[28] He was talking about dictatorships in West African countries, but it seems to work just as well right here in America in circumventing the left's media dictatorship.

Book publishing has long been another method for the ruling class to take in one another's laundry and give each other jobs. Vast agglomerations of money are deployed to publish and promote liberal authors. National magazines and newspapers give hallucinatory reviews of books by their fellow liberals and snub books by conservatives. Ludicrous uncompensated advances are made to support liberal authors, and liberal jeremiads make it to print without the most cursory fact-checking.

Meanwhile, the entire information industry works overtime to suppress conservative books. The left's control of the monopoly media has its greatest crossover effect on books. While the radio and Internet can bring conservatives to people's homes with the flick of a dial or modem, conservative books have to clear three sets of liberal censors before making their way to readers. First the books have to be published. Then the public has to know the book exists. Finally, potential readers have to find a bookstore where they can buy it. All this is complicated by the fact that publishers don't like conservative books, the major media ignore them, and bookstores refuse to stock them.

But, frustratingly, liberals can't stop Americans from buying conservative books. Once a book has been published, even monopoly control of the establishment media can't repeal the free market. Inasmuch as mainstream publishing houses would prefer to ignore the free market entirely and publish only books with the hectoring anger of a *New York Times* editorial, publishers hide sales figures. Arbitron ratings are public, Nielsen ratings are public, movie box office numbers are public, but book sales are treated like Coca-Cola's secret formula. Try finding out how many copies of Frank Rich's flop of a book *Ghost Light* sold.

Still, some facts are available on the public record and they add up to a grim picture. Mistakes can be made even in industries not driven by ideological zeal. But in publishing it's striking how it's always the same mistakes. Though regularly rejected by the big publishers with marketing muscle, conservative books keep ending up on the best-seller lists. The best-seller lists themselves are biased against conservative books by virtue of excluding books sold through Christian bookstores—about one third of all bookstores—as well as books sold through book clubs.[29]

Not all books by conservatives are best-sellers, but conservative books are vastly more popular with book consumers than they are with book publishers. Indeed, the empirical evidence does not contradict the thesis that conservatives read books and liberals don't. While the typical nonfiction best-seller is about cats or diets, substantial, serious books by conservatives have sold well for half a century. The average nonfiction book sells about five thousand copies, and a best-seller is generally one that sells thirty thousand copies or more. These are the sales figures for some conservative classics:

Conservative Best-Sellers	Copies Sold
Friedrich Hayek, *The Road to Serfdom* (1944)	206,000
William F. Buckley Jr., *God and Man at Yale* (1951)	69,700
Whittaker Chambers, *Witness* (1952)	unknown
	(became an instant best-seller)
Russell Kirk, *The Conservative Mind* (1953)	37,750
Ayn Rand, *Atlas Shrugged* (1957)	4,132,000
Barry Goldwater, *Conscience of a Conservative* (1960)	3,500,000
Phyllis Schlafly, *A Choice, Not an Echo* (1964)	3,000,000
Edward C. Banfield, *The Unheavenly City* (1970)	+100,000
William E. Simon, *A Time for Truth* (1978)	unknown
	(sold more than 150,000 in hardcover)
Milton Friedman, *Free to Choose* (1979)	1,240,000
George Gilder, *Wealth and Poverty* (1981)	350,000
Francis August Schaeffer, *A Christian Manifesto* (1981)	312,000[30]

Among the *New York Times* best-sellers only since 1999 and only out of tiny little Regnery Publishing are: David Limbaugh's *Absolute Power: The Legacy of Corruption in the Clinton-Reno Justice Department;* Bill Sammon's *At Any Cost: How Gore Tried to Steal the Election;* Bill Gertz's *Betrayal: How the Clinton Administration Undermined American Security;* Bernard Goldberg's *Bias;* Barbara Olson's *Final Days;* Ted Nugent's *God, Guns & Rock and Roll;* Bob Zelnick's *Gore: A Political Life;* Barbara Olson's *Hell to Pay: The Unfolding Story of Hillary Rodham Clinton;* Roger Morris's *Partners in Power: The Clintons and Their America;* Patrick J. Buchanan's *A Republic, Not an Empire;* David Schippers's *Sellout: The Inside Story of President Clinton's Impeachment.*

There is a reason *Pravda* once called Henry Regnery "the most dangerous man in America."[31]

The reluctance of the mainstream publishing houses to publish conservative books stems from two factors: (1) the public seems to like them; and (2) they are often profitable for the publisher. Unable to learn from the second kick of a mule (or the third, fourth, or twentieth), the elite media invariably describe the frequent conservative best-sellers as "surprise best-sellers." It's been the same surprise for twenty years. Excluding alternative phraseologies such as "a bigger hit than anticipated" (Dan Quayle's *Standing Firm: A Vice-Presidential Memoir*)[32] or "an unexpected success" (*The Real Anita Hill*), here is a partial list of conservative books that have been described in the mainstream media as "surprise best-sellers" (italics added):

"Another *surprise national bestseller* is *Senatorial Privilege: The Chappaquiddick Cover-Up*. . . . in fact, president Al Regnery says it's been No. 1 most of the summer."

Washington Post[33]

"*The Closing of the American Mind* . . . became a *surprise best seller*"[34] and "Allan Bloom's *surprise 1987 bestseller, The Closing of the American Mind* . . ."[35]

New York Times

Alan Bloom "detonated a cultural bomb when he published the *surprise best seller The Closing of the American Mind.*"

Newsweek[36]

". . . such *surprise bestsellers* as Dinesh D'Souza's *Illiberal Education* and David Brock's exposé *The Real Anita Hill* . . ."

United Press International[37]

"*The Bell Curve*, by Charles Murray and Richard Herrnstein, a *surprise best-seller* . . ."

Report Newsmagazine[38]

"*Parliament of Whores* remains a *surprise best seller.*"

Newsweek[39]

"The hilarious *Politically Correct Bedtime Stories: Modern Tales for Our Life & Times*, by James Finn Garner has become a *surprise best seller.*"

USA Today[40]

"Last year, Chicago writer James Finn Garner's *Politically Correct Bedtime Stories* became a *surprise bestseller.*"

U.S. News & World Report[41]

"*The Death of Common Sense: How Law Is Suffocating America*, a scathing indictment of regulatory law and a *surprise best seller.*"

New York Times[42]

"The book, *Unlimited Access*, with its fierce and often undocumented critique of the Clinton White House by retired FBI agent Gary Aldrich, is a *surprise best-seller.*"

National Public Radio[43]

". . . in [Robert Bork's] new, *surprise best seller, Slouching Toward Gomorrah.*"

Chicago Tribune[44]

"Inspired by *The Book of Virtues*, a *surprise best seller* edited by former Secretary of Education William Bennett . . ."

Buffalo News [Dallas Morning News][45]

"Stephen E. Ambrose's *Undaunted Courage*, a scholarly history book that extols the accomplishments of dead white males, was the *surprise best seller* of 1996."

Newsweek[46]

". . . the *surprise bestselling* impeachment guidebook *High Crimes and Misdemeanors* . . ."

U.S. News & World Report[47]

"[The Conservative Party British prime minister's] 774-page memoir, titled *John Major: The Autobiography* . . . is already a *surprise best seller* in Britain."

USA Today[48]

"[*Flags of Our Fathers*, the story of the six young men who raised a flag on Iwo Jima] is the *surprise runaway nonfiction best seller* of the season."

New York Times[49]

". . . the *surprise best-seller The O'Reilly Factor: The Good, the Bad, and the Completely Ridiculous in American Life* . . ."

Entertainment Weekly[50]

"Books by conservatives are hot these days, but it still comes as a *surprise* to see that Bernard Goldberg's *Bias* has bounced to the top of the *New York Times best-seller* list."

Time[51]

The surprise of conservative books repeatedly showing up on the best-seller list evidently never gets any less surprising. Growing weary of all the surprises, the left is itching to silence conservatives once and for all.

No conservative book will have a major rollout on the *Today* show, be excerpted in *Vanity Fair,* lead to an appearance on *Conan,* or merely be politely reviewed in the *New York Times.* Conservative books will not be assigned to mammoth college lecture courses and their purchase subsidized by student loans. Their authors will never be hailed as geniuses and poets and feted at Manhattan cocktail parties. Leaving nothing to chance, liberals also hide conservative books. The hiding-books trick—long well-known to conservatives—eventually became comical enough to be written up in the *New York Times.*

The publisher of David Brock's *The Real Anita Hill* (written when Brock was a conservative) told of wandering through bookstores in Harvard Square and finding "every feminist book you can think of . . . prominently displayed." Brock's book, which was then number three on the *New York Times* best-seller list, was "hidden in obscure corners as though it were a piece of pornography." And that was when it was available at all.[52] The owner of now-deceased Shakespeare & Company Booksellers on the Upper West Side of Manhattan proudly admitted to hiding Brock's book. He noted the store also "carr[ied] *Mein Kampf*, although we don't display that prominently, either."[53]

Despite liberals' little tricks, *The Real Anita Hill* was a best-seller. It was called "sleaze with footnotes" on the op-ed page of the *New York Times.*[54] *The Nation* proclaimed that "no reputable publishing house should have touched" the book.[55] It was denounced as a fraud and a scam in the *New Yorker* by Jane Mayer and Jill Abramson, who later wrote their own book flacking for Hill. (Brock's critical treatment of Anita Hill would sell about 40 percent more than Mayer and Abramson's book fawning over Anita Hill.[56])

The popularity of Brock's book with book buyers—"despite generally negative reviews"[57]—came as a total shock to liberals. It always does. Criticism of Anita Hill would never see the light of day on the nation's op-ed pages or network news: Who was buying all these books?

Publishing houses react to conservative authors like Linda Blair to holy water. Yet and still, people keep reading conservative books and somehow they keep landing on the *New York Times* best-seller list. If books by minorities were treated the way books by conservatives are, the nation would be consumed by wailing and gnashing of teeth in reaction to the manifest prejudice of the publishing industry.

There are many happy stories of books rejected by big-name publishers that, when finally published, become runaway best-sellers. A suspiciously large number of these stories involve conservative books. Imitating an Alzheimer's joke, every successive conservative best-seller genuinely is a "surprise best-seller" to publishers. By contrast, it's hard to think of a single liberal book whose commercial appeal eluded publishing houses—even those that went on to spectacular failure.

In 1989, every major New York publishing house turned down Leo Damore's *Senatorial Privilege,* about Senator Edward M. Kennedy's 1969 auto accident at Chappaquiddick. Only ideology-driven insanity could explain how New York publishers would refuse to recognize the commercial potential of such a book. After Regnery Publishing put it out, Damore's book immediately shot to number one on the *New York Times* best-seller list, and remained on the list for twenty weeks. In response to the Cinderella story of *Senatorial Privilege,* the *New York Times* rushed in to deny "that the big publishing houses practice censorship" or follow a narrow "ideological line." As the *Times* explained: "They do not."[58] With that, the inquiry was complete.

Also having nothing to do with ideological agendas was the publishing world's reaction to William F. Buckley's *God and Man at Yale* back in 1951. The University of Chicago's Great Books Foundation broke its contract with Regnery merely for having published the book, stripping Regnery of a lucrative textbook series. Was that evidence of an ideological agenda?[59]

For another couple of decades, conservative books spurned by the big publishers kept reliably turning up on the best-seller list. Finally, even the *Times* wearied of denying that political censorship was at work. In 2001, *Flags of Our Fathers* by James Bradley spent forty-four weeks on the *New York Times* best-seller list after having been rejected by twenty-seven New York publishing houses. This time, the *Times* gingerly raised the possibility of a "subliminal reason" leading to publishers' consistent rejection of certain types of books. As the *Times* put it: "Most book editors and publishers were culturally formed by the 1960's and 70's and seem to suffer that Manhat-tan–West Coast ambivalence if not aversion to things military."[60] Military books, one publisher explained, are seen as "Middle America books, which is still a hard sell to editors." (This is opposed to the easy sell of having no military and getting used to planes flying into your skyscrapers.)

"Middle America" means you—you reading this book. After Rush Limbaugh's first book, *The Way Things Ought to Be,* had spent fifty-four weeks at the top of the *New York Times* best-seller list, a *Times* book reviewer sought to explain the author's peculiar popularity by saying Lim-baugh's "appeal is to a part of middle America—call it the silent majority or the American People or the booboisie."[61] That is how New York publishers think of people who buy books.

Still puzzling over the ceaseless surprise of conservative books on the best-seller list, in January 2002 the *New York Times* was shocked again: "I was startled to learn," a reporter wrote, "that five books appealing to polit-ical conservatives, a third of the total, will be on the *New York Times* hard-cover nonfiction best-seller list on Jan. 20 and that one of them will be No. 1."[62]

Casting about for an explanation of the conservative dominance of the best-seller list despite the fact that this had been true for generations, the *Times* attributed it to conservative authors' "broadcasting celebrity." Being permitted to give opinion commentary "from the right!" within a McGovernite universe—where George Stephanopoulos, Jesse Jackson, Lesley Stahl, Dan Rather, Katie Couric, and Bryant Gumbel are deemed objective reporters, and William Safire (voted for Clinton) and David Ger-gen (worked for Clinton) are considered "conservatives"—is what gives conservatives their mysterious edge in book sales.

The number one book that week, *Bias* by Bernard Goldberg, the *Times* reported, had been turned down by many "mainstream publishers." Once again, Regnery was left to publish another runaway best-seller. Faced with the hard evidence that by publishing conservative books, Regnery had been able to produce a mind-bogglingly high percentage of best-sellers, the *Times*'s demented conclusion was: "Where Regnery has the missionary zeal as well as the profit motive, mainstream houses publish books by conser-vatives (or nearly anyone) mostly for the profit." Ah! So the real reason mainstream publishers refuse to publish an entire category of popular best-selling books is savvy business judgment.

Liberals pretend to believe that when two random hoodlums kill a gay man in Oklahoma, it's evidence of a national trend, but when a million people buy a book, it proves absolutely nothing about the book-buying public. These great opponents of "intolerance" are so fanatically intolerant of conservatives they will sacrifice the bottom line to prevent conservative books from being published.

Gigantic book advances go to all sorts of authors—liberal historians, liberal feminists, liberal celebrities, liberal Clinton aides, liberal fighter pilots, liberal comedians. But you can be sure that enormous advances that turn out to be enormous mistakes will never be lavished on any of those "surprise best-sellers." Book advances are pure wealth transfers to liberal gabbers.

Feminist Naomi Wolf is regularly given mammoth advances, averaging half a million dollars apiece,[63] for such intriguing themes as how Naomi lost her virginity.[64] Despite colossal media interest more appropriate to the Second Coming, the actual books sell relatively poorly.

In its characteristic understatement, the *New York Times* called Wolf's first book, *The Beauty Myth,* about how women are victimized by the cosmetics industry (men)—I quote—"one of the most important books of the 20th century."[65] It was given an adulatory write-up in a coveted *New York Times* book review. It was listed among the *Times's* recommended "Summer Reading 1991: Books for Vacation Reading." It was among the honored "Notable Books of the Year 1991." Of course *The Beauty Myth* also made the *Times's* "And Bear in Mind" ("Editors' choices of other recent books of particular interest")[66] special listing for books (by liberals) that the *Times* feels ought to be on the best-seller list but aren't.

Eventually, the endless press attention bumped Wolf's book to the lower end of the best-seller list for three weeks—coming in at numbers 16, 13, and 13. Also on the *New York Times* best-seller list at about the same time were Dinesh D'Souza's *Illiberal Education*—which spent fifteen weeks on the list—and P. J. O'Rourke's *Parliament of Whores*—which spent thirty-eight weeks on the list.

O'Rourke's book got a 146-word blurb from the *Times,* and D'Souza won a rare (for a conservative) *New York Times* book review—which said dourly of D'Souza's runaway best-seller: "There is a place for good muckraking, but this book does not fill it."[67] With no establishment press flacking whatsoever, D'Souza's book spent five times as long on the best-seller list (and at much higher numbers) than Wolf's book. For his next book D'Souza got an advance of $150,000. For Wolf's next book, Random House paid her an advance of $600,000.

Though Wolf's next book, *Fire with Fire,* also didn't sell well, her insipid feminist scribblings produced another media rapture. (Insights from her book worth $600,000: "The rape crisis center starved for lack of fun."[68]) Needless to say, it was reliably included among the "Notable Books of the Year"[69] and again the next year as one of the "New & Noteworthy Paperbacks."[70] It was reviewed in the *Times* and mentioned in a dozen columns there as well. Sadly, having the *New York Times* doing publicity for her wasn't enough to bump Wolf onto the best-seller list this time. But that didn't put an end to her half-million-dollar book advances.

The head of Random House cited Wolf as an author he was "proud" of—irrespective of book sales.[71] (A few years later, the *New Yorker* reported Random House had lost $50 million in unearned advances.[72]) Making money is less important in the book business than publishing liberals editors can be "proud" of.

In the first of his many establishment rewards for having worked for a Democrat president, who was later impeached and disbarred, George Stephanopoulos was given a $2.75 million advance by Little, Brown for his book, titled *All Too Human.* Another monopoly media rapture ensued. Stephanopoulos was interviewed about his book on NBC's *Today* show (twice!), ABC's *Good Morning America, CBS This Morning,* CNBC's *Tim Russert Show,* CNN's *Larry King Live,* Fox News's *Special Report with Brit Hume,* Fox News's *The Crier Report,* CBS News's *Saturday Morning.* His book was the topic of dozens of other programs. He had an appearance on *Late Night with Conan O'Brien.* Stephanopoulos's book was excerpted in *Newsweek* three days before it was released. It was written up in six separate articles in the *New York Times* alone the first week it came out—and another dozen times over the next month. That level of publicity is enough to make Britney Spears a star.

The media swoon put Stephanopoulos's book on the *New York Times* best-seller list for fifteen weeks, five of those at number one. (D'Souza had received an advance of $25,000 for his book that spent fifteen on the best-seller list, though, admittedly, not at number one.) On the best-seller list at the same time as Stephanopoulos's *All Too Human* was Bill Gertz's *Betrayal*—another Regnery book—which spent seven weeks on the list. This was also without being excerpted in *Newsweek,* reviewed in the *Times,* or featured on the Conan O'Brien show, the *Today* show, *Good Morning*

America, or *CBS This Morning.* It was certainly without a $3 million advance.

And so it goes. Matt Drudge's book, *The Drudge Manifesto,* received no monopoly media attention—no adulatory book reviews in the *Times,* no appearances on the morning shows, the late-night shows, or any network shows at all. Yet the book sailed onto the *New York Times* best-seller list and remained there for four weeks. Released concurrently with *The Drudge Manifesto* was a book by *Nightline*'s Ted Koppel. Koppel got a *Times* book review and appearances on the *Today* show and *Larry King Live* to promote his book, which barely made the list for one week. It must be the "broadcasting celebrity" of conservatives that propels their books onto the bestseller list.

Kelly Flinn, a liberal heroine for being both an adulteress and a girl Air Force pilot, got a $1 million advance for her book, *Proud to Be.* The same liberals in the publishing industry who feel "ambivalence if not aversion to things military"—as the *New York Times* put it[73]—were enthralled by this modern-day Bathsheba. The reading public was not, and the book bombed.[74]

In the appropriate liberal comedian category, Whoopi Goldberg received a whopping $6 million advance for her book. It briefly graced the bottom of the best-seller list (at numbers 15, 10, 15, and 9) in what the *New York Times* called a "dizzying tumble from grace."[75]

The one near-exception to the rule that only liberals are eligible for mind-boggling advances is David Brock, who received an enormous advance for his book on Hillary Clinton. This was hardly undeserved inasmuch as his previous book had spent eleven weeks on the *Times* best-seller list (while being slammed by the critics). But between the advance and the publication of the book, Brock became a liberal. His book crashed and burned when it was spurned by conservative readers. Thus, the Brock exception merely demonstrates the axiom that conservatives read books and liberals don't—an unalterable fact that will never, ever be acknowledged by mainstream publishers.

Though publishers incessantly complain that big advances are often not repaid in book sales, they refuse to acknowledge a half-century of marketing research demonstrating that conservative books tend to sell quite well while liberal books require major blockbuster promotion merely to avoid publishing disasters. Liberals compete for advances in the millions of dollars. Conservatives are happy to be published at all.

In addition to lucrative advances for books that don't sell, liberal writers can always be assured of a position on the op-ed page of any of various major newspapers, where a writer need be popular only with his editors. Liberals succeed by impressing an oligopoly of fellow liberals rather than winning in the marketplace of ideas.

Arthur Hoppe annoyed readers of the *San Francisco Chronicle* with his pompous liberalism three to five times a week for forty years. In one of Hoppe's crowd pleasers he wrote that when he heard American troops were bogged down in Vietnam, "I nodded and said, 'Good.' And having said it, I realized the bitter truth. Now I root against my own country." Letters denouncing Hoppe for his anti-Americanism, even threatening newspaper cancellations, never made Hoppe's position at the *Chronicle* any less secure. Though it was asserted that Hoppe had a "loyal, loving following," there is no evidence of much of a following outside of the *Chronicle's* editorial board. All eight of Hoppe's books bombed.[76]

Anthony Lewis's bitter left-wing screeds were published biweekly, year after year, decade after decade in the *New York Times* for half a century. This is despite a dearth of evidence that anyone read them. Though he occupied prime real estate on the op-ed page of the Newspaper of Record, only one of Lewis's four books ever became a best-seller. Lewis did get a favorable mention for his book *Make No Law* on the *Times's* "And Bear in Mind" list of editors' recommendations.[77] That same week, two authors who could never hope for positions as regular *New York Times* columnists were on the best-seller list—D'Souza and O'Rourke.

It would be interesting to compare liberals and conservatives on a grid— one axis for "number of words published in elite newspapers" and the other axis for "weeks on a best-seller list."

In reviews that are often as compelling as their books, unsuccessful liberal authors use their premiere positions in the pages of the monopoly media to describe best-selling conservative authors as follows:

- Windbags, no-talent hacks, and laughably inept flops (the *Washington Post's* Tom Shales, none of whose books ever made any best-seller list, on Bernard Goldberg's number one book, *Bias*, on the *New York Times* list);
- Smear artists who are repulsed by female sexuality (Frank Rich, whose book *Ghost Light* was a midlist failure, on David Brock's best-selling *The Real Anita Hill*[78]);

- Writers of "hatchet" books (*Newsweek* columnist Jonathan Alter, whose books were commercial failures,[79] on Barbara Olson's best-selling *Hell to Pay*[80]);
- A blowhard recycling his radio monologues in a rant of opinions, gags, and insults with a few facts or near-facts, who applies ad hominem ad nauseam, unsubtle slobberings and slaverings, sprinkled in like the meat in last week's stew (*Times* book reviewer Walter Goodman, whose own books flopped, on best-selling champion Rush Limbaugh).

Conservative books may be snubbed in the elite media, hidden by bookstores, and regularly spurned by major publishers, but at least with books, we know who the public wants to read.

While publishing houses are understandably wary of conservative books that instantly skyrocket onto the *New York Times* best-seller list, the evidence suggests they are a bit overanxious to publish liberals. In the rush to provide the public with yet more liberal bilge, editors apparently dispense with fact-checking.

Books that become publishing scandals by virtue of phony research, invented facts, or apocryphal stories invariably grind political axes for the left. There may be publishing frauds that are apolitical, but it's hard to think of a single hoax book written by a conservative.

Perhaps the most famous left-wing hoax was *I, Rigoberta Menchu*. Menchu's purported account of her torment at the hands of the Guatemalan military was uncritically accepted by the left, and used as a bludgeon against the Reagan administration for sending aid to Guatemala. Menchu herself met with State Department officials "to urge an end to American aid to Guatemala."[81] Her alleged autobiography won the Nobel peace prize, was translated into twelve languages, inspired fifteen thousand scholarly papers, and was required reading at colleges across America. Menchu was the recipient of fourteen honorary doctorates.

And then it was exposed as a hoax by anthropologist and Guatemalan expert David Stoll of Middlebury College, who examined archival material and interviewed survivors of the events described by Menchu. He found that her book was a fantasy—an utter fraud from beginning to end. Thus, for example, on the very first page of her Nobel Prize–winning book, Menchu claimed to be an uneducated, illiterate peasant. Indeed, the book had to be translated from tapes of Menchu's oral history. It turned out Menchu had attended prestigious boarding schools run by nuns. She claimed to have engaged in arduous low-wage labor in coffee and cotton fields as a child. In fact, she belonged to a relatively prosperous farming family. She vividly described being forced to watch family members starve or burn to death. These events, too, never occurred.

As one of Menchu's native countrymen described it, "The book is one lie after another, and she knows it."[82] Stoll's refutation of Menchu's account was later confirmed by the *New York Times.*[83]

Menchu first denied the allegations of a hoax, then blamed the attacks on racism, and finally blamed the co-author to whom she had dictated her story. (A check of the tapes indicated the lies were Rigoberta's, not the translator's.)

The director of the Norwegian Nobel Institute brushed off the scandal, saying "all autobiographies embellish to a greater or lesser extent." There was, he assured the public, "no question of revoking the prize."[84]

Another prize-winning hoax was the anti gun *Arming America: The Origins of a National Gun Culture* by Michael A. Bellesiles. He claimed to have reviewed more than ten thousand probate and criminal records to make the stunning claim that only about 14 percent of men owned guns in colonial America and most of those guns were unusable. America's gun culture, he said, was "an invented tradition." The jacket flap on his book boasted: "This is the N.R.A.'s worst nightmare." Neither his publisher nor the reviewers needed to know more. Bellesiles's conclusion was instantly and uncritically embraced by the elite media despite questions raised about his research by Second Amendment scholars such as Gary Kleck, Glen Reynolds, and Don Kates.

Arming America was granted a major pre-release promotion in the *New York Times* "Week in Review" section entitled "The Lock and Load Myth: A Disarming Heritage." The article boasted, "Mr. Bellesiles's book may change the terms of the debate."[85] Upon its publication, the book was giddily reviewed in the *Times* by Garry Wills, who gushed, "Bellesiles has dispersed the darkness that covered the gun's early history in America." He praised Bellesiles for marshaling "overwhelming evidence" that proved America's view of the gun was a "superstition" as pervasive "as any that affected Native Americans in the 17th century."[86]

Charlton Heston wrote a letter to the editor complaining of Wills's overeager acceptance of Bellesiles's "ludicrous argument."[87]

Naturally, *Arming America* was repeatedly included in the *Times*'s "And

Bear in Mind" list as well as the annual "Notable Books" list for books by liberals, where Bellesiles was again hailed for having "rattle[ed] some time-worn myths."[88] *The New York Review of Books* raved that Bellesiles had "done us all a service if his book reduces the credibility of the fanatics who endow the Founding Fathers with posthumous membership in what has become a cult of the gun."

The trustees of Columbia University awarded Bellesiles one of the three 2001 Bancroft Prizes in American history and diplomacy for *Arming America*.[89]

But after a year of praise and awards and glorious press for *Arming America*, it turned out Bellesiles had fabricated his research. Other scholars had tried to review Bellesiles's research, but the data didn't match. Often the records he claimed to have reviewed didn't exist. There were literally hundreds of errors and invented facts in Bellesiles's book. He claimed to have reviewed San Francisco probate records for 1849 to 1859. It turned out all those records had been destroyed by a fire in the earthquake of 1906.[90]

When questioned about his research, Bellesiles said he couldn't respond because his notes had been lost in a flood in his office at Emory University. (Other faculty members found that claim incredible.) When factual errors were found on his website, he claimed it had been hacked. When a sympathetic colleague offered to search through the probate records on his own time and duplicate Bellesiles's work in order to defend him, Bellesiles never returned his call.

Another liberal publishing fraud, *Fortunate Son: George W. Bush and the Making of an American President,* was pulled from the shelves shortly after publication when the author, whose book relied on his personal credibility, turned out to be a convicted felon. The author, Jim Hatfield, made the extravagant claim that he had nailed down Bush's alleged cocaine conviction—a long-rumored incident that had eluded scores of talented and battle-worn journalists. St. Martin's Press released the book just as George W. Bush was embarking on his presidential campaign in 1999.

It raised no flags at St. Martin's Press that top-flight investigative reporters from the mainstream media—where nine out of ten reporters voted for Clinton—had unearthed no evidence of the purported cocaine bust. An unknown, unpublished author who refused to divulge his sources struck New York liberals as completely credible. He claimed to have the goods on George Bush.

Though the author of *Fortunate Son* was not known in publishing circles, it turned out he was well known to law enforcement. He was a two-time convicted felon, still on parole for a solicitation of murder conviction. For his most recent criminal conviction, Hatfield had paid a hit man $5,000 to kill his female supervisor, because—according to a witness—"he was enraged about the fact that this incompetent woman was his supervisor."[91]

The *Washington Post* described the careful vetting process for a book that would accuse a presidential candidate of having a criminal record: "Nobody at St. Martin's had met the author until he arrived for the abortive book promotion last October.... No fact-checking was done. Nobody insisted on knowing Hatfield's sources or on securing supporting material for his sensational charges."[92]

Hatfield claimed the Bush family had purged the supposed cocaine bust from the record, but could produce not a shred of evidence. He had no date for the conviction, no arresting officer, no judge, no county, no general description of his "sources." *Slate Magazine* soon caught Hatfield describing one of his alleged sources as spitting tobacco into "the ever-present Styrofoam cup"—contradicting an earlier claim that he had talked to his sources only by telephone. The *New York Times* rushed in with a defense of the ex-con author, noting that novelists "John Bunyan, Cervantes and Dostoyevsky all did time." Not only that, but the *Times* proclaimed: "Perhaps if politicians were more forthcoming, they would be smeared less."[93] It was Bush's fault that a convicted felon was libeling him.

St. Martin's withdrew the book when Hatfield's solicitation of murder conviction was revealed.[94] Hatfield had received a $25,000 advance—not huge but quite a bit more than the typical advance paid to first-time conservative authors whose books end up on the best-seller list.

The *Washington Post*'s explanation for St. Martin's flirtation with the ex-con's apocryphal exposé on Bush was fascinating. It seems that "publishers often care more about getting books to market and less about accuracy."[95] Again, the profit motive at work! The same "profit motive" that incomprehensibly causes publishers to reject conservative best-sellers also induces publishers to dispense with the most cursory fact-checking for left-wing fairy tales written by convicted felons.

Other books subjected to the rigorous fact-checking methods of publishers about to drop a stink bomb on a conservative include one that said Richard Nixon was a wife-beater[96] and another that accused J. Edgar

Hoover of being gay and showing up at Mafia parties in drag—startling facts that somehow eluded the rabidly anti-Hoover press of the day.[97]

One of the more lascivious stink-bomb books was Kitty Kelley's 1991 *Nancy Reagan, the Unauthorized Biography.* Kelley accused both Reagans of having affairs and of smoking pot in the governor's mansion in the late sixties. The former first lady was said to have carried on a long-term affair with Frank Sinatra in full view of the White House staff. (Her husband awarded Sinatra the Presidential Medal of Freedom in 1985.) Kelley was paid what was at the time the largest book advance ever paid for a nonfiction book.[98]

Kelley's book was almost entirely unsourced—and the sources Kelley did provide repeatedly denied her claims. As George Will wrote in the *Washington Post,* Kelley's book exhibited raw "malice, crudeness, mendacity, and ignorance."[99]

Yet her book was treated as hard news at the *New York Times* in the heavy-breathing account of then-reporter Maureen Dowd.[100] A few years hence, Dowd would be hooting that the Starr Report demonstrated only Ken Starr's "cravings for ecstasy."[101] Not only was the Starr Report concerned with felonies rather than idle gossip, it was at least based on proven facts rather than unsubstantiated gossip. But the Starr Report was "pornography" (though what Clinton did wasn't "sex"). Kitty Kelley's purple prose about the Reagans' alleged sexual trysts was literally front-page news at the *New York Times.*

In addition to a bumper crop of vicious and unsourced books defaming conservatives, books by feminists are often a treasure trove of invented statistics.

Confirming the feminists' well-known facility with numbers, Naomi Wolf absurdly claimed in *The Beauty Myth* that 150,000 women die each year from anorexia. Comparing death by anorexia to the Holocaust, Wolf fumed: "How would America react to the mass self-immolation by hunger of its favorite sons?" Gloria Steinem repeated the alleged anorexia statistic in her book *Revolution from Within.*

Christina Hoff Sommers, author of the 1992 book *Who Stole Feminism,* went to the trouble to call the National Center for Health Statistics (NCHS) to find out that there are approximately one hundred deaths from anorexia each year. Noting that anorexia occurs in an extremely narrow demographic, affecting almost entirely white, upper-middle-class, over-achieving women,

Hoff Sommers wryly observed that if 150,000 women had been dying every year from anorexia, "at Wellesley College graduation you would need to have ambulances on hand the way you do at major sports events."[102]

Now consider: Only about two million people die of all causes in the United States each year. Auto accidents claim the lives of about forty thousand people annually—including pedestrians.[103] How on earth did the purported 150,000 anorexia deaths slip past the editors—to say nothing of the authors themselves?

In a classic liberal sneer, the *New York Times* sniffed that some of Regnery's anti-Clinton books would not "be likely to pass muster at an assembly of scholars."[104] No examples were cited nor evidence adduced for this assertion. Such jeers say no more—and are intended to say no more—than that the *Times* disapproves of conservative books. I've just listed a half-dozen mendacious liberal books. What do they have?[105]

On the off chance anyone would dare cite former FBI agent Gary Aldrich's book *Unlimited Access* as of questionable veracity, there is no evidence that Aldrich was wrong. Indignant denials by the Clinton administration do not constitute disproof. To the contrary, Clintonian denials have historically constituted confirmation.

Even with advance review,[106] the only story the White House disputed in Aldrich's book was his claim that Clinton used to sneak out of the White House in the backseat of a car for extramarital trysts at the Marriott Hotel. Aldrich, who obviously had a great many sources at the White House, never budged from his claim that he had a solid source for the story, whom he would not identify because of the source's continued employment with the FBI. In light of events since the release of Aldrich's book, leading to Clinton's impeachment, contempt citation, and disbarment, Aldrich appears to have been vindicated with a whoop.

Liberals don't believe there is such a thing as "fact" or "truth." Everything is a struggle for power between rival doctrines. They express boundless credulity for the claims of communist regimes. ("You must admit Cuba has an excellent health care system!") They respect totalitarian regimes for their power to enforce the "truth" at the end of a gun. And they respect the truth in America as it is enforced in the pages of the *New York Times.* Only a disregard for both market forces and the truth can explain why publishing houses keep rushing liberal hoax books to print, while doggedly refusing to publish "surprise best-sellers."

U nable to compete and running out of book-advance money to provide liberals with lifetime sinecures, the left is increasingly desperate to censor conservatives outright. It was easy enough before the Internet. Newspaper editors, TV executives, and publishers could simply refuse to hire or publish conservatives. They could jam liberalism down our throats on every television broadcast, morning show, late-night comedy program, and large-circulation newspaper and magazine in the country.

But the Internet has undermined the major media's capacity to enforce a strict party line. It is not a coincidence that conservative books, always strong sellers, have experienced a boom since books became available on the Internet. Even the left's precious "campaign finance reform" can only stop conservatives from buying space in the mainstream media outlets. On the Internet, speech is free—and liberalism can't survive the competition. The same relentless competition of the Web that annihilated the commercial dot.coms has produced near-dominance of the Internet by conservatives.

In a ranking of the nine most-visited websites in the "Politics & New Media" category, conservative sites regularly outnumber liberal sites. Though the rankings vary from month to month, the list for March 2001 is typical: Four of the nine are conservative websites: drudgereport.com (number 2), townhall.com (number 4), freerepublic.com (number 6), and reagan.com (number 9). Only two are liberal websites, coming in at numbers 5 and 8.[107]

Similarly, conservative think-tank sites are consistently over-represented in the top nine "think tank" websites.[108] Thus, for December 2000, six of the top nine most-visited think-tank sites were conservative groups; only one was liberal.[109] One month later, in January 2001,[110] the conservative Heritage Foundation was number one, the libertarian CATO institute number two, and Pete Dupont's National Center for Policy Analysis, number four. There were only two liberal think tanks in the top nine.

The effect of the Internet on the left's capacity to shape the truth cannot be exaggerated. Consider a few truths forced into the open by the Internet.

- *Newsweek* had a tape of an intern discussing her affair with the president of the United States, but the magazine decided to sit on the story that reflected poorly on a Democratic president. Later that night, the story ran on the Internet, broken by the Drudge Report.

- For decades, the *New York Times* had allowed loose associations between Nazis and Christians to be made in its pages. Statements like these were not uncommon: "Did the Nazi crimes draw on Christian tradition?"[111] ... "the church is 'co-responsible' for the Holocaust"[112] ... "Pope Pius XII, who maintained diplomatic ties with Hitler, ... "[113] Then out of the blue one day in 2002, the *New York Times* ran a prominent article describing the Nazis' virulent crusade against Christianity. That very week, evidence from the Nuremberg trials detailing Nazis' crusade against Christianity had been posted on the Internet.[114]

- When a Nigerian student went on a shooting spree at the Appalachian Law School in January 2002, he was stopped by two armed students. In an online article posted on the *New York Post*'s website, economist John Lott wrote that of the 280 stories posted on NexisLexis in the week after the attack, only four mentioned that it was students pointing their own guns at the gunman that ended his rampage. "Much more typical," Lott said, "was the scenario described by the *Washington Post,* where the heroes had simply 'helped subdue' the killer. The *New York Times* claimed the attacker was "tackled by fellow students."[115] In a Google search of the Web, the vast majority of stories about the shooting focused on how the shooting spree was stopped by armed students—as well as on the major media's refusal to report that fact.[116]

- The *New York Times*'s economic columnist, Paul Krugman, the only known economist who hates the free market, ferociously attacked the Bush administration for having received campaign contributions from Enron.[117] Andrew Sullivan revealed on his website that Krugman himself had been paid a $50,000 "consulting fee" by Enron. After receiving his Enron "consulting fee," Krugman finally had kind words to say about one running dog lackey of the capitalist system. In a 1999 *Fortune* magazine column, he enthusiastically compared Enron to Goldman Sachs, the gold standard of investment banking, and gushed that Enron was "making freewheeling markets possible."[118] The fact that Enron had bought more influence with Krugman than it did with Bush—or as Krugman phrased it: "the people Enron put in the White House"[119]— would likely not be known but for Sullivan's relentless pursuit of the matter on his website. True to form, Krugman eventually responded by attributing Sullivan's attacks to a right-wing conspiracy.

- After enduring decades of liberal sneering about Star Wars, the Pentagon tested the technology and shot a missile out of the sky at 11:09 P.M. on July 14, 2001. The next day, less than two months before a terrorist attack on America, the *New York Times* ran a major front-page, two-inch headline, nine thousand-word article . . . on the Florida election.[120]

The successful dry-run of a missile defense system was mentioned in a short item on page 12 of the Newspaper of Record.[121] It didn't matter. The night before, news of the successful test of Star Wars had been blasted all over the Internet. (Drudge Report headline moments after the test: "IT'S A HIT!")

This is why liberals are in a panic about the Internet. They believe conservatives should be prevented from speaking. Thus, the same pious blowhards who love to prattle about the sacrosanct First Amendment when the speech at issue is obscene or treasonous are constantly issuing lunatic demands for regulation of America's most dangerous Samizdat media: the World Wide Web.

Over the years, the *New York Times* has bemoaned "a disappointing" Supreme Court decision upholding a local ordinance requiring go-go dancers to wear pasties;[122] it has denounced Mayor Giuliani for "grossly distort[ing] the First Amendment" by threatening to withdraw taxpayer money from a pornographic exhibit of the Virgin Mary;[123] it has criticized the "Child Online Protection Act" for requiring credit cards for pornographic websites as a violation of our First Amendment rights.[124] But University of Chicago law professor Cass Sunstein's book *Republic.com,* detailing the bright side of censorship, won fulsome praise from the *Times.*[125] Sunstein had proposed censoring only the Internet. The *Times* is ever-vigilant against deft manipulations of the First Amendment to protect the likes of Matt Drudge.

Sunstein's book argued that the Internet had created the intolerable situation of allowing the reading public choice. As Sunstein darkly put it: "Consumers are able to see exactly what they want." This must be stopped. His point—in his own words—was that "a commitment to consumer sovereignty may well compromise political sovereignty." A clearer statement of left-wing fascism is hard to come by. Whose "political sovereignty" will be compromised exactly?

Though Sunstein strained preposterously to suggest that it is not just conservative websites that threaten democracy as we know it, his "both sides" argument was transparently phony. The dangerous world he imagined consisted of "liberals watching and reading mostly or only liberals; moderates, moderates; conservatives, conservatives; neo-Nazis, neo-Nazis."

How, precisely, would a conservative go about eliminating liberal points of view from his life? You would have to be a survivalist in Idaho to escape the liberal sound chamber. As a start, one would have to cut out public schools, colleges, the evening news, sitcoms, movies, children's cartoons, book reviews, *Lifetime: TV for Women,* Katie Couric, Bryant Gumbel, *People* magazine, *Vanity Fair,* the *New York Times, Time, Newsweek,* and, indeed, all major newspapers and magazines.

It isn't compartmentalization that liberals are worried about, it is the capacity of Americans to escape the Orwellian drivel. Restricting oneself to only leftist propaganda, day in and day out, simply requires taking no action. Like the mass-marketing solicitations advise: You do nothing! Don't tune in to Rush Limbaugh, don't subscribe to *Human Events,* don't seek out conservative websites.

But Sunstein's insight that the Internet allowed people "to limit their exposure to like-minded viewpoints" raised a red flag at the *New York Times.* That's not free speech, it's conservative kooks! The *Times* was rapt with admiration for the idea of censoring the Internet and hailed Sunstein for raising "important and troubling questions about the effects of the Internet on a democratic society."

Unlike child pornography and totally nude dancing—which are the very heart of the First Amendment—the *Times* noted the Internet offers "a powerful new weapon to fringe groups and reinforces extremism." The Internet must not be permitted to interrupt important commentary that preserves the political sovereignty of liberalism. Among the important commentaries that could be disrupted by the Internet are these:

"I had heard that [Reagan] was a very open-minded, broad-minded person, that he cared about human rights . . . but the record is abysmal."
Lesley Stahl, *CBS News* White House correspondent on Howard Cosell's
Speaking of Everything, **April 10, 1988.**[126]

"Medical care was once for the privileged few. Today it is available to every Cuban and it is free. Some of Cuba's health care is world-class. In heart disease, for example, in brain surgery. Health and education are the revolution's great success stories."
Peter Jennings, ABC's *World News Tonight,* April 3, 1989[127]

"The North Pole is melting . . . something that has presumably never before been seen by humans and is more evidence that global warming may be real and already affecting climate."
The *New York Times,* August 19, 2000[128]

"A front-page article on Aug. 19 and a brief report on Aug. 20 in The Week in Review *about the [North Pole] misstated the normal conditions of the sea ice there. . . . The reports also referred incompletely to the link between the open water and global warming. The lack of ice at the pole is not necessarily related to global warming."*

The *New York Times,* **Correction, August 29, 2000**

"[T]he media consortium . . . decid[ed] on October 22—for the sake of national unity in the current political crisis—not to release an in-depth analysis of the Florida election . . . which, according to inside sources, gave the state election to Al Gore."

Keith Kelly, the *New York Post,* **December 5, 2000.**[129]

(The media consortium study was not completed for another year, at which point it was promptly released, showing that Bush had won on any count.)[130]

"Elvis, the first rock star. Clinton, the first rock star President. . . . Clinton had a talent for convincing anyone listening to him that he was speaking only to them, just as Elvis convinced someone in the 100th row that he was singing only to them. Presley drew on black culture for inspiration. Clinton draws on black culture for solace."

CNN political analyst Bill Schneider, *Inside Politics,* **August 16, 2001**[131]

By disrupting the constant drumbeat of liberal propaganda—Reagan was a brute, Cuba has excellent health care, Santa's home is melting, Gore won the election, and Clinton is Elvis—the Internet had become a threat to "democracy."

The first chapter of Sunstein's book was posted on Freerepublic.com— a website that is wildly popular on the basis of the now-discredited "consumer sovereignty" principle. One Freeper responded, "I've been exposed to a massive excerpt from *Republic.com,* a book written by a liberal, on a conservative niche website. Without that conservative niche site, which I visit often, I would not have read his stuff."[132]

With only slightly more subtlety than Professor Sunstein, in 1996 *Time* magazine noted with alarm that a computer user can "totally customize his or her daily supply of information."[133] This "suspect" development meant that news was "moving away from the universal." If the universal experience of liberal hectoring was not so unpleasant, Americans might not have turned to the Samizdat media with such zeal. The new "individualized" nature of information, *Time* said, means "news is no longer a common experience."

See, that's just the sort of thing conservatives are talking about. The "news" never was a "common experience" for people who didn't think Ronald Reagan was a contemptible dunce.

Time expressed alarm that news sources now included the likes of Rush Limbaugh and Internet websites. (MTV was thrown in for cover.) Like-minded Americans were meeting and communicating with one another! And not just any Americans. As *Time* explained, these were paranoid right-wing kooks. If liberals were not already scared out of their wits, the magazine stated that "right-wing militia groups"—i.e., mainstream conservative chat rooms—were being "nourished by their own books, periodicals and E-mail lists." Though stopping short of Professor Sunstein's call for regulation of the Internet, *Time* did raise questions about what this meant "for our understanding of the world around us, for our sense of community."

Hillary Clinton has also expressed concern about the "accessibility and instantaneous information on the computer."[134] Too much free speech! This was in a press conference on February 11, 1998—or two weeks after Matt Drudge broke the Monica Lewinsky story being suppressed by *Newsweek*. Not surprisingly, Mrs. Clinton raised the need for some "kind of editing function or gate-keeping function" for the Internet. Saying, "It is just beyond imagination what can be disseminated," Mrs. Clinton said, "we are all going to have to rethink how we deal with this." There are, she announced, "competing values." To wit; her electoral viability versus the First Amendment. So the First Amendment's got to go, the children need her.

Celebrated First Amendment lawyer Floyd Abrams also never saw the dark underbelly to free speech until the Drudge Report. Abrams was quoted in the *Wall Street Journal* saying, "If one were rewriting libel law today, one would try to write it to assure that the false statements of Matt Drudge were treated as libel." More likely you'd rewrite the First Amendment to take account of Floyd Abrams's clients. Abrams has defended the false statements of:

- ABC[135]
- NBC[136]
- *Fortune* magazine[137]
- Consumer Reports[138] and
- political candidates[139]

Matt Drudge evidently cries out for a higher standard of accuracy than every other information source in America. In any event, Drudge seems to be meeting the new special high standard of accuracy reserved for the Drudge Report. His only alleged misstatement that was ever tested in a court of law concerned a statement about Clinton aide Sidney Blumenthal, for which Blumenthal sued Drudge for libel. The case ended with Blumenthal paying Drudge money.

A Clinton-appointed federal judge actually made a finding of fact that Drudge is "not a reporter, a journalist, or a newsgatherer." *Hustler* magazine is journalism protected by the First Amendment.[140] *Penthouse* and the *National Enquirer* are journalism protected by the First Amendment.[141] Indeed, even the *New York Times* is deemed "journalism" protected by the First Amendment. The dean of the Columbia Graduate School of Journalism noted with some consternation that "no journalist or journalism organization protested after this federal judge took it upon himself to determine who can be called a journalist."[142]

To the contrary, media "experts" treated Drudge like a cancer that had to be excised so real journalists could get on with the important business of calling Reagan stupid. Joan Konner, publisher of the *Columbia Journalism Review,* said Drudge is "by no reasonable measure working in the public interest." Marvin Kalb, then-head of the Shorenstein Center on the Press at Harvard, dismissed Drudge as "a conveyor of gossipy information."[143]

When defending pornographers, lawbreakers, or traitors, one of the left's favorite clichés[144] is from Justice Powell's opinion in *Gertz v. Welch:* "Under the First Amendment, there is no such thing as a false idea. However pernicious an idea may seem, we depend for its correction . . . on the competition of other ideas."[145]

Liberals love the sound of the ringing peroration "there is no such thing as a false idea." But the moment they are confronted with ideas other than their own—on the Internet, on radio, and in books—liberals discover boatloads of false ideas. Not only that, but "the competition of other ideas" turns out to be nothing but trouble. In a true competition of ideas, it turns out the American people are appalled by theirs. So now they tell us a robust, free, unregulated marketplace of ideas is a threat to "democracy."

SEVEN

THE JOY OF ARGUING WITH LIBERALS: *YOU'RE STUPID!*

If liberals were prevented from ever again calling Republicans dumb, they would be robbed of half their arguments. To be sure, they would still have "racist," "fascist," "homophobe," "ugly," and a few other highly nuanced arguments in the quiver. But the loss of "dumb" would nearly cripple them. Like clockwork, every consequential Republican to come down the pike is instantly, invariably, always, without exception called "dumb."

This is how six-year-olds argue: They call everything "stupid." The left's primary argument is the angry reaction of a helpless child deprived of the ability to mount logical counterarguments. Someday we will turn to the *New York Times* editorial page and find the Newspaper of Record denouncing President Bush for being a "penis-head."

The "you're stupid" riposte is part of the larger liberal tactic of refusing to engage ideas. Sometimes they evaporate in the middle of an argument and you're left standing alone, arguing with yourself. More often, liberals withdraw figuratively by responding with ludicrous and irrelevant personal attacks. Especially popular are non sequiturs that are also savagely cruel. A vicious personal smear, they believe, constitutes a clever counterargument. Your refusal to submit to name-calling means you were overwhelmed by the force of their argument that you are a penis-head.

George Bush doesn't actually have to be a penis-head for some portion of voters to believe absolutely, without hesitation, that he is a penis-head. That's the beauty of controlling all major sources of news dissemination in

America. It ensures that liberals will never have to learn how to argue beyond the level of a six-year-old.

Indeed, almost all liberal behavioral tropes track the impotent rage of small children. Thus for example, there is also the popular tactic of repeating some stupid, meaningless phrase a billion times: *Arms for hostages, arms for hostages, arms for hostages, it's just about sex, just about sex, just about sex, dumb, dumb, dumb, money in politics, money in politics, money in politics, Enron, Enron, Enron.* Nothing repeated with mind-numbing frequency in all major news outlets will not be believed by some members of the populace. It is the permanence of evil; you can't stop it.

The power of brainwashing by repetition is powerfully illustrated in the case of the Clarence Thomas–Anita Hill battle. Immediately following the hearings, 69 percent of women believed Thomas rather than Hill. (A *Newsweek* reporter wrote in the liberal *New Republic* magazine that, among co-workers who knew both Thomas and Hill, the vote was: Thomas, "20-to-1.")[1]

But over the course of the next year, Hill was endlessly praised in the mainstream media, showered with dozens of awards, and invited to speak at once-prestigious organizations, such as Yale Law School and the American Bar Association.[2] Her heroism—and Thomas's perfidy—was flogged on TV sitcoms such as *Murphy Brown* and *Designing Women* (the latter ironically produced by Linda Bloodworth-Thomason, friend of real sexual harasser Bill Clinton).[3] Hill was made *Glamour* magazine's Woman of the Year and featured in a Ted Turner documentary, *A Century of Women*—with fair and balanced commentary by liberal Senator Barbara Boxer.[4] Needless to say, Hill was sympathetically stroked by Katie Couric on the *Today* show.

One year later, with no new facts, no new hearings, no new evidence—but a *lot* of media propaganda—only 44 percent of women believed Thomas over Hill. After watching the hearings, 73 percent of people said the Senate had treated Hill fairly. One year later only 49 percent thought so.[5]

Repetition alone doesn't win elections (and is demonstrably incapable of producing a twitch of interest in "campaign finance reform"). But constant liberal browbeating demonstrably can persuade large numbers of people that Republicans are dumb, irrespective of cold, hard facts. Also angry, mean, intolerant, inflexible, and judgmental—unlike the welcoming charm and noted flexibility of, say, Hillary Clinton.

Another infantile trope of the left is to deny the relevance of analogies and categories, so you can never trap them. No matter how apt it is, no matter how clearly it exposes the poverty of their logic, liberals always say analogies have "changed the subject": *We were talking about Paula Jones, so I don't know where Anita Hill came from.* Each case must be treated as if it just emerged from the ether, analyzed in a vacuum apart from any conceivable larger principle.

Liberals also refuse to acknowledge the meaning of "labels," which are nothing more than truths liberals don't like. They especially hate the word "liberal." Everyone knows it's an insult to be called a liberal, widely understood to connote a dastardly individual. Consequently, liberals are constantly insisting that the word is utterly meaningless. (In contradistinction, evidently, to phrases like "right-wing," "ultra-conservative," and "religious right," which are treated as terms of near-scientific accuracy.) Indeed, the surest sign that one is dealing with a liberal is his refusal to grant meaning to the word "liberal."

The argument that "liberal" conveys no meaningful information is always stated in terms of the great variation among liberals. There is more variation among dogs than among liberals, but that doesn't mean the word "dog" has no meaning. No one demands a twenty-minute exegesis on the differences between a poodle and a Great Dane before acknowledging that the word "dog" has meaning. Similarly, there are tall liberals, short liberals, cowardly liberals, even more cowardly liberals—but there is still an essential dogness to all of them.

Humans could not communicate if liberal objections to labels were applied across the board—which is precisely the point. Liberals argue by creating semantic bedlam: They conceal conservative arguments like furtive children hiding contraband from Mother under the bed. Conservatives have a point of view; there's no reason to be frightened of hearing it stated in an artful form.

The goal of modern propaganda "is no longer to transform opinion but to arouse an active and mythical belief."[6] The myth of the "dumb" Republican is no more rational than a cultural belief in voodoo or rain dances. It keeps not raining, but the people still believe in it. Your own cultural myths are never recognizable as such; otherwise they wouldn't be cultural myths.

In other contexts, especially university admissions, liberals deem IQ a meaningless construct and the SAT test a racist, sadistic ploy. But the wholly subjective opinion of liberal journalists about a Republican's IQ is treated like holy gospel. Though IQ is an ephemeral quality absolutely indiscernible to university admissions officers perusing student SAT scores, the *Washington*

Post managed to locate a Harvard professor who was able to comment thoughtfully on Bush's intelligence.[7] Liberals acknowledge the concept of IQ only in the cases of Republican presidential candidates and murderers on death row. (The retarded should not be executed! Nor should anyone else.)

The myth of dumb Republicans permits only one narrow exception: When not defined by their monumental stupidity, Republicans must be scarily weird. The far-less-popular scarily weird caricature has been applied, for example, to Nixon, Dole, and Gingrich.

Liberalism's High Priests in the media provided insistent cues that Newt Gingrich was supposed to be portrayed as "mean," not "dumb." The "weirdo" caricature was stated most forthrightly in a *Newsweek* headline that called Gingrich "Spiro Agnew with Brains."[8] It was also indicated by *Time* magazine, putting him on their cover as Scrooge. Weeks later, showing the fierce independent thought that dominates liberal discourse in America, *Newsweek* put him on their cover as the Grinch. (The idea was, welfare was Christmas, and Gingrich was trying to steal it. After the Scrooge's welfare reform turned out to be a fabulous success, it became Clinton's initiative, his signature reform, his good idea.)

So powerful are liberal myths, that they often lead to spiritual visions among the media elite. The apocryphal stories typically acquire the status of fact by neurotic repetition in Maureen Dowd columns. Among many other widely accepted apparitions, Attorney General John Ashcroft is absurdly said to fear calico cats and Dan Quayle was alleged to have apologized to an audience in Latin America for not studying his Latin more. (Noticeably, nobody could ever seem to produce a videotape of many famous Dan Quayle gaffes.)

The Dumb Republican/Smart Democrat myth lives in a world devoid of rational thought and logical consistency. It never occurs to anyone to ponder why the Republican Party would pursue such a crazy strategy of consistently running really dumb guys for office—much less president. Or why the Democratic Party insists on tapping presidential candidates who are so mind-bogglingly smart they can never connect with the average voter.

Yet the compulsion to describe every Republican president as an idiot has been part of the left's re-education efforts for over half a century. Coolidge was dumb, Eisenhower was dumb, Ford was dumb, Nixon was dumb (overshadowed by his pure evil), Quayle (standing in for his boss) was dumb, Reagan was dumb, Bush (43) is dumb.

Coolidge presided over peace and prosperity, was successful with Congress, and wildly popular with the public. But he was supposed to be an idiot. In the most titanic military accomplishment since Alexander the Great, Dwight Eisenhower marshaled the greatest military alliance in history, masterminded the D-Day invasion, and smashed the Nazi war machine. Liberals go around calling people fascists—well, this is the guy who beat them. Dumb, dumb, dumb. Gerald Ford had been an All-American football player and graduated from University of Michigan and Yale Law School. Yet he was indelibly known as a clumsy dolt. He was not nearly as dumb, however, as Ronald Reagan, the bumbling old guy who won the Cold War.

George Herbert Walker Bush (41) was shielded from the "dumb" argument not by his stellar résumé, but by his lightning rod vice president. (Liberals cannot fight a two-front war.) Consequently, though Bush was portrayed as a simpleton who couldn't talk, the most vicious attacks were trained on Dan Quayle. Whatever you can say about Quayle, he's smarter than Tom Daschle. George Bush (43), with degrees from Yale and Harvard, is ridiculed for his stupidity by Hollywood starlets whose course of study is limited to what they've learned from bald sweaty little men on casting couches.

Maybe some Republicans (Ford) were a little dumb, but liberals don't even try to make distinctions. Not distinctions with a tenuous connection to reality, that is. As a rule of thumb, only Republicans dumb enough to lose to a Democrat have a shot at ever being called smart. Thus, under what classification scheme, precisely, is Bob Dole more intelligent than Ronald Reagan? Yet Dole was rarely called dumb. His candidacy was dead in the water before it began.

"Stupid" means one thing: "threatening to the interests of the Democratic Party." The more conservative the Republican, the more vicious and hysterical the attacks on his intelligence will be. Liberals have not only run out of arguments, they've run out of adjectives.

Consistent with this definition of "dumb," the current idiot Republican is always dumber than all the dumb Republicans who preceded him. Bush is dumber than Dan Quayle, who was dumber than Ronald Reagan, who was dumber than Dwight Eisenhower and Calvin Coolidge. Astonishingly, the left's propagandistic purposes have recently demanded even Reagan's rehabilitation in order to attack George W. Bush's intelligence with greater vigor. This is nuance in liberal argumentation: dumb and dumber.

College dropout Michael Moore expressed the party line on relative

Republican IQs, saying, "Once you settle for a Ronald Reagan, then it's easy to settle for a George Bush, and once you settle for a George Bush, then it's real easy to settle for Bush II. You know, this should be evolution, instead it's de-evolution. What's next?"⁹

That's easy. What's next is a Republican even dumber than George Bush!

But if you can remember what happened the day before yesterday, it never adds up. If the last Republican was the dumbest person in the history of mankind, at some point it becomes metaphysically impossible for the next Republican to keep being even dumber. On the bright side, the constant upgrading of former Republican presidents keeps historians in business. They can always go back and produce shocking new evidence that some previous Republican president, chosen at random, was not a dimwit after all. At least it's nice to know that all Republican presidents will eventually see their IQs skyrocket.

Historians have concluded only fairly recently, for example, that both Coolidge and Eisenhower were quite shrewd and perfectly content with the sophisticates of their days ridiculing them as idiots. This follows decades of sneering at both presidents for failing to live up to the standards of FDR, who was obviously great because he spent eight years failing to get the country out of the Depression but then had the skill and foresight to allow the nation to be taken by surprise at Pearl Harbor.

Just before the 2000 election, *Slate* columnist Robert Wright referred to the recent revisionism on Eisenhower, saying his "voluminous personal correspondence shows beyond doubt that he was vastly smarter than either Reagan or Bush."¹⁰ That's an interesting formulation. The only baseline Wright acknowledges is "Reagan or Bush." Only Republican presidents are subject to having their intellects questioned. Why not Truman and Kennedy—Eisenhower's immediate predecessor and successor?

Truman got the country into a war in Korea, and couldn't get us out for two and a half years. Eisenhower was elected and ended the war in six months. Kennedy got the country into a war in Vietnam after the disastrous Bay of Pigs invasion and then sat passively by while the Russians built the Berlin Wall. So how does Eisenhower's intelligence compare with those two guys? It's as if comparisons with a Republican's immediate predecessor and successor are inherently invalid because it wouldn't be right to comment on the relative competence of a Democrat.

Remember how stupid Reagan was? *New York Times* editor Howell Raines famously pronounced that Reagan was so stupid, he couldn't tie his shoes.[11] Now get this: Quayle was even dumber! (And what were Raines's SAT scores again?) Michael Kinsley attacked Quayle in 1988, saying he was "outdoing even Ronald Reagan's" gaffes.[12] In 1992, the year of Quayle's next run, cartoonist Matt Groening, creator of *The Simpsons,* said Quayle "is more stupid than Ronald Reagan put together."[13] But then, guess who turned out to be even *dumber* than Quayle? That's right: George W. Bush! In twenty years, he'll be the smart one.

Senator John Kerry (D-Mass.) attacked Bush during the 2000 presidential campaign—or "questioned Mr. Bush's intelligence," as the *New York Times* somberly put it—by calling him dumber than . . . Dan Quayle. Kerry said, "All over this country people are asking whether or not George Bush is smart enough to be president of the United States." And the "scary" thing is, "one of the people asking me was Dan Quayle."[14]

Columnists sneered that Bush was the biggest "overprivileged frat moron to appear in the public eye since star-spangled superdunce Dan Quayle,"[15] and that if Bush could "hold his own" with Quayle, they could form the candidacy of "dumb and dumber."[16] Another columnist stated that Bush "could be considered just another Dan Quayle"—except Quayle was at least a good golfer.[17]

Even the highly accomplished tutu model, Ron Reagan Jr., got in on the act, scoffing that Bush was "probably the least qualified person ever to be nominated by a major party. What is his accomplishment? That he's no longer an obnoxious drunk?" If he weren't family, Ron Jr. would have called his father a worthless idiot, too.

The left's single most impressive use of the "dumb" argument was against Ronald Reagan. Trying to document the widespread belief that Reagan was dumb would be like trying to document a general societal animosity toward the flu. Reagan's stupidity was touted in late-night jokes, Broadway plays, the nation's editorial pages, and morning TV shows. It was pervasive, unquestioned, something all cultured people simply took for granted. A lesser man would have been destroyed by the relentless attacks.

More enraging than the media's gibes about Reagan's stupidity were their patronizing expressions of phony concern about Reagan's mental acuity. Reagan's supporters were called upon to assure *New York Times* reporters that Reagan is "not a stupid person at all."[18] As with all liberal smear campaigns, eventually the slur became its own reality.

In the 1980 presidential campaign, Jimmy Carter's reported strategy was to portray Reagan as "untested, old, dumb, simplistic, [an] actor, naive, inexperienced, Republican, right wing,"[19] as *National Journal* reporter Ronald Brownstein put it. When Walter Mondale ran against Reagan four years later, Brownstein said the Mondale campaign had "dusted off" the old Carter list, dropping only the "inexperienced" charge.[20] Even the *New York Times* expressed exasperation with Mondale for adopting as his sole debate strategy "calling Ronald Reagan dumb."[21]

Mondale's daughter Eleanor campaigned for her father wearing a button that said NO MO'RON FOR PRESIDENT. Mondale said she was "terribly afraid about what is going to happen to this country."[22] With only slightly more nuance, Mondale himself said: "What we need is a President who's in touch with reality."

Former governor Edmund (Pat) Brown made the compelling point that "anybody that's for Reagan is stupid."[23] Reagan was called an "amiable dunce" by Clark Clifford (who by contrast, was "an unctuous sleazeball," as Andrew Ferguson put it).[24]

In 1982, Mike Royko wrote in the *Chicago Sun-Times:* "No matter how you look at it, Reagan has managed to goof things up in record time."[25] In a 1986 column (comparing Reagan to Muammar Qaddafi) Pete Hamill spoke of Reagan's "fuzzyheaded political ideology" and his tendency to reduce "political thinking to dumb slogans."[26]

Shortly after Reagan won the largest electoral landslide in history, Gore Vidal quipped, "President Reagan's library burned down, both books. The tragedy was, he had not finished coloring the books."[27] In contradistinction to the anti-Reagan bile of college dropout Michael Moore, Vidal's remark was at least a joke. It's just that it's always the same joke. In an attack too pointlessly complicated to quote in full here, Richard Cohen of the *Washington Post* wrote: "Picture Ronald Reagan. Okay, now picture him as a giant knee. . . . He really is a knee-jerk conservative."[28]

University professors filled letters-to-the-editor sections with snotty jeers at stupid old Reagan, such as one that referred to "the simpleminded pronouncements of grandpa Reagan."[29] A joke popular with the liberal sect throughout the Reagan years was "George Washington couldn't tell a lie, Nixon couldn't tell the truth, and Ronald Reagan can't tell the difference."[30]

Toward the end of Reagan's amazingly successful second term, American Enterprise Institute's William Schneider authoritatively announced—as Schneider announces all liberal clichés—that the Reagan presidency was eight years of "simpleminded bromides."[31] There was even a Broadway play written by Garry Trudeau of *Doonesbury* fame, the theme of which was:

Reagan is dumb. (When the play bombed, the failure was attributed to the Reagan character's being too lovable.[32])

Throughout the Reagan years, opposition to any administration policy—any policy at all—never had to be explained beyond calling it dumb. Since all sophisticated people knew Reagan was stupid, the proposition that his policies were stupid because he was stupid was, ispo facto, a good argument. Republican Vin Weber (R-Minn.) objected to Reagan's proposed education cuts by calling the cuts "dumb." Representative Henry Gonzalez (D-Tex.) said the denial of a visa to Nicaraguan leader Tomas Borge was an example of Reagan showing his "mental senility"—as opposed to one of those other types of senility.[33] When then-Senator Al Gore was campaigning for president in 1988, he attacked Vice President Bush for supporting some Reagan policies that were "unfathomably dumb."[34] Opponents of Reagan's proposal to privatize Amtrak explained that the idea was "dumb."[35] New York Mayor Ed Koch said Reagan's plan to eliminate federal mass-transit subsidies was "the dumbest thing I've heard of in years."[36] Columnist Mike Royko said that, in the opinion of "several hundred of the nation's top scientists—physicists, engineers, mathematicians and others," Reagan's missile defense system was "a dumb idea."[37]

And this is how liberals developed their formidable debating skills.

Another classic from the Reagan-Is-Dumb genre was an op-ed piece in the *Washington Post* attacking Reagan for his proposal to disband the Council of Economic Advisers. The article thoughtfully explained: "[N]othing is so downright dumb as the consideration President Reagan is giving to junking the Council of Economic Advisers."[38] All in all, you weren't likely to learn much from the column if your reaction to Reagan's proposal wasn't already *"How in God's name are we going to get along without the Council of Economic Advisers!"* The article included the powerful testimony from "one of the two surviving members of the CEA" who strenuously opposed the elimination of his job.

But not to lose sight of the main point, the article stressed that Reagan was dumb. His plan to eliminate the invaluable CEA reflected "a more general distaste at the White House for alternative ideas, especially from economists and academics of all kinds." Strictly speaking, this *was* an alternative idea: Instead of having the CEA (old idea), Reagan was going to get rid of it (new idea). But whatever—Reagan's idea of eliminating the CEA was dumb because Reagan was dumb.

Foreign dignitaries quickly adapted to the native culture by telling reporters they, too, thought Reagan was dumb. *New York Times* columnist James Reston wrote that visiting NATO officials had "no confidence" in President Reagan and questioned his "knowledge of the facts."[39] To really drive the point home, Reston noted that the foreign ministers were "highly intelligent" and "make elegant toasts." The elegant toastmasters believed "diplomacy is an exercise in compromise," and that "compromise is the goal." Reagan, by contrast, "thinks it's a struggle between winners and losers." Scaring the wits out of liberals everywhere, Reston reported that Reagan's "objective is to win." And then when Reagan did win the Cold War, they said he was lucky.

It's always the same story about delightful sophisticates sneering at Republican presidents; the actual Republican is utterly fungible. Thus, in an eerie coincidence, the *New York Times* made the shocking discovery that foreign leaders were smirking about another "dumb" Republican president seventeen years later. (The *Times* has a sensitive barometer for these things.) Maureen Dowd reported that many foreign leaders held President Bush in disdain: "Gerhard Schröder thinks that he and W. had no communication when they met, and that W. had trouble remembering his name. Tony Blair has to call Bill Clinton to find a sympathetic ear."[40]

Most embarrassing for Bush, Dowd said snide remarks were being made about Bush at a recent Georgetown cocktail party. Robert McNamara, mastermind of America's defeat in Vietnam, was sniping about Bush's handling of the Chinese plane crisis. Bush, it seems, had departed from the prized McNamara dispute-resolution technique, which consists of starting a ground war in a jungle, losing the war, condemning millions of people to live under a communist tyranny, and then casually announcing twenty-five years later that you knew the war was doomed from the start. McNamara probably makes elegant toasts, too.

When Reagan was up for a second term in 1984, liberals deftly switched their argument from "dumb" to "senile." Since they always thought Reagan was an idiot, only the finely honed talents of skilled American reporters could detect the subtle distinction between innate stupidity and age-related senility. Without irony, the *Washington Post* reported: "Democrats, usually sensitive about raising the issue, openly suggested that Reagan, 73, was too old to serve another four years."[41]

Striking a particularly smarmy note, the *Economist* advised Reagan to "think hard" before running again. Nothing personal, but he was senile. For reasons having to do with his "virtues as much as his manifest faults as a president," the *Economist* was foursquare against a second term. "By hanging on in old age Mr Reagan might undermine his legacy more than if he leaves it persuasively behind him now."

When Reagan began his (spectacularly successful) second term, he was seventy-three years old. A majority of the Justices on the Supreme Court were older than he was, including liberal icons William Brennan, seventy-seven; Thurgood Marshall, seventy-five, and Harry Blackmun, seventy-five.[42] Yet there was no media hysteria over the senile old guys deciding life and death issues from the Supreme Court, no campaign to get those old coots to hang up their stirrups.

Attempting to duck charges of ageism, the media began deploying old people for the Reagan senility watch. Naturally, the *New York Times* led the way. In June 1984, the paper ran an article by George W. Ball, undersecretary of state in the Kennedy and Johnson administrations. Ball was—it was duly noted—seventy-four years old.[43] In an incredibly creepy column, Ball ("who is 74 years old") ran through Reagan's chances of dying during the next four years. Apparently, the actuarial tables indicated that Reagan had only "a two-thirds chance" of living for four more years. Becoming increasingly macabre, Ball ("who is 74 years old") noted that Reagan's chances were "even less" if he were re-elected since in this century "one-eighth of our dead Presidents were assassinated."

All in all, it was a column that would have provoked a visit from the Secret Service during the Clinton administration.

The "real hazard," said Ball ("who is 74 years old"), was not that Reagan would be assassinated, but that he "will become ill, senile or slow in thought and reactions." Frighteningly, he might be unable to surrender to the Soviet Union with the alacrity desired at the *New York Times*.

Ball ("who is 74 years old") went on to describe in unseemly detail a paralytic Democrat president, Woodrow Wilson, who functioned "only marginally and fitfully" and was unable to sign or veto legislation (an appalling amount of which managed to become law anyway). Ball excused Wilson's blithering senility on the grounds that we had just won World War I—"fortunately"!—and the nation was safe from foreign attack. And happily, the Wilsonian peace lasted until the consequences of Wilson's partition of Germany led like night into day to World War II.

But that was different: Wilson was a Democrat. Or as Ball phonily distinguished the cases, in 1984 "we face an antagonist armed to the teeth with nuclear weapons." Citing his own experience as an advisor to President John F. Kennedy when Kennedy almost got us all killed during the Cuban missile crisis, Ball wrote: "How could we deal with a Soviet Union whose leaders knew that the only man empowered to push the nuclear button was too ill to think or act decisively?" Of course, if they read the *New York Times,* Soviet leaders already thought Reagan was too stupid to "act decisively."

Ball concluded soothingly: "God help our country if we ever have to face such a tragic mess!" You wouldn't want a senile old guy like Reagan handling the Cold War. If he had been any more spritely, Reagan might have dispatched Red China, too.

Not long after the *Times*'s old-geezer attack, the *Washington Post* found its own septuagenarian to attack Reagan.[44] To seem less vicious than he was, the *Post*'s septuagenarian styled his attack on Reagan's mental acuity in the folksy, condescending tone young people find so irritating. He described the crippling effects of old age, saying, "one 73er, perhaps, has a better feel for another" and "one 73-year-old can see those telltale signs of slowing down in another." Drawing analogies from his own mental breakdown to the acumen of the man who was about to win the Cold War, he said: "We 73-year-olds simply don't think as fast as we used to; it's more of an effort when we try." He proclaimed Reagan "not dumb but—well, 73 years old."

When they weren't running articles by old people relating how they tend to misplace car keys around the house, the media raised the senility issue by reporting on the emergence of an "issue." Like other phony liberal concerns, "the age issue" only was an "issue" because the blabocracy kept harping on it.

Most peculiarly, a spate of general-interest articles on senility began to pop up in large-circulation magazines. In the ten months before the 1984 election, *Newsweek, Time, Ladies' Home Journal,* and *U.S. News & World Report* all ran major pieces on senility.[45] That's too many to be a coincidence. The LexisNexis archives yield only one magazine article on senility (*U.S. News & World Report*)[46] in 1976; zero in 1980; zero in 1988;[47] zero in 1992; one in 1996 (*Time* magazine);[48] and one in 2000 (*Maclean's*).[49] In other words, the same number of magazine articles on senility were published in 1984 alone as in all other presidential election years combined in the last quarter of the twentieth century.[50]

Fortunately, it turned out that forty-nine states preferred a senile old man to a Democrat. Amid unusually high voter turnout, Reagan was re-elected in the largest electoral college total ever. He went on to end the Soviet Union, preside over a booming economy, and translate his immense popularity with the public into another landslide election for his vice president (who then squandered it all by raising taxes). This is what liberals mean by "senile."

Years later, the media was still muttering about what a dope Reagan was. On September 27, 1999, NBC's host Katie Couric opened the *Today* show by chipperly announcing, "The Gipper was an airhead. That's one of the conclusions of a new biography of Ronald Reagan that's drawing a tremendous amount of interest and fire today."[51] She was referring to the recently released Edmund Morris book, *Dutch: A Memoir of Ronald Reagan.* The next day, Matt Lauer opened the *Today* show saying, "Good morning. For the first time, President Bush is responding to the controversial new biography of Ronald Reagan and, in particular, the author's assertion that Reagan was a great president but an airhead."[52] After quoting President Bush attacking the "airhead" characterization as "grossly unfair and untrue," Lauer observed that another thing the author seems to say "is that the Reagans were not all that crazy about the Bushes."

When Morris finally came on the *Today* show to respond, he denounced the claim that his book called Reagan an airhead as "brutal and grossly unfair. I did not call him an airhead."[53] Explaining that he had simply written that on a first meeting, Reagan seemed "an apparent airhead," Morris observed that the "whole course" of his book "makes quite obvious that that first impression was wrong." To Couric's follow-up question, "So you do not believe today that Ronald Reagan was an airhead?" Morris said, "Oh, good God, no. He was a very bright man."[54]

Years after Reagan liquidated Lenin's revolution, biographer Lou Cannon pontificated that Reagan "was wonderful about Jack Benny and worthless on the subject of Lenin."[55] Good thing he wasn't "wonderful" on Lenin, or the Red Army might be goose-stepping through Toronto about now.

Summarizing the wildly successful Reagan years, *Washington Post* reporter Haynes Johnson wrote a book suggesting Reagan had sleepwalked through history—a thesis coyly alluded to in the title of his book, *Sleepwalking Through History: America in the Reagan Years.* Ponderous windbags wrote earnest book reviews observing that Johnson did not "specifically" say that Reagan was the one doing the sleepwalking.[56] (How about *Sleazeballing Through History: The Clinton Years?*) But as John Kenneth Galbraith admitted in his *New York Times* review of Johnson's book, Johnson made the case that Reagan was the sleepwalker "over and over again." Galbraith pompously added, "This is as it should be."[57]

The irrevocable fact that the American people adored Reagan posed a problem for liberals. They had very clearly explained that Reagan was dumb, mean-spirited, frightening, and so on. But, still, Americans loved him. Even during the media's nightly flogging of Iran-Contra, Reagan's approval ratings fell only 5 percentage points, from 80 percent to 75 percent.[58] This was "the biggest ever recorded" drop in Reagan's public approval rating.[59] A majority of Americans continued to approve of the job he was doing as president, and 79 percent of Americans said they "like him personally."

Eventually liberals threw in the towel on persuading the public to hate Reagan and instead trained their hostility on the American people. From the beginning, this had been the logical consequence of the left's attacks on Reagan. The self-appointed Party of the People hated the People because the People kept voting for Reagan.

A book reviewer for the *Washington Post* commented on the Reagan era by impotently demanding to know "just how dumb, how submissive Americans really are." He speculated that the public was "hypnotized by the fluctuations of Reagan's left eyebrow."[60] Citing "many observers," *Newsday*'s Jonathan Schell said that during the Reagan era "we Americans" (a preposterous conceit) "began willfully to deceive ourselves about the world in which we live and about our place in it."[61] Still in a huff about Reagan's triumphant popularity, Schell fumed: "A nation that has enclosed itself in a bubble of illusion is at risk of sudden, startling inundations of facts from the real world."

Reagan was elected by the American people in two presidential landslides—the second was the largest electoral college total in history. And then the ripe old fellow single-handedly won the Cold War, ending the forty-year threat of nuclear annihilation and finally freeing liberals of their grave responsibility to frighten small children with tales of a coming nuclear holocaust. He cut taxes, ended inflation, and presided over a booming economy. In a Gallup poll taken in February 2001, respondents ranked Ronald Reagan as America's "greatest" president, beating out George Washington, Abraham Lincoln, and the left's beloved Franklin Delano Roosevelt.

If that isn't enough for liberals to stop calling you stupid, it makes you wonder if maybe it isn't something else about Republicans they don't like.

Another Republican who failed to meet the exacting IQ standards of the media is President George W. Bush. The image of Bush as an "airhead"—as the *New York Times* nonjudgmentally put it[62]—has been lovingly nurtured by the media. During the 2000 presidential campaign, the media was issuing daily updates on the Bush intelligence issue, which, as usual, had become an "issue" solely by virtue of the media's perseverating that it was an "issue."

In a seething rage that Bush does not defer to important Ivy League intellectuals so treasured at Establishment headquarters, the *New York Times* called Bush "determinedly nonintellectual"—an anti-intellectualism he "has resolutely cultivated." The *Washington Post* framed the Bush IQ "issue" this way: "Call it a recurring plume of doubt that hangs in the air like cigar smoke. Sometimes framed as depth, sometimes intellect, sometimes gravitas. Does George W. Bush have the candlepower to be a great president? Is George W. Bush bright enough to steer the country in times of crisis? Is George W. Bush a lightweight?"[63] *Time* magazine elaborated: "The implicit charge is less that he's stupid than that he's incurious, proudly anti-intellectual."[64]

This was in contrast to John McCain, who graduated fifth from the bottom of his class at the U.S. Naval Academy,[65] but was beloved by liberals and, therefore, never had his intellectual curiosity questioned.[66]

Dozens of columnists—chosen not for their leadership qualities, but presumably for their facility with words—used the "sharpest knife" cliché to describe Bush, such as an article in *U.S. News & World Report* that asked: "Is George W. Bush not the sharpest knife in the drawer?"[67] Demonstrating her own superior intellect, *Boston Globe* reporter Mary Leonard described Bush as not "the sharpest knife in the drawer" twice within the same month.[68] (It is long past time that reporters attacking Republicans as "dumb" be required to run SAT scores with their bylines, starting with Pinch Sulzberger at the *New York Times.*) In the LexisNexis archives, there is not a single use of the wildly original "sharpest knife" expression to describe Al Gore.

Liberals' idea of intellectual engagement is Bill Clinton's adolescent cramming in all-night slumber parties, leaving the place littered with pizza rinds and women's panties. Describing Gore's love of complex ideas, *Newsweek* admiringly observed that his office "is strewn with pizza cartons and Diet Coke cans."[69]

In a campaign profile of George Bush's college years, the *Times* quoted numerous real people—including famed Clinton flack Lanny Davis—testifying to Bush's superior intellect. Still, the article repeatedly insinuated that Bush was an idiot by use of the *Times*'s signature unsubstantiated asides. Thus the *Times* vaguely referred to conceptual Yale classmates "who frowned on Mr. Bush, seeing him as an airhead party boy." Also, the *Times* reported on impressions that seemed to exist: "Few, if any, professors seem to have left a mark on him, or he on them."[70]

Other evidence that Bush was dumb consisted of his failure to argue with the press about their querulous descriptions of him as dumb. After relentlessly calling Bush stupid, the media began psychoanalyzing his reaction to being called dumb. *Time* magazine reported: "[His] body tenses. He turns his face forward, his eyes narrow and he gazes out the windshield at the long road ahead."[71] Could it be . . . he was weary of being asked the same moronic questions about his intelligence?

Further probing Bush on the issue of just how dumb he was, the *Washington Post* reported: "It becomes apparent rather quickly that this is not a comfortable interview, and not a comfortable subject, for George W. Bush."[72] What precisely is the proper reaction to having one's intelligence questioned a billion times daily?

Gore was never asked if he was "too dumb." He was, however, asked whether Bush was too dumb. As reported by the AP, Gore "convulsed in laughter while taking a drink of Diet Coke . . . grabbed a towel to hold against his mouth then, finally swallowing, insisted the tape recorder be stopped for an off-the-record observation." And then Gore lost to the dumb guy—becoming the first incumbent president or vice president ever to lose a presidential election during peacetime and a good economy.

Most preposterously, the *New York Times* reported—as if it were news—"With his grades and college boards, Mr. Bush might not have been admitted [to Yale] if he had applied just a few years later."[73] *"Might not have been admitted"?* What on earth does that mean? Bush also "might not have been admitted" if he had dropped out of high school and become a Gangsta Rapper. It so galls Northeastern liberals that Republican George Bush went to an Ivy League school, they can't resist publicly fantasizing about an alternative universe in which Yale rejects him.

When not daydreaming about Republicans being rejected from Yale, the media spends its time enforcing the party line on dumb Republicans with Stalinist zeal. The tiniest deviation from liberal Scripture will be ferreted out and the apostate will be held up to ridicule by the liberal clergy. *New York Times* reporter Frank Bruni came in for public rebuke for an article in which he noted that Bush was "plenty bright." The whole point of the article was to suggest that Bush's allies were overplaying the intellectual disdain card and that Bush seemed to want "to have it all ways."[74]

Newsweek seized on the "plenty bright" locution to accuse Bruni of having fallen under Bush's spell. Bush was "manipulating reporters," *Newsweek* declared, "charming them."[75] And none were more susceptible than Frank Bruni—"probably the most influential beat reporter on the plane." The Bush magnetism, it was darkly suggested, had worked its magic. "Importantly for Bush," *Newsweek* said, Bruni had called Bush "plenty bright."

It probably wasn't really all that "important for Bush," actually. If the electoral viability of any Republican candidate turned on what *Times* reporters said about them, there would never be any Republican presidents.

Still, insinuating that Bush was "plenty bright" was bald-faced heresy. Consider that the "plenty bright" phrase had appeared in an article that accused Bush of coming across as a "self-satisfied boob." It recited a string of insults to Bush's intelligence from a (truly stupid) Republican, Governor Gary Johnson of New Mexico.[76] The subtitle of the article was "Ignorance Is Bliss." But Bruni's minuscule deviation from the party line required a public shaming ritual.

After having spent months dutifully creating an "issue" about a Republican's intelligence—nourishing it, protecting it from dissenting opinions, writing about it from this angle and that angle, taking it out and polishing it up again—the press then jumps on the smallest misstatement by a Republican on the grounds that it reinforces "impressions." Trading anonymity for instant celebrity, Andy Hiller, political correspondent for WHDH-TV in Boston, sprung a pop quiz on Bush early in the presidential campaign. The reporter demanded that Bush name the leaders of India, Pakistan, Chechnya, and Taiwan.

Bush exasperately refused to answer two world leader questions, gave the name of one leader, and described another. (Inasmuch as this was during the Clinton era, many Americans were frankly relieved at Bush's response, hoping that if we couldn't name their leaders, perhaps they couldn't name ours.) The media reacted as if Bush had been unable to locate Canada on a map. On the morning of November 15, 1999, this was major headline news across America:

"Pressed by a Reporter, Bush Falls Short in World Affairs Quiz"
New York Times

"Bush Fails Boston Reporter's Surprise Quiz in Interview"
USA Today

"Bush Names 1 of 4 World Leaders in Questions from Reporters"
Dallas Morning News

"Bush Fails Surprise Foreign Affairs Test"

Boston Globe

"Bush Flunks Reporter's Pop Quiz"

Atlanta Journal-Constitution

"Pop Quiz on World Leaders Trips Up Bush"

Philadelphia Inquirer [77]

George Stephanopoulos recited the DNC talking points memo as part of his objective analysis on ABC's *Good Morning America.* It seems the quiz incident raised an "underlying question" about Bush's qualifications and suggested that Bush was not "sure-footed": "There have been questions about George Bush's experience with foreign policy and his knowledge. He hasn't been surefooted on foreign policy this campaign ... When the war in Kosovo came up, he wasn't surefooted in his responses. I think his campaign now is going to have a very hard time calming people down about whether Governor Bush is up to this."[78]

This was 1999—the Republican primaries hadn't even gotten under way yet. (To his eternal credit, MSNBC's Brian Williams began questioning Clinton flack Paul Begala about the quiz, saying: "I assume you are going to tell us here, tonight, that the Bill Clinton of Little Rock, Arkansas, of 1991 and '2 knew every name of every foreign leader.")[79]

The pop quiz dominated the talk shows for days, including the Sunday morning political shows and every major newspaper and magazine in the country. Bush was directly questioned about it on ABC's *This Week.*[80] There was palpable joy on the *New York Times* op-ed page. In one of literally hundreds of articles on the incident, *Time* magazine described the pop quiz as a "critical moment" for Bush. *Newsweek* reported that the Bush campaign was "spin doctoring madly."[81] The *Washington Post* uncritically quoted Gore campaign officials comparing Bush's performance on a meaningless pop quiz to Gore's claim to have invented the Internet.[82] Not knowing this week's leader of Cameroon was the equivalent of pathological lying.

Andy Hiller, the wise-ass local reporter who sprung the pop quiz on Bush, was giddily feted as if he had just invented cold fusion. It was such a galling spectacle that even the *New York Times* expressed "hope" that the incident would not "tempt other journalists away from a deeper, more probing style of questioning."[83]

On the off chance that the public had missed the point, the media quickly sketched out the larger themes. Fascinatingly, these were the exact same themes the press sees with any Republican presidential candidate: (1) It reinforced "impressions" that Bush was dumb; and (2) it raised questions about how Bush reacted under fire. Thus, in a typical exegesis on the pop quiz, a *Kansas City Star* columnist said the pop quiz raised doubts about "Bush's most glaring weakness." It showed that "the frat boy born with a silver spoon still has something to prove."[84]

Over at the *New York Times,* they were mainly upset about Bush's facial expressions. Despite the incredible importance of the facial expression issue, *Times* columnists gave diametrically opposed descriptions of what Bush's facial expression was. Maureen Dowd wrote: "His interview smirk—that anti-intellectual bravado—was jarring."[85] On the very same page, the very same day, *Times* op-ed columnist Thomas Friedman described Bush's reaction as the exact opposite of a smirk: "It was the Quayle-in-the-headlights look."[86] So which was it? Cocky smirk or stupid, frightened stare? Whatever. The main point was the quiz was major news. The media's own lunatic overreaction turned the story into World War III.

Contrarily, the press maintained radio silence on stories embarrassing to Gore. For example—as long as we're on the subject of world leaders—Al Gore couldn't pick George Washington out of a lineup. In a highly publicized stop at Monticello during Clinton's 1993 inaugural festivities, Gore pointed to carvings of Washington and Benjamin Franklin and asked the curator: "Who are those guys?" He was surrounded by reporters and TV cameras when he said it. Only one newspaper, *USA Today,* reported the gaffe.[87]

The pop quiz soon raised a delicate matter even more urgent than Bush-bashing: How many answers should the opinion makers lyingly claim they could have gotten right? Eventually, the blabocracy bravely settled on "only two" as the appropriate answer. This was probably because Zbigniew

Brzezinski, President Carter's National Security advisor, admitted he would have known the answer to only two. Noticably, only two well-known commentators admitted that they could have identified only one of the world leaders (the same one Bush got): George Will and Chris Matthews. Say what you will about Will and Matthews, neither can be accused of lacking intellectual confidence.

On NBC's *Later Today,* the hostesses interrupted news on "surprise" recipes and home-designing tips to ridicule Bush for his ignorance. Host Asha Blake ("Her goal? To find foods and a lifestyle that give her energy")[88] sneered: "Somebody running for presidential office, a presidential candidate, should know the names of foreign leaders." On a break from her busy brain-surgery schedule, *Later Today* co-host Jodi Applegate complained: "I mean, it's not like he's being asked about some obscure leader in some obscure country."[89] Zbigniew Brzezinski: two; George Will: one. Telegenic half-wits don't even know enough to know what smart people are supposed to know.

A fairly extensive LexisNexis search turns up only two people who claimed they could have named all four leaders—a Democrat pundette on Fox News's *Hannity and Colmes* named Jenny . . . and Al Gore.

The media's fanatical obsession with Bush's minor slips of tongue says nothing about Bush's intelligence and everything about how liberals demean their political opponents rather than argue with them. Every human being occasionally stumbles over words. Only Republicans have their stumbles giddily repeated ad nauseam, analyzed and used as epithets, until more Americans can recite a simple slip of tongue by a Republican than can place the Civil War in the correct century. You would think the geniuses in the media had never made a mistake themselves. The often lengthy and hilarious "corrections" section of the *New York Times* belies that impression.

The *New York Times* launched one of its typical substantiveless sneers at George W. Bush's intelligence when he first considered running for president in March 1999: "Mr. Bush has embarked on a cram course that could be titled 'What you need to know to run for President.' . . . There may never have been a 'serious' candidate who needed it more."[90] A "correction" issued four days later stated that the last sentence was not supposed to appear in the article, but was a "message between editors after the article was written" that somehow ended up in the article text.[91]

Throughout impeachment, commentators were constantly calling Clinton "Nixon," and to this day say "impeach" when they mean "remove" (as

in, "President Clinton was not impeached"). Months after he finally left office, impeached former president Clinton was introduced by a member of the
New-York Historical Society as "Richard Nixon."[92] Over on NBC, John
McLaughlin—no slouch—made what came to be a very common slip, referring to Whitewater as "Watergate."

Even TV personalities with TelePrompTers and earpieces who only have
to speak coherently for an hour a day are constantly making verbal slips that
would never be forgotten if they had passed the lips of George Bush on his
fourteenth campaign stop in a single day. Turn on a TV news program right
now and you'll see one.

After the first 2000 presidential debate, CBS's Bob Schieffer remarked,
"[I] think George Bush's weakest moment—when—when he turned on
Bush's character."[93] The next day NBC's Tom Brokaw confused the $4.6 tril-
lion estimated surplus with the rather more substantial $25 trillion spending
estimate. Interviewing Bush, Brokaw said, "Almost everyone who is an
authority in this area says that both you and the vice president are way too
optimistic when we talk about this $25 trillion surplus, that there's a very
good possibility that we'll never get to that number."[94] When Bush merely
confused "billion" and "trillion" in the heat of a presidential campaign, the
Washington Post leapt on the slip to proclaim that Bush had "bolstered" his
critics.[95]

Word stumbles by Democratic politicians are hard to come by, inasmuch
as they are not recycled endlessly in peevish Maureen Dowd columns.
Democrat errors are buried, forgotten, ignored, and lied about. Sometimes
they are even falsely attributed to Republicans. When absolutely forced to
report on a Democrat's gaffe, the media insistently include a Republican's
error as well, so that it can be reported that both candidates are idiots.

One of the more outrageous examples of the media cushioning a Democrat's error with an alleged Republican comparable error concerned Clinton's
bungling incomprehension of what the Patriot missile does. In a campaign
speech on September 8, 1992, Clinton said: "We come up with great ideas
and then turn them into things like the Patriot missile, which will go through
doors and down chimneys."[96] This was an extremely embarrassing error
about missile technology. The Patriot missile is a purely defensive missile: It
is a surface-to-air missile designed to shoot down incoming missiles, not
objects on the ground, like chimneys.

If it were possible for "impressions" to be "reinforced" about Democrats, Clinton's mistake might have been said to reinforce impressions that he

knew nothing about the military. National defense was arguably even more important than the proper spelling of "potato." Dan Quayle quickly rejoined that Clinton had "confused the Patriot with the cruise missile. Bill Clinton knows less about national security than I do about spelling."[97]

This is how the mainstream media reported on Clinton's gaffe and Quayle's retort: The *Los Angeles Times* said, "Quayle had to extract both feet from his own mouth. He too had the wrong missile."[98] *Time* magazine said: "Quayle tweaked Clinton for referring in a speech to Patriot missiles going 'down chimneys' during the Gulf War. Ha, said Quayle: 'Bill Clinton knows less about national security than I do about spelling!' The weapons, said Quayle, were cruise missiles. Join the club, Dan. They were smart bombs."[99] CNN's Frederick Allen said that "neither side had much luck when it came to discussing national security," because "[a]ctually, these things are called smart bombs—which gives them a distinction from the candidates."[100]

Who was right? The combined intellectual firepower of the *Los Angeles Times, Time,* and CNN—or Dan Quayle? The answer is: Dan Quayle. Neither the cruise missile nor smart bombs literally go down chimneys—but in theory, both could, and about equally well.[101] Thus, when talking about weapons that can "go down chimneys and through doors," it would be accurate to refer to either cruise missiles or smart bombs. By contrast, the Patriot missile—identified by Clinton as going down chimneys—has nothing whatsoever to do with precise targeting. But the media was so determined to call Quayle an idiot, they could not bear reporting that Quayle had caught Clinton making a mistake. So they simply lied and reported that Quayle was wrong, too.

If accurately correcting a Democrat makes you an idiot, God help any Republican who misplaces a syllable. In the 2000 presidential election, the *ABC News* website carefully catalogued Bush's every word slip in a section titled "The English Patient." There was no "One Flew Over the Cuckoo's Nest" section for Gore's incessant lies. Indeed, the misstatements of Democrats are extremely difficult to come by inasmuch as no record of them is meticulously compiled by media watchdogs.

Shockingly though, Democrats are not infallible, either. Here are a few Democratic blunders that somehow made their way into the public record:

Bill Clinton: "This is still the greatest country in the world, if we just will steel our wills and lose our minds."[102]

Bill Clinton: "They've managed to keep their unemployment low although their overall unemployment is high."[103]

U.S. Senator Barbara Boxer: "Those who survived the San Francisco earthquake said, 'Thank God I'm still alive.' But, of course, those who died, their lives will never be the same again."[104]

Former Attorney General Janet Reno: "I always wait until a jury has spoken before I anticipate what they will do."[105]

Al Gore: "A zebra cannot change its spots."[106] (In a speech on the Senate floor on September 1991, later edited in the Congressional Record.)

British Prime Minister Tony Blair: "The people going into action are in far more danger than me."[107] (On the relative safety of his family and soldiers being sent to Afghanistan, October 11, 2001.)

Hillary Clinton: "I'm having a great time being presi—"[108] (On July 19, 2001, denying she intended to seek the presidency.)

Bill Clinton: "I'd like for you to have more, rather than less, sooner, rather than later." (On January 22, 1998, meaning he would never cough up any information whatsoever until threatened with a subpoena.)

Al Gore: "I always had a very vivid and clear sense that men and women were entirely and completely equal—if not more so."[109]

Gore tried to pass off his "equal if not more so" stumble as a hilarious joke, and that is how the media obediently reported it. Except the joke would have been: *Women are equal, if not more so,* not *men and women are equal, if not more so.* Otherwise, it's only a joke about bad grammar. Bush could have just as plausibly passed off his verbal slips as jokes about verbal slips.

Gore also told a union gathering that his mother used to sing lullabies to him as an infant including "Look for the Union Label." Then it turned out that song had been written in 1975, when Gore was twenty-seven. Gore misspoke. Therefore—pursuant to the rigorous IQ standards imposed by the media—Gore is a moron.

For truly appalling grammar, nothing beats Hillary's scandal patois. Legal troubles always seem to bring out the hillbilly in her. During the *60 Minutes* interview when the Clintons lied to the country about Gennifer Flowers, Hillary's ersatz Arkansas twang was virtually unlistenable: "I'm not sittin' here, some little woman, standin' by my man like Tammy Wynette. I'm sittin' here because I love him, and I honor what he's been through and what we've been through together, and, you know, if that's not enough for people, then, heck, don't vote for him."

Particularly grating is Hillary's Valley Girl penchant for saying "real" when she means "really." When asked at a press conference on Whitewater about her failing health care plan, she began: "I think that's a real important question."[110] During the lying *60 Minutes* interview, she said: "I think it's real dangerous in this country if we don't have some zone of privacy for everybody."[111] The only solace is knowing that listening to that must have been like nails on a blackboard for every single *New York Times* reporter.

Meanwhile, *Vanity Fair* actually psychoanalyzed Bush's misstatements, purporting to have proved him dyslexic. This was absolutely *not* liberals avoiding real issues. To the contrary, Bush's occasional misstatements were a matter of grave national importance. As author Gail Sheehy explained, dyslexics "develop rigidity, needing the comfort of following a known path."

By total happenstance, this is exactly what liberals say about all conservatives, with or without any phony "dyslexia" diagnoses. The left's dogmatic refusal to acknowledge any facts that contradict their ideology—such as the now dispositive data on concealed carry laws—is known as thinking "outside the box." In a charming populist touch, Sheehy claimed Bush's Christianity was a symptom of his mental defect. It seems Christianity filled a psychological need for "structure and a spiritual discipline" common to many dyslexics. Citing "experts," Sheehy proclaimed that Bush's apocryphal "dyslexia" could affect his performance as president.

If liberals truly believed verbal fluency were determinative of IQ, why did they call Reagan dumb? The peculiar liberal obsession with verbal facility as a proxy for IQ seemed to recede a bit when the "Great Communicator" was president. Instead of hailing Reagan as the greatest genius ever to inhabit the White House, his very facility with words was derided as the vocational faculty of a hackneyed actor.

When he was over eighty years old, having left public life four years earlier, Reagan made an incredibly minor slip during his speech to the 1992 Republican National Convention. The refrain to his speech was a quote from John Adams: "Facts are stubborn things." Reagan stated the refrain flawlessly a half dozen times, but in one single rendition of it he said: "Facts are stupid things—stubborn things, I should say."

That one-syllable slip quickly became the greatest Republican error since Watergate. Reagan's monumental idiocy in making a minor slip has been cited in at least four books[112] and flogged in seventy-seven news stories on LexisNexis. Soon liberals began embellishing on the word slip to claim

Reagan had got the quote wrong—claiming it was not a verbal slip but a "misquotation." This called for snippy remarks from all the Adams experts in the media.

A book review in the *New York Times* noted that "many famous and successful people had little regard for history, . . . cf. Ronald Reagan, 'Facts are stupid things' et passim"[113] (meaning "and throughout"). An article in the *Dallas Morning News* said Reagan had "misquoted John Adams," saying Reagan's "version" was "Facts are stupid things."[114] A column in the *Los Angeles Times* suggested Reagan was "making up something stupid on his own."[115]

Bush occasionally misspeaks and therefore he's an idiot. Reagan spoke mellifluously, which proved he was an idiot, except the one time he finally fumbled a word—which also demonstrated he was an idiot. You can't win with these people; all a Republican can do is die.

On the left's theory that misspeaking is a searing gauge of intelligence, Gore was an imbecile. "Subliminable," for example, is a lot closer to "subliminal" than "was the inspiration for *Love Story*" is to "knew the guy who wrote *Love Story*." Bush may stumble over his words on occasion, as does every human. At least he never claimed he fought at the Alamo.

Liberals are not only incapable of explaining a conservative position, they censor conservative views from their media. Instead of arguing substantive issues, liberals prefer to drone on and on about the larger cosmic meaning of Bush saying "subliminable." It's as if they believe allowing an articulate statement of the conservative position to escape into the world will put a religious hex on them. Until you can intelligently articulate the other side's position, you are not an adult. You are a liberal.

For those easily duped by media propaganda, there would be no more staggering surprise than George W. Bush's masterful response to a devastating terrorist attack seven months after he took office. Never was the myth of a "dumb" Republican shattered with such dispatch. Stupid old Reagan won the Cold War, but that took time. It was the gradual, if inevitable, outcome of Reagan's massive defense buildup, military invasions, support for anti-communist insurgents around the globe, and, finally, walking away from the table at Reykjavik.

Unfortunately for liberals, a surprise attack on America on September 11, 2001, would test George W. Bush like no other president in United States history. It was precisely the risk of something like a terrorist attack happening that sent the media into anxious reveries about Bush's performance on Andy Hiller's pop quiz. How on earth could Bush be expected to handle a national crisis if he couldn't name the Prime Minister of Swaziland? (Dr. Barnabas Sibusiso Dlamini.)

Bush's alleged weaknesses—subjected to side-splitting ridicule throughout the campaign—were precisely those that would be most severely tested in the crucible of war. Contrary to urgent news bulletins throughout the campaign, Bush was a masterful leader. War was where the rubber met the road and Bush was the consummate wartime commander. The media's campaign portrayal of Bush as "not the sharpest knife in the drawer" was not simply wrong in the sense of being untrue. It was the opposite of true. The media had lied and now everyone knew it.

Far from smirking bravado, Bush exuded calm deliberation. He didn't overreact with a quick ostentatious display of pyrotechnics, as Democrats are wont to do. Indeed, in a direct rebuke to the Clinton administration, Bush pointedly said: "When I take action, I'm not going to fire a $2 million missile at a $10 empty tent and hit a camel in the butt. It's going to be decisive."

The very opposite of an incurious frat boy, Bush inspired the nation and showed the world America's resolve. In one of the most eloquent speeches in American history, he proclaimed, "As long as the United States of America is determined and strong, this will not be an age of terror. This will be an age of liberty here and across the world."

Describing a new and confusing enemy, Bush said we have "seen their kind before": "They are the heirs of all the murderous ideologies of the twentieth century. By sacrificing human life to serve their radical visions, by abandoning every value except the will to power, they follow in the path of fascism, Nazism, and totalitarianism. And they will follow that path all the way to where it ends: in history's unmarked grave of discarded lies."

The dyslexic retard delivered the speech flawlessly. *New York Times* columnist Bob Herbert called it "a near-perfect speech."[116] (For someone who hangs out with a bad crowd, Herbert's first impulses are almost always good.)

Most impressively, in word and deed, the president emboldened a jittery nation: "The course of this conflict is not known, yet its outcome is certain. Freedom and fear, justice and cruelty, have always been at war. And we know that God is not neutral between them. . . . Fellow citizens, we will meet violence with patient justice, assured of the rightness of our cause and confident of the victories to come. In all that lies before us, may God grant us wisdom and may He watch over the United States of America."

America had a leader who said what he meant and meant what he said—and just in the nick of time. Having cleared out the pizza boxes, women's panties, and other detritus of the Caligula administration, the country was finally being run by grown-ups again. The entire administration was a smooth, purring machine. Bush had assembled an astonishingly talented team of advisors, and placed each in the perfect position. The nation could sleep well at night.

The incurious frat boy would go on to demonstrate the value of real intelligence, courting world leaders with his charm and resolute determination. Importantly, Bush instantly forged a crucial alliance with the leader of a Muslim nation that had its own share of Islamic terrorists, but which bordered on Afghanistan. That leader was General Pervez Musharraf of Pakistan. One wonders how President "Jenny" would have done sealing that delicate deal: Musharraf, of course, was one of the leaders Bush had been unable to name in the celebrated TV reporter's pop quiz.

The media's relentless campaign of portraying Bush as a frivolous ne'er-do-well had culminated just days before the election when Senator Joseph Lieberman, Gore's running mate, solemnly raised the prospect of war. This was supposed to be an argument in favor of Al Gore. "When I think of a solitary figure standing in the Oval Office, weighing life and death decisions that can affect the security of our country and the stability of our world, I see Al Gore."[117]

But when war came, liberals were forced to confront their own demons, realizing with unmitigated relief that Al Gore was not the man "standing in the Oval Office." Not long after the attack, the *New York Times* talked to a series of "prominent Democrats"[118]—mostly off the record for obvious reasons. Uniformly, the Democrats sang Bush's praises, and conceded that Gore would have been a disaster. Though Bush had been ceaselessly derided for his inability to talk, Democrats were now giving rave reviews to Bush's wartime pronouncements and questioning "whether the former vice president would have been as nimble at communicating to the public."[119]

These prominent Democrats also heaped praise on Bush's advisors and "questioned whether Mr. Gore would have surrounded himself with as experienced a foreign policy team as Mr. Bush." Shuddering at the thought of Gore's foreign policy advisors "running a war against Afghanistan," one former "top" Clinton appointee "criticiz[ed] the qualifications of those he expected to be Mr. Gore's foreign policy team."[120] A "staunch" Gore supporter and former Democratic senator griped that Gore "would have tried to micromanage everything."[121]

If you got your news from the news, all this would have come as a bolt out of the blue. Bush's most impressive qualities included every single point for which he had been demeaned during the campaign. When Bush was running for president, the typical news report on his leadership abilities went something like this: "He flunked a foreign leaders pop quiz, doesn't know a Greek from a 'Grecian,' was a C-average college student, can't remember what, if anything, he liked to read as a boy, and admits that, even today, he doesn't care to read weighty books on public policy, a subject that would seem a natural for the governor of the second-most-populous state."[122] (Incidentally, "public policy" isn't a "subject." And he was a C-average *Yale* student—back in the days when it was still possible to get a C at Yale.)

Astonishingly, Bush had even been mocked for his advisors. *New York Times* columnist Thomas Friedman put the case this way: "A lot of people say that Mr. Bush, while he knows little foreign policy, has hired smart advisors. Oh, really? Well what happens when his two smartest advisors disagree?"[123]

Somehow that devilish conundrum worked itself out. There was no question that it was he who was calling the shots. It was he who made the central decision to go after the entire Al-Quida terrorist organization after CIA director George Tenet raised the "sobering thought" that Al-Quida was a "60-country problem."[124] Not Secretary Donald Rumsfeld, not National Security Adviser Condoleeza Rice, not Secretary of State Colin Powell.

Recall that the pop quiz had been treated like the Rosetta stone of presidential qualifications. *USA Today* reported that Bush's performance on the pop quiz had intensified "concerns" that he "lacks the intellectual heft to be commander in chief."[125] Showing great prescience, the article also complained that Bush had made matters worse by appearing to "put a positive spin on last month's military coup in Pakistan."[126] This was the coup that installed General Musharraf—who became America's indispensable ally in the war on terrorism.

New York Times columnist Friedman had claimed the pop quiz was important because it told us how Bush "feels" about these countries.[127] Good call. Another *Times* columnist, Maureen Dowd, said Bush should have seen it coming: "The question has been hanging out there for months about whether Bush the Younger knows enough about the world to deal with all the loons, coups and wars that spring up like twisters across the post-cold-war plains."[128]

Time magazine triumphantly proclaimed that "the quiz was as much a test of his political radar as of his foreign-policy smarts." That article also made the inane argument that Bush was in no position to complain about "a media ambush" because his own education reforms required "testing what students know before allowing them to advance to the next grade."[129]

This must have struck *Newsweek*'s Jonathan Alter as a devastating critique since he made the same incredibly weird point a week later. It was "ironic," Alter said, that Bush had criticized social promotion in schools and now he would "be tested repeatedly by the press on his knowledge of foreign policy" where there would "be no social promotion."[130]

Obviously, some portion of the population knew it was being lied to all along—and some portion of the population knew it was doing the lying. But there are also many people who mechanically adopt any and all fashionable platitudes. They will look you straight in the eye, every four years for their entire insipid lives, and insist that the Republican de jour is "stupid." (Cher on Bush: "He's stupid."[131])

When America was attacked, even that segment of the populace had to pull itself away from Lifetime TV for five minutes to watch the president. And, suddenly, the media had some 'splaining to do. The Oracle of Delphi was fast losing credibility. Liberals couldn't just own up and admit they had lied about Bush (Coolidge, Eisenhower, Reagan, and Quayle). So instead, they began promoting an "Invasion of the Body Snatchers" theory of Bush's performance in wartime. It seemed like a perfectly plausible story to claim war had miraculously transformed a dopey, smirking frat boy into . . . SUPER BUSH! The only alternative was for the media to admit they had lied.

Thus the *New York Times* earnestly reported that Bush had been "transformed."[132] He had begun "coming of age as president."[133] Another *Times* article claimed, "You could almost see him growing into the clothes of the presidency."[134] Universal receptacle for liberal clichés, Richard Cohen of the *Washington Post* rolled out all the excuses in a single column, saying Bush had "grown," "rise[n] to the occasion," "gained confidence," and "seemed emboldened by the heroism of others."[135]

In case it was still not clear that this was definitely not the *same* George W. Bush the media had relentlessly called an idiot and probably dyslexic, the *New York Times* observed that Bush had found "the eloquence that has eluded him so often in the past."[136] Another *Times* reporter detected in Bush a "spontaneous new intensity" and a "new resolution" in his voice.[137] Democratic Representative Richard A. Gephardt remarked on how strong Bush had been—"these last few days."[138] Bush's eloquent speeches were called "a surprising development for a president who has often seemed rhetorically challenged."[139] After praising Bush's speech, *Times* columnist Bob Herbert duly noted that Bush "seldom wanders into the precincts of eloquence."[140]

Bush wasn't the only Republican who was mysteriously transformed by the war. Shortly before he became a national sex symbol, Secretary of Defense Donald Rumsfeld was the subject of gleeful sneering by *New York Times* columnist Maureen Dowd, who wittily called him "Rip Van Rummy." Proclaiming that "poor Rummy" was hopelessly out of touch,[141] Dowd snipped that he was "clueless about the press." In a reappearance of smirking foreign leaders, she fretted that "the Russians wonder if he's slept through the last decade." The "urgent question," the supercilious *Times* columnist announced, was "just how conscious of the world around him Rip Van Rummy is." In a ringing peroration, Dowd declared that Rumsfeld—as well as Vice President Dick Cheney—do "not know anything about how the world works." The "most striking thing is how out of touch they act."

Remember this when they call the next Republican "clueless."

EIGHT

CLEVER IS AS CLEVER DOES:

THE LIBERAL DILEMMA

In a single *New York Times* profile, a presidential candidate was repeatedly quoted using such expressions as "That's no good for sure" and "Isn't she cool?" Telling a reporter he wanted to discuss "big think" ideas, he stammered, "I can't say this, it's going to sound so weird." That was intellectual colossus Al Gore. Naturally, this led the *New York Times* to query: "Is Gore too smart to be president?" Mr. Gore's "challenge," the *Times* explained in that very article, is "to show that he is a regular guy despite a perceived surplus of gravitas, which at least some Americans seem to find intimidating." Or as Gore himself eruditely put it: "weird."

This is one of the grave injustices of the world: Democrats can run ridiculous and insubstantial men for important national offices and no one will ever know because the media won't report it. It is as unthinkable to describe a Democrat as stupid as it is to describe a Republican as smart. The adversary press will finish a Democrat's sentences for him, defend his arguments, provide substantiation for his ludicrous claims, and refuse to report his mistakes.

Gore is only the most recent Democratic mediocrity to dazzle media shills with his genius. Whenever the public fails to be similarly dazzled, the media leaps in to explain that the Democratic mediocrity is "too smart" to connect with ordinary voters. Thus, a columnist in the *Los Angeles Times* ruefully explained in the media's formulaic excuse, Gore was "too smart for [his] own good." Sadly, the "best and brightest student"—that's Gore here— "doesn't always get to be class president."[1]

One of the first Democrats to have his vast unpopularity with voters attributed to his soaring intellect was Adlai Stevenson. Widely known as a lover of literature, with an erudite wit, Stevenson was supposed to be the thinking man's president. Though it was blindingly obvious at the time that Stevenson was a boob—certainly clear to the American people who continually rejected him for president—only later was Stevenson discovered to be a lowbrow who rarely read books. When he died, only a single book was found on his nightstand: *The Social Register.*[2]

This has been a fifty-year game of the Emperor's New Brain, in which only true intellectuals (the media) are capable of discerning a Democrat's profound intellect. *U.S. News & World Report* wearily recounted the Herculean efforts the Clinton campaign was forced to undertake to conceal Clinton's towering intellect. His campaign staff "took great pains to 'dumb down' Clinton."[3] The author snippily added that this "won't be Bush's problem." *Time* magazine also addressed the question of how Clinton dealt with the problem of being so brilliant. "In politics, it's not smart to seem too smart. Bill Clinton uses his intellect to dazzle audiences, but he does it in an inclusive way. He articulates things people know but can't quite express."[4] The same article somberly reported that Hillary "was the Woman Who Knew Too Much."[5] She "sometimes can't help intimidating" voters with her grasp of the issues.

Other Democrats alleged to have been disadvantaged by their oversize intellects include Jimmy Carter, Walter Mondale, Michael Dukakis, and Bill Bradley. Also every other Democrat you've ever heard of.

Dukakis was so smart he was unaware of his wife Kitty's twenty-six-year addiction to diet pills.[6] As the *Los Angeles Times* reported, Dukakis "said he did not know of her habit until she underwent treatment in 1982." In light of Dukakis's renowned "attention to detail," the *Times* said, "even [Kitty's] sister was surprised at his professed ignorance."[7] He also displayed his towering intellect by advising Iowa farmers during the 1988 campaign that they should be growing Belgian endive.

Walter Mondale cleverly informed the voters in the middle of a campaign that he was going to raise their taxes. He also deftly sent his media strategists out to explain that the guy who had just walloped him in a debate was a senile old weakling.[8]

Jimmy Carter was so intelligent, he claimed to have been attacked by a killer rabbit during the 1980 campaign.[9] In a nationally televised debate with

Reagan, Carter smartly said that, in preparation for the debate, he had solicited the opinion of his teenage daughter Amy on nuclear war.

Senator Bill Bradley, Democrat of New Jersey, was well known to newspaper readers everywhere by his unofficial first name "Cerebral." The *Boston Globe* reported that unless "the cerebral Bill Bradley" caught on, "Gore appears to be the candidate."[10] The *San Francisco Chronicle* said the "cerebral Bradley wants to talk about his many ideas about tax policy and defense restructuring."[11] The *St. Louis Post-Dispatch* described Bradley's run-of-the-mill, tax-and-spend liberalism as "his cerebral approach to politics."[12] The *Boston Globe* said Bradley exuded "cerebral self-deprecation."[13] And CNN political analyst and *Los Angeles Times* columnist Ron Brownstein informed CNN viewers that Bradley was "cerebral."[14]

It was too much intellect for one man. Eventually, Bradley's soaring IQ began to infect his supporters and liberal colleagues. In the sort of major puff piece that makes Republicans nervous, the *New York Times Magazine* hailed half-wit "moderate" Republican Senator Susan Collins (Me.) as "reminiscent of Bill Bradley"—because she is "too cerebral."[15] CNN's William Schneider[16] and the *Los Angeles Times*[17] both reported that Bradley voters, too, were "cerebral."

But then—whoops!—it turned out Bradley got a 485 on his verbal SATs.[18] That's "cerebral" for a Democrat. Dumb George Bush got a 566, which was lower than Gore's 625—but a lot higher than Bradley's 485. (For those of you who took the SAT after 1994, all these scores would be higher under the new inflated scoring system.[19])

Let the record reflect that an octogenarian former Republican president who makes a two-syllable slip in an otherwise flawlessly delivered convention speech is an idiot, but a Democratic presidential candidate who gets a 485 on his SATs is "cerebral." The "cerebral" Bradley's very non-Princetonian SAT score was not discovered by *Time*, *Newsweek*, or the *New York Times*. They were too busy with the hard-hitting investigative work of calling Bush dumb. Mr. Cerebral's SAT score was outed on the Internet.

Even after the truth was out, the serious media barely alluded to the mammoth hole that had been blown in Bradley's "cerebral" image. Those that did mention it cited Bradley's low score as part of the burgeoning case that Bush was dumb or, alternatively, that the test was dumb. It being a metaphysical impossibility for a Democrat to be dumb, this was the only other possible explanation for Bradley's low score. The *New York Times* dropped the bomb in the Education section of the paper, concluding that *both* Bradley's and Bush's scores "offer two more pieces of evidence that the SAT is not an exceptional predictor of success." The headline on *U.S. News & World Report*'s article on Bradley's scores was incomprehensibly titled "Who's the dimmest dim bulb?" Jay Leno joked, "The bad news is that Bush may be the smart one." The *Washington Post* said that Bradley's low score "cannot be good news for the people who run the Educational Testing Service," since it raised old charges that the test "does not reflect real aptitude or accurately predict success."[20]

The media's designation of all Democrats as smart and all Republicans as dumb had finally been contradicted by cold, hard evidence. But instead of exposing media bias, the facts had to be shoehorned into a different theory.

If Bush is a dope with a 566 on the verbal SAT, but a 485 makes a Democrat "cerebral,"[21] what were Pinch Sulzberger's SAT scores? Liberals whose principal argument against Republican after Republican is that they are all idiots should put up or shut up. We want the scores of every reporter who ever sneered at the intelligence of Reagan and Bush. Especially Maureen Dowd and Howell Raines.

While we wait, let's consider the media's most stunning accomplishment since persuading the public that Adlai Stevenson was not a bilious blowhard: turning Al Gore into a genius. Even with years of practice, this was quite a feat. Among Gore's "big think" ideas was his proposal to ban the internal combustion engine. In the 2000 presidential campaign, he paid a feminist $15,000 a month to teach him how to be a man. He said he created the Internet. He claimed to be the inspiration for *Love Story*. He described his childhood (spent in the penthouse apartment of the Fairfax Hotel) as "cleaning out hog waste, clearing land with an ax, and plowing hillsides with a team of mules." Gore couldn't identify George Washington and Benjamin Franklin at Monticello.

In a 1994 speech, Gore got the country's national motto backward, saying, "*E Pluribus Unum*—out of one many."[22] He called Chicago Bulls forward Michael Jordan "Michael Jackson." (This last mistake was written up in the *Washington Post* in an article that attributed the error to George Bush and was titled "Bush's Gaffes Are Back as Debates Near.")[23] When it was Bush's mistake, the misstatement was big news, but when it turned out Gore had said it, it proved absolutely nothing and was promptly forgotten.

Rather, the question on every journalist's mind was, Will Gore's "brainy earnestness . . . deny him the larger prize"? (*USA Today*).[24] Or as the *New York Times* put it (citing the thoughts of "many"): "Many perceive that Mr. Gore is too smart for his own good."[25] In the unique analysis of *U.S. News & World Report,* "Gore is very smart, but he is almost too smart."[26]

In case Gore's robust intelligence had somehow failed to impress the public, the media issued repeated updates on the fact that Gore was smart. Amid vague citations to "voters," the *New York Times,*[27] *USA Today,*[28] the *Los Angeles Times,*[29] and the *National Journal,*[30] among many many others, all proclaimed Gore is "smart." Gore's subtle intellect was vividly captured by journalists Maureen Dowd[31] and David Gergen,[32] both of whom wrote: "Gore is smart."

These were, of course, the understated descriptions of Gore's intellectual prowess. More common was hallucinatory overstatement. *Newsweek* gasped that Gore was "thinking about complexity theory, open systems, Goethe and the absence of scientific metaphors in modern society."[33] Bloomberg News said Gore was impatient "with those a few IQ points short of genius" (which evidently included George Bush, who was said to be "no genius").[34]

One of the formulaic benedictions for Gore was that he is "the smartest kid in the class"—as he was described in dozens of articles in the year 2000 alone.[35] (This was in dramatic contrast to Bush, who, in addition to not being the "sharpest knife in the drawer," also "ain't the smartest kid in the class," according to the *New York Times*—quoting others to maintain reportorial distance.[36])

Being the "smartest kid in the class" was not all sunshine and song. To be sure, it meant Gore was smart (!). But it was also supposed to explain why voters seemed not to like him: He was just too damned smart. Except it turned out, again in the harsh light of facts, just because no one liked him didn't mean Gore was "the smartest kid in the class." Far from it. Gore's real school records were abominable. In high school, Gore received mostly Cs and Bs in English and history. He got all Cs in French. Only in art classes did Gore earn straight As. (And he took a lot of art classes.) Gore was admitted to Harvard—but he was the son of a prominent United States senator when applying to college.

Oddly, it was Bush who was routinely accused of having sailed through life on his father's name. But the truth was the reverse. The media was manipulating the fact that—many years later—Bush's father became president. When Bush was admitted to Yale, his father was a little-known congressman on the verge of losing his first Senate race. His father was a Yale alumnus, but so were a lot of other boys' parents. It was Gore, not Bush, who had a famous father likely to impress college admissions committees.

Having gotten in to Harvard at least in part on the basis of his father's prominence, Gore did not redeem himself. In his sophomore year at Harvard, Gore got one D, one C-minus, two Cs, two C-pluses, and one B-minus. This, the *Washington Post* reported, "placed him in the bottom fifth of the class for the second year in a row."[37] Gore's grades that year "were lower than any semester recorded on Bush's transcript from Yale." Conforming to the *New York Times* stylebook on how to report negative information about a Democrat, the *Post* slipped in an untrue and irrelevant potshot at Bush. The *Post* headline was: "Gore's Grades Belie Image of Studiousness; His School Transcripts Are a Lot Like Bush's."[38]

After college, Bush earned an M.B.A. from Harvard; Gore failed out of divinity school and dropped out of law school at Vanderbilt University. Gore failed five of his eight classes at divinity school. Here's a question for modern philosophers: How many classes does a Democrat have to fail in order not to be called "smart"?

Bolstering the media's message that Gore was very smart—maybe too smart—during the Democratic National Convention, an endless stream of Gore's friends and relatives took the stage to issue personal testimonials about what a clever jokester Gore was in private. By the end of it all you had to marvel at how well Gore had kept that amazing wit under wraps. He must reach Olympian heights when he's alone in the bathtub.

His convention speech-of-a-lifetime did bear witness to how his enormous cleverness seems to dissipate whenever anyone was watching. In the verbal equivalent of George Bush Sr. looking at his watch during the 1992 townhall debate, Gore could not read his speech fast enough. He just kept rushing through his windbag of a speech and stepping on his applause lines as if he wanted to spit out the whole garbled mess as quickly as possible and get back to the bathtub where he really hits his humor stride.

Bush couldn't name three foreign leaders? Gore couldn't name his own positions. On *Meet the Press,* Tim Russert asked Gore for his position on a bill that would prohibit the execution of pregnant women on death row. Gore's response was—and I quote—"I don't know what you're talking about." Russert tried restating the question several times, but Gore kept insisting he would need to know "the circumstances." The only pertinent "circumstances" were fully contained within the question: A pregnant woman is on death row. Would you be for a law preventing her execution until she gives birth? Gore didn't know.

The good part of being a Democrat is that you can commit crimes, sell out your base, bomb foreigners, and rape women, and the Democratic faithful will still think you're the greatest. The bad part is that you must effortlessly follow the party orthodoxy, which is completely impenetrable to human logic. Adhering to Democratic Party principles, the correct answer is, Kill the fetus and spare the murderess. Since Democrats can't just come out and say that, the situation obviously called for hostile evasion. Though he had spent years studying with the master, Gore could not produce the proper Clintonesque dodge: I've already answered that, this legislation is politically motivated, it's a private matter between the woman and "her God," the question has been propounded by a vast right-wing conspiracy, and I didn't do it.

Gore once claimed the biblical story of Cain and Abel was a parable about the dangers of pollution. Not original sin, not murder, not envy: pollution. "Indeed," he wrote in his magnum opus, *Earth in the Balance,* "the first instance of 'pollution' in the Bible occurs when Cain slays Abel." According to Gore, God was hopping mad about Cain polluting. Cain had "defiled the ground" with Abel's messy blood. Murder is one thing, but polluting really got God's goat. In Gore's view, the Bible inveighs against global warming and the internal combustion engine, but has nothing of any relevance to say on the matter of killing the unborn.

When pressed by the *New York Times* to expand upon his singular interpretation of the Cain and Abel story, Gore explained that God's original rebuff of Cain's offering of the fruit of the ground (which set off Cain's murderous jealousy—and the first recorded case of pollution) was simply "a metaphorical reference to the move from a herding to an agricultural economy."

I don't know. God works in mysterious ways and all, but His repudiation of agriculture products doesn't seem like the most lucid manner of promoting an agricultural economy.

In the second presidential debate, Gore segued directly from global warming to Scripture: "In my faith tradition, it's written in the Book of Matthew, where your heart is, there is your treasure also. And, I believe that we ought to recognize the value to our children and grandchildren of taking steps that preserve the environment in a way that's good for them." Skipping right past that preposterous "faith tradition" locution—a PC phrase for a religion you were brought up in and that voters have heard about but that you don't actually, technically speaking, in the narrow sense, believe—the book of Matthew emphatically does *not* say what Gore said it says.

The vice president's bungling misquote didn't just reverse Christ's words, but also reversed His meaning. Christ's real quote comes in the middle of a teaching warning that man "cannot serve God and mammon." He is commanding us to abjure "treasure upon earth," and instead to build "treasures in heaven." So when Christ says, "Where your treasure is, there will your heart be also," it's an admonition that if your treasure is anyplace but with God, then your heart cannot be with God (and you'll burn in hell).

To mangle Christ's quote into "where your heart is, there is your treasure also" and to suggest that the environment should be our treasure was not just stupid, it was aggressively anti-Christian. Gore's rendition sounds like some inspirational saying a guidance counselor might put on his office wall—"If you love soccer, follow your heart! . . . Where your heart is, there your treasure shall be! . . . Go for it!" Christ's whole point was that if your heart is with soccer (the environment, mammon, whatever) and not with Him, you're going to burn in hell. Hell ought to have gotten Gore's attention. All that burning probably causes pollution.

Gore spent much of his campaign denying any memory of his legally questionable fund-raising. Even Gore's campaign staff at the *New York Times* remarked on how often Gore's memory—"considered to be quite excellent—fails." When asked on Fox News how it was that his subpoenaed White House E-mails got lost, the Inventor of the Internet protested that he was "not an expert on computers."[39]

Of his Buddhist temple fund-raiser, Gore said: "I'll tell you what I learned from it, which is that we need campaign finance reform." So, by virtue of breaking the law, he was in a better position to reform it?

The easiest path to being recognized as a genius in America is to become a completely predictable, run-of-the-mill, redistributionist Democrat. Then no matter how dumb you are and how many ludicrous lies you keep telling, the media will only remark on your dazzling brilliance. Gore explained that it wasn't a "fund-raiser," it was an "event to raise funds." He's a modern Wittgenstein!

In the classic "adversary media" approach, during the 2000 presidential campaign *Good Morning America*[40] rigorously grilled both Bush and

Gore on a misstatement made by Bush. To provide some context, at this point in the campaign Gore had claimed the following: He had discovered Love Canal (in fact, it had already been declared a national disaster area by President Carter months before Gore noticed it); his father was voted out of office for his courageous stand on civil rights (though his father voted against the 1964 Civil Rights Act); his mother sang him a union lullaby in his crib (this is highly unlikely inasmuch as his father had just cast a major anti-labor vote and the song didn't exist until Al Jr. was twenty-seven years old); he was a co-sponsor of the McCain-Feingold campaign-finance reform bill (an impossibility since he never served in Congress with Senator Feingold); he had taken "a risk" in asking the former prime minister of Russia to get "personally involved" in Kosovo (though President Boris Yeltsin of Russia had already designated Mr. Chernomyrdin as special envoy to the Balkans weeks earlier); he created the Internet (see *infra*); and had been the inspiration for *Love Story* (yikes!).

Thus, the question put to Gore on *Good Morning America* was this:

JACK FORD: Governor Bush was asked a question about hate crimes law in Texas. And as—as part of his answer, he stressed the fact that three men had been sentenced to death as a result of the killing of James Byrd. Well, it turns out that he's wrong. Only two men were sentenced to death there. Is that the type of error, the type of mistake that the Bush campaign has—has criticized you for making?

Bush's misstatement was also the topic of Ford's interview with Bush:

FORD: You had said during the course of your response in the debate that the three people involved in the death of James Byrd were going to get the ultimate penalty, death penalty.

GOV. BUSH: Yeah. Unfortunately, I was wrong. Two of them are going to get the ultimate penalty.

FORD: Two will get the death penalty.

GOV. BUSH: Three maybe should have.

FORD: Yeah.

GOV. BUSH: But the jury decided otherwise.

FORD: The question that people will ask now is—is that, however, the kind of error that you've criticized the vice president for making?

GOV. BUSH: Of course not. No.

FORD: Why not?

GOV. BUSH: I'm telling you right now it's two instead—instead of three.

Ford then asked Bush if he was an inexperienced dope. Ford probed Bush on "questions about your experience, the fact that you never held a job that dealt with foreign policy" and "questions . . . about your intelligence, your ability to grasp presidential issues."[41]

Gore was asked: "As the vice president of the United States, you've had a distinguished career in the House and in the Senate, and yet you find yourself on stage in front of family members and tens of millions of people with a moderator asking questions about your integrity and your credibility. Does that hurt?"

Does that hurt? Can you imagine this question being asked of a Republican? No—can you imagine this question being asked of an adult?

After Ford had vigorously cross-examined both candidates on Bush's misstatement, asked Bush if he was stupid, and Gore if he "hurt," former Clinton hatchetman George Stephanopolous wrapped up with ABC's signature objective political analysis.

The fact that Gore claimed to have invented the Internet was never mentioned on any *Good Morning America* broadcast, except a few times when Bush referred to it.[42] Nor was it discussed on NBC's *Today* show. Also not mentioned on either *Good Morning America* or the *Today* show were Gore's claims about Love Canal or *Love Story* or his inability to identify George Washington at Monticello. This is not meant to suggest any other morning shows did cover Gore's misstatements. These just happen to be the only searches I ran. Indeed, Gore's astonishing claim about being the prime mover on the Internet might not ever have been heard on any ABC morning broadcast if Bush hadn't raised Gore's delusional Internet claim in his own campaign ads. Those ads were mentioned on ABC news segments in order to denounce Bush for "attacking Al Gore."[43]

Gore's inanities became well known only through the voice of non-elite America—and only because Gore's misstatements were so raucously funny. Gems like Gore's claiming to have invented the Internet tended to capture the imaginations of FM disc jockeys, sports announcers, and late-night comedians. While media blowhards raved about Gore's colossal intellect, every time the public actually heard Gore, they laughed at him for being such a dork.

It's always so great to see the reaction of normal Americans to Democrats unfiltered by the courtier press. The dichotomy didn't start with Gore. The classic media/human split concerned Clinton's truth telling. Law professors and legal pundits ponderously described President Clinton's grand jury testimony as "legally accurate." The D.C. grand jury laughed out loud when they heard it.

Jimmy Carter won "Best in Show" for his nuclear arms consultation with Amy the night before a presidential debate. The next day, the *New York Times* debate analysis began: "The Presidential debate produced no knockout blow, no disastrous gaffe and no immediate, undisputed victor."[44] Though the humor of Carter's high-level consultation with a little girl totally eluded the media, it did not go unnoticed in other quarters. Placards proclaiming "Amy for Defense Secretary" began turning up at campaign events. Comedian Bob Hope said Amy's interest in nuclear weapons began when "Uncle Billy gave her a Raggedy Ann doll with a nuclear warhead." Hope continued: "The only difference between Billy Carter and Jimmy Carter is that Billy has a foreign policy."[45]

It took several days of hooting by the American people for the *Washington Post* to figure out that Carter's "Amy" gaffe had been "the joke of the campaign."[46] The *New York Times* never did figure that out. Eventually the Amy consultation was briefly mentioned in the sports pages but only because former Dallas Cowboys quarterback Roger Staubach kept peppering his NFL football analysis with, "I was talking to my daughter Amy about it."[47] (In the *Times* deadly earnest style: "The remark was similar to one that the President made during his debate against Ronald Reagan last week regarding his daughter's fears about nuclear proliferation."[48])

The *Times* has a more delicate gauge for blunders by Republicans. President George H. W. Bush's evidently monumental misstep of looking at his watch during a 1992 debate with Bill Clinton was mentioned on the *Times*'s front page the next day.[49] It was described again in three more election articles that week.[50]

The same journalist/American dichotomy occurred every time the public got a gander at Al Gore, unfiltered by the media propaganda machine. Like Tolstoy's unhappy families, Gore was always strange, but he was strange in different ways. In the first debate, he was his natural self—little

Miss-Know-It-All (*"Yugoslavia, as they call Serbia plus Montenegro"*). In the second debate he overcompensated and became Norman Bates in the last scene of *Psycho*. Gore was so tightly wound, you could almost hear him thinking, *I hope they are watching, they will see, they will see and say, "Why, she wouldn't even hurt a fly."*

Naturally, therefore, the entire nation was on tenterhooks waiting to see what new weirdness Gore would unleash during the third debate. It was brownnoser Tracy Flick from the movie *Election*. Even the audience was laughing at Gore for his ridiculous pomposity. Bush was in on the joke, laughing and winking at audience members as Gore grew increasingly insufferable. It was in that final debate that Bush said Gore's budget would require three times the spending Clinton had proposed. Gore butted in, as he was wont to do, with this dazzling retort: "That's in an ad, Jim, that was knocked down by the journalists who analyzed the ad and said it was misleading." The journalists, Gore proclaimed, "are the keepers of the scorecard."

Oh—"the journalists." The "journalists" said Bush's ad was misleading. The same journalists who had been browbeating the nation with the information that Gore was an intellectual titan. In fact, Gore's auxiliary staff in the media hadn't said what Gore claimed they said. (The only mention of the ad was in the *New York Times,* which supported Bush's statement about Gore's spending plans, but nitpicked that the ad's ten-second description of Bush's plan was "somewhat misleading."[51]) So Fibber McGee's citation of the "journalists" referred to a stupid quibble made by a partisan newspaper about a nongermane point in Bush's ad.

For every media lie (Gore is a genius), there is invariably a second, auxiliary backup lie sheltering the first lie (the media exaggerates Gore's mistakes). Thus, while the major media censored Gore's incessant misstatements with an iron fist, they simultaneously criticized themselves for being so tough on Gore. There was a virtual cottage industry in phony self-criticism about their maltreatment of poor, put-upon Al Gore.

CBS Evening News, for example, mentioned Gore's Internet bluster only once—in order to denounce media coverage of Al Gore as having been "dominated by trivia."[52] It was just that sort of trivia that had been carefully avoided at ABC, NBC, and CBS. The typical mention of Gore's Internet boast was this from ABC's *World News Now:* "After months of promising not to go negative, the Bush campaign is going negative. . . . It's not about the issues, it's about Gore's character ... Why this ad now? ... It worked for Bush once before, going negative."[53]

An example of hard news coverage about a serious issue was Bush's mispronunciation of "subliminal." That was not paltry "trivia" like Gore claiming to have invented the Internet. Bush's word slip merited three separate mentions on *CBS Evening News* shows. It was also a news item on NBC's *Today* show[54] and ABC's *World News Tonight*.[55]

The *Washington Monthly* complained of "exaggerations or even publishing outright falsehoods about Gore." Gore's college roommate set up a supposedly nonpartisan website called "The Daily Howler" to expose the media's ceaseless attacks on Al Gore.[56]

An immaterial misquote in Gore's lie about Love Canal was seized upon as an example of how Gore couldn't get a fair shake from the media. The Love Canal incident began when Gore told a high school audience that he "found" Love Canal. He explained how he was led to Love Canal by a letter he received from a high school girl alerting him to toxic waste in Toone, Tennessee: "I called for a congressional investigation and a hearing. I looked around the country for other sites like that. I found a little place in upstate New York called Love Canal. Had the first hearing on that issue, and Toone, Tennessee—that was the one that you didn't hear of—but that was the one that started it all."[57]

The problem was that Gore's hearings were held in March 1979—well after Love Canal had been declared a national disaster area. Indeed, it was one of the major news stories of 1978, with front-page stories showing hundreds of people being evacuated from Love Canal. But Gore's lie became the prime example of how the media maliciously twisted Gore's statements.

It seems that the *Washington Post* and the *New York Times* had misreported Gore's last sentence as: "*I* was the one that started it all"—as opposed to "*that* was the one that started it all." This was the only part of Gore's statement that anyone ever claimed the newspapers got wrong. The thing is, changing "I" to "that" didn't change what Gore had said from being "false" to being "true." He plainly said that after his Toone, Tennessee, hearings, he had "looked around the country" and "found" Love Canal. "That," he said, "started it all." Neither "I" (Gore) nor "that" (his Toone, Tennessee, hearings) started anything regarding Love Canal.

Still, a nongermane misquote from Gore's Love Canal boast was supposed to demonstrate the press's unfair attacks on Al Gore. Headlines on articles about the "misquote" proclaimed: "Gore More Victimized Than

Guilty of Falsehoods, Press Critics Say."[58] An article in the *Atlanta Journal and Constitution* ruefully said the misquote was "a textbook example" of how people "have come to view the veracity of candidates and reporters."

Writing in the *Washington Monthly,* Robert Parry claimed the Love Canal "flap" was created when the press "misquoted" Gore and then was "amplified endlessly by the rest of the news media."[59] The "endless" amplification consisted of Gore's misstatement never passing the lips of anyone on *NBC* or *CBS News* and being mentioned one time on ABC. That was when Clinton aide George Stephanopoulos observed that Gore's misstatement was merely "a senator's slip" and that Gore had "fixed" it (by accusing the press of misquoting him, apparently).[60]

Historian Douglas Brinkley accused the media of engaging in a game of *gotcha* with the Love Canal incident. He claimed Gore "could argue that he was talking about the Tennessee site being the one that he found."[61] To restate the facts, Gore said: "I found a little place in upstate New York called Love Canal."

Also preposterously billed as a "myth" by the watchdog media was Gore's claim that he had invented the Internet. *New York Times* columnist Paul Krugman asserted, "True, Mr. Gore didn't invent the Internet—but then, he never said he had."[62] *Slate*'s Mickey Kaus pronounced Gore's Internet boast "minor, and excusable."

You see, technically, precisely what Gore said was this: "I took the initiative in creating the Internet." This is supposed to be *completely* different from claiming he had "invented" the Internet. In point of fact, "create" is a synonym for "invent." Any thesaurus will quickly confirm this. If Gore said he took the initiative to create, develop, devise, or produce the Internet, all of those would be false. An accurate paraphrase is not untrue simply for being a paraphrase. If Gore had said he invented the Internet in French, he still would have said he invented the Internet and it still would have been preposterous.

Gore's phraseology just happened to be more inept and convoluted than "invent." Indeed, Gore's inelegant speaking style invariably allowed his flacks to claim Gore was being "misquoted" when his lies were restated with greater clarity than he had been able to muster. Their position was that Gore could only be accused of lying if his lies were restated verbatim (which is at least an improvement over having to produce DNA evidence before accusing a Democrat of lying).

Gore's claim to have "taken the initiative to create the Internet" was based on his having joined with a majority of senators, a majority of House members, and the president to support government funding for the Defense Department's development of the Internet. Voting to fund the National Endowment of the Arts doesn't make you an artist. (Though, come to think of it, receiving a grant from the NEA doesn't make you an artist, either.)

Nonetheless, the media repeatedly asserted that Gore's claim to have invented the Internet was a "myth." (*He said "create"!*) It is a "myth" that had thrived despite the major media's blackout. Liberals think that if they never admit to lying, there is no proof that they are lying. Gore misspoke, invented facts, and told lies. Thus, he was a genius—too damned smart to connect with ordinary voters. Also, the media was picking on him. Only Bush's occasional slip of tongue was major news. Gore's forked tongue proved nothing—except that the Bush campaign was mean for mentioning it.

This gives you some idea why the media is in a perpetual snit about "campaign finance reform." They believe attacking politicians should be the sole prerogative of the press. A paid campaign ad might reveal unflattering information about a Democrat the media had been hiding.

S H A D O W B O X I N G

T H E   A P O C R Y P H A L

" R E L I G I O U S   R I G H T "

[Propaganda] proceeds by psychological manipulations, by charac-
ter modifications, by the creation of feelings or stereotypes useful
when the time comes. . . . The two great routes that this sub-
propaganda takes are the conditioned reflex and the myth.

JACQUES ELLUL, *Propaganda*[1]

Like all propagandists, liberals create mythical enemies to justify their
own viciousness and advance their agenda. There is no bogeyman that strikes
greater terror in the left than the apocryphal "religious right." The very
phrase is a meaningless concept, an inverted construct of the left's own Mar-
quis de Sade lifestyle. It functions as a talismanic utterance to rally the faithful against anyone who disagrees with the well-organized conspiratorial left.

Despite the constant threat of the "religious right" in America, there is
evidently no such thing as the "atheist left." In a typical year, the *New York
Times* refers to either "Christian conservatives" or the "religious right"

166

almost two hundred times.[2] But in a LexisNexis search of the entire *New York Times* archives, the phrases "atheist liberals" or "the atheist left" do not appear once. Only deviations from the left-wing norm merit labels.

The point of the phrase "religious right" or "Christian conservative" is not to define but to belittle. It informs the reader that the object of the sobriquet is presumptively insane by saying he is a member of it. The "religious right" serves the function of Emmanuel Goldstein in Orwell's *1984:* "The program of the Two Minutes Hate varied from day to day, but there was none in which Goldstein was not the principal figure. He was the primal traitor, the earliest defiler of the Party's purity. All subsequent crimes against the Party, all treacheries, acts of sabotage, heresies, deviations, sprang directly out of his teaching."[3]

Though neither "religious" nor "right" nor even "religious right" are inherently insulting terms, they are thrown out as if they are accusations. The media is repelled by the people it believes these terms describe. Just as some people once spat out the word "Jew" as an insult (causing polite people to start using convoluted euphemisms like "person of the Hebrew faith"), "religious right" has become a slur by usage. In one of the most astonishing uses of "religious right" to mean "lunatic," the *New York Times* explained that after September 11, 2001, leaders in Saudi Arabia were hesitant to crack down on militant clerics for fear that it "would have inflamed the religious right."[4] In addition to jihad, do crazed homicidal Muslims support the devolution of power to the states?

Presumably demonstrating the sort of warm ecumenical tolerance the religious right would do well to emulate, California Congressman Vic Fazio calls Christian conservatives the "fire-breathing Christian radical right."[5] President Clinton's kindly Surgeon General Joycelyn Elders referred to citizens opposed to her condom distribution project as "the un-Christian religious right, selling out our children in the name of religion."[6] Discussing the movie *Chocolat,* set in prewar France, the Reverend Jesse Jackson claimed it was a parable about the religious right: "You can just see the religious right narrowly defining the rights of others."[7]

If you threw a glass of cold water on a liberal in the middle of a sound sleep, he'd jerk awake denouncing the religious right.

During the 2000 election, the *New York Times* praised John McCain for attacking the religious right, saying his message was "badly needed" and "cannot be dismissed."[8] Though the editorial did gently chastise McCain for having "withdrawn an earlier characterization of them as 'evil,' " it went on to denounce the religious right for exercising a "bullying influence" on politics. Unlike the calm persuasion on display daily at the *Times,* the religious right was eroding "the spirit of tolerance."

It is a thesis of long standing at the *New York Times* that the "religious right" is tyrannical because it has opinions at odds with the editorial page of the *Times.* In 1996, *Times* columnist A. M. Rosenthal denounced the religious right delegates (the "religious right" is now a state) for supporting Bob Dole at the Republican National Convention—provided they "control what he and the party do and say and where the party is going. That is agenda number one."[9] Apparently other delegates were eagerly hoping to have their issues buried or forgotten by the party.

On a 1994 radio program titled "Christian Conservatives Defend Their Politics" (try to imagine a program called "Liberal Jews Defend Their Politics") National Public Radio host Bob Edwards raised the issue of the religious right's vast influence over the Republican party, saying "Christian conservatives showed their strength" by helping nominate a Republican gubernatorial candidate whose "platform is almost identical to the agenda of the Christian Coalition."

Of course, another explanation for the similar "agendas" is that "Christian conservatives" have fairly conventional Republican views. The media might as well refer to anyone who favors lower marginal tax rates as the "Tax Nuts" and darkly warn of the growing influence of Tax Nuts on the Republican Party. News items would begin noting sinisterly that the Republican Party platform on taxes mirrors the agenda of the Tax Nuts. Gradually, some Republicans would gingerly state their support for a reduction in the marginal gains tax rate while loudly proclaiming that they hold the Tax Nuts in contempt and denouncing the undue influence of the Tax Nuts on the Republican Party. Reductions in the base points for calculating the capital gains tax would take on sinister connotations by virtue of association with the Tax Nuts.

Implicitly—sometimes quite explicitly—the devil-words "religious right" connote irrationality, inflexibility, simplemindedness, and judgmentalism. In 1993, the *Washington Post* informed its readers that the religious right—or the "Gospel lobby"—is composed of people who are "largely poor, uneducated and easy to command."[10] A correction the next day admitted there was "no factual basis for that statement." Attempting its own definition of the religious right, the *New York Times* reported in 1986,

"Evangelical Christians are more easily led than other kinds of voters." The *Times* cited a college professor as its authority.[11]

Without the pretend-accuracy, *San Francisco Chronicle* columnist Arthur Hoppe described the religious right as a woman named Maude who wants "to slog through the snow down to the Grange to pray for Pat Buchanan."[12] Unlike Maude, Hoppe explained, left-wing sophisticates are "far too busy sampling restaurants, discussing films, or discovering the inner epicurean." This sneering account of "Maude" was intended to explain how such a comically ridiculous bunch as the "religious right" kept winning at the polls. "Maude"—imaginary Maude—has nothing else to do, Hoppe explained: "Maude doesn't jog, cruise the Internet, read Danielle Steel, play golf or otherwise waste her time." (Or apparently "sample" restaurants.)

Revealingly, Hoppe added, "These folks certainly have a right to their beliefs." Gee, thanks. Free speech is always a wildly counterintuitive concept for liberals. They believe free speech is something liberals magnanimously bestow on others. No matter how loathed Dan Rather is on the right, it would never occur to any conservative to proclaim that Rather, personally, on his own time, has a "right to his beliefs." Having generously conceded that religious conservatives have a "right to their beliefs," Hoppe immediately demanded to know "What can be done to save the country from this dedicated minority?"

A guest on National Public Radio described the religious right as "a very, very vocal minority with a lot of money that's doing most of the unconstitutional stuff out there." This was in contradistinction to the majority "who really don't want to bother with how I believe and really don't want to bother with forcing anybody to do anything that's against their will."[13]

So the religious right is a "very, very small minority" whose goal is to force people to do things "against their will," populated by an army of "easily led" corn pones. They are "fire-breathing," sell out "our children in the name of religion," and enjoy "narrowly defining the rights of others." Also "evil."

It's hard to imagine that such an intolerant bunch would have much leverage no matter how "vocal" they are. But according to the frequent "religious right" updates in the press, this revolting minority possesses a staggering amount of influence—all the while operating under the watchful eye of a hostile media. So powerful is the left's imaginary enemy, that Norman Lear, a multimillionaire TV producer, was said to have "walked away from his prime-time kingdom" to found People for the American Way for the sole purpose of "combat[ing] the political influence of the religious right."[14] (Imagine the Sturm and Drang if a conservative group purported to represent "the American Way.")

Referring to the "powerful influence" of the religious right, the *Los Angeles Times* has estimated its strength at "a third or more of the primary vote in many states."[15] *The Economist* magazine put it at about a fifth.[16] In 1998 *Fortune* magazine called the Christian Coalition alone the seventh most powerful lobbying group in Washington.[17]

None of the figures about the religious right ever add up. The facts marshaled to demonstrate that this scary group is bent on total domination of America instantly collapse under the most cursory examination. And the members of the scheming religious right cannot be identified beyond the description of a fictitious character named Maude.

Eventually, the *New York Times* set its logicians to cracking how a small minority intent on forcing people to do things against their will could wield such vast power. The key to the disproportionate influence of the religious right—despite its universal unpopularity at the *Times*—was (1) money, and (2) a predilection to engage in bloc voting. These Christians, according to the *Times,* were using "bloc voting and substantial financial resources to single out politicians in both parties who do not share their religion-based views." (Is that "Maude" with the deep pockets?) This set them apart from other Americans who tirelessly promote politicians who disagree with them.

For twenty years, evangelical Christians had been portrayed as toothless hicks preaching for a nickel in the Ozarks. Then—seamlessly, without remark on the shift in the Orwellian propaganda—they were transformed into Howard Hughes money men, expertly manipulating the system. Overnight, the Beverly Hillbillies became the Boys from Brazil. In fact, there is no possible method of calculating political contributions that supports the *Times*'s thesis about the "substantial financial resources" of Christian conservatives.

Using Federal Election Committee data, the Center for Responsive Politics compiled this list of the top twenty Political Action Committee (PAC) contributors to federal candidates, during the 1999–2000 election cycle:

National Association of Realtors $3,423,441
Association of Trial Lawyers of America $2,661,000
American Federation of State/County/
     Municipal Employees $2,590,074
Teamsters Union $2,565,495

National Auto Dealers Association $2,498,700
International Brotherhood of Electrical Workers $2,470,125
Laborers Union $2,255,900
Machinists/Aerospace Workers Union $2,188,138
United Auto Workers $2,155,050
American Medical Association $2,028,354
Service Employees International Union $1,871,774
National Beer Wholesalers Association $1,871,500
Carpenters & Joiners Union $1,869,920
National Association of Home Builders $1,824,599
United Parcel Service $1,755,065
United Food & Commercial Workers Union $1,743,652
National Education Association $1,717,125
Verizon Communications $1,677,617
American Bankers Association $1,657,615
American Federation of Teachers $1,599,555

A search of "Christian Coalition" turns up $250,000 donated by Pat Robertson in the 1997–1998 election cycle. In the "Ideological/Single-Issue PAC" category, "Abortion Policy/Pro-Life" groups gave $482,789 to federal candidates in 1999–2000—compared with $1,159,966 from Pro-Choice PACs.

The total for all "Republican/Conservative" PACs combined was $2,599,663. That's less than the contributions from a single trial lawyers' PAC. It is comparable to the individual donations to the Democrats from about a half dozen individual union PACs.

From January 1, 1999, through June 30, 2000, three unions made soft money donations of approximately $2 to $3 million apiece to the Democrats. (Service Employees International Union, $2,853,250; American Federation of State County & Municipal Employees, $2,568,600; Communications Workers of America, $1,995,000).[18] In the same time period, the entire category of "Ideology/Single-Issue givers" from Christians to Sierra Club members contributed just over $1 million to Bush and Gore combined.[19]

But the slush fund champion of the 2000 campaign was a group that is arguably even more annoying than Christian conservatives—lawyers.[20] According to the director of the Center for Responsive Politics, lawyers were the biggest political contributors in the 2000 election cycle "no matter how you look at it."[21] By September 2000, trial lawyers alone contributed more than $7 million to the Democrats and $13,500 to the Republicans.[22]

Yet, the "substantial financial resources" and "bullying influence" of the Legal Left was never alluded to, much less decried, in the *New York Times.*

So how did the editors of the *Times* settle on "substantial financial resources" as the source of the religious right's inordinate influence on national politics? Are there any facts supporting the *Times*'s thesis? Did it occur to anyone at the *Times* to check? No. As usual, the editors were speculating wildly and irrationally on the basis of their own freakishly narrow, insulated lives. No one at the *New York Times* knows anyone who could possibly be described as either "religious" or "right." Thus, the frequent popularity of traditional values at the voting booth in national elections—and the unaccountable devaluation of the interests of Manhattan heroin addicts and transvestites—is a total mystery, suggestive of a sinister plot. It must be money!

But for pure detachment, nothing beats the *Times*'s accusation that the religious right engages in "bloc voting."[23] Unless you are a Manhattan liberal, the suggestion that Christian conservatives bloc vote more than other groups—say, blacks, Jews, Hispanics, women, or editors of the *New York Times*—will instantly strike you as highly suspect. To begin with, whatever else "religious right" means, the absolute bare minimum requirements are: (1) religious and (2) right. Having defined "religious right" as people who are right-wing, the *Times* then denounces them for being right-wing. The "Scientologist right" probably leans toward Republicans, too. Only in an environment of ideological fanaticism can a tautology be passed off as analysis.

Still and all, voters who identified themselves as "white religious right" (14 percent) were less predictable voters than people who identified themselves as either "conservative" or "liberal" without qualification (totaling 29 percent and 20 percent of the population, respectively). In the 2000 election, the "white religious right" chose Bush over Gore 80 percent to 18 percent. Self-identified conservatives voted for Bush 81 percent to 17 percent and self-identified liberals voted 80 percent to 13 percent for Gore.[24] Apart from the promising development of 14 percent of the population cheerfully identifying themselves as a liberal cuss word, it isn't particularly startling that 80 percent of people who call themselves politically "right" tend to vote Republican.

Eliminating the tautological aspect of the "religious right," and getting straight to the heart of the matter—Christians "bloc vote" less than almost any other imaginable cohort. Quite a bit less, actually. In order of magnitude and based on the 2000 presidential election, the biggest "bloc voters" were blacks (Gore, 90 percent; Bush, 8 percent); Jews (Gore, 79 percent; Bush, 19 percent); Hispanics (Gore, 67 percent; Bush, 31 percent); and unmarried women (Gore, 63 percent to 32 percent). Non-Cuban Hispanics voted for Gore by 75 percent, contravening Milton Himmelfarb's famous quip that Jews live like Episcopalians and vote like Puerto Ricans.

By contrast, Christians are the least predictable voters of almost any demographic group. Protestant voters went for Bush 55 percent, compared with 43 percent for Gore. This was almost identical to the breakdown among white people (54 percent to 42 percent) and men (54 percent to 43 percent). Catholics were the most evenly balanced, voting for Gore over Bush by a razor-thin 49 percent to 47 percent. According to a poll cited in the *Dallas Morning News,* even among Evangelicals, only 41 percent are registered Republicans, with about 30 percent apiece registered Democrats or Independents.[25]

If you wanted to know who someone voted for in the 2000 election, any one of these demographic factors would give you more information than knowing the person is a white Protestant:

Black	Gore, 90 percent to 8 percent
Jewish	Gore, 79 percent to 19 percent
Hispanic	Gore, 67 percent to 31 percent
Unmarried women	Gore, 63 percent to 32 percent

Compare that to white Protestants, who voted for Bush by 62 percent to 32 percent.[26] Even people who self-identify as "white religious right"—a narrow category of aggressive conservatives who enjoy annoying Northeastern liberals—bloc vote less than blacks, and bloc vote about the same as Jews. But you never read about blacks or Jews being "easily led" or exercising undue influence by their infernal "bloc voting." To the contrary, when blacks bloc vote 90 percent for the Democrats, it's the Republicans' fault for somehow not "reaching out" to minorities. But when white Protestants show a slight preference for Republicans, it's supposed to demonstrate something nefarious about the Protestants.

Meanwhile, the media continue to issue hysterical Klan-watch updates about the "religious right," as if these phrases conveyed information of taxonomic precision. Thus, a few months after the presidential election in which 90 percent of blacks and 79 percent of Jews bloc voted for Al Gore, an op-ed in the *New York Times* purported to sketch the views and feelings of "Christian conservatives." Steven Waldman, editor of an Internet site about religion, prattled on about "Christian conservatives" as if it were a small, closely held corporation. According to Waldman, Christian conservatives are intolerant, threatening to George Bush, and suspicious of "pluralism."[27]

How about an op-ed piece purporting to analyze what "white people" believe? What are their hopes and dreams? Is there any internal debate among white people over the Bush presidency? Do many white people accept a "limited form of pluralism"?

Beyond the basic building blocks of "religious right"—Christians who tend to vote Republican—the meaning of "religious right" remains maddeningly obscure. Considering that McCain's message denouncing the religious right was such an important one, a message worthy of amplification on the editorial page of the *New York Times,* the message might be a little clearer. Even a witch hunt requires a working definition of the witch. Are you a member of the "religious right" if you want your taxes cut and believe in a Supreme Being? Or must one also support elimination of the National Endowment for the Arts? Is an unseemly enthusiasm for the NEA's elimination the defining characteristic?

In fact, according to the careful analysis of the *New York Times,* the NEA is a major bête noir of the apocryphal "religious right." The *Times* has reported on several occasions that "the agenda of the religious right" includes "elimination of the National Endowment for the Arts."[28] Is that now the definition of the "religious right"? It's never explained.

Despite its founding expressly to "combat the political influence of the religious right," "People for a Small Sliver of the Malibu Way" is maddeningly elusive in defining the enemy. Its website denounces every known conservative from Judge Robert Bork to Rush Limbaugh. The only definition of the "religious right" that ever holds up is "Republicans Liberals Don't Like." In this sense, it is the molecular opposite of "moderate Republican."

One could go mad trying to nail down even the leaders of this vast and terrifying conspiracy. Four Republicans who have been frequently identified in the media as "leaders" of the religious right are Pat Robertson, Jerry Falwell, Pat Buchanan, and Gary Bauer. No meaningful classification scheme would ever lump these men together. Falwell endorsed George Bush Sr. over Robertson for president. Robertson endorsed Senator Bob Dole over Pat Buchanan for president. Bauer endorsed John McCain—even as McCain viciously attacked Falwell and Robertson as "agents of intolerance" and "forces of evil." Pat Buchanan defended Falwell—but not Robertson—against McCain's attacks.

The point of throwing these men together as leaders of the religious right is not to explain or clarify. It is simply to say, "We don't like them." They are no more or less alike than any other four Republicans chosen at random—excluding those dubbed "moderate Republicans," who are all identical. The only commonality among the four is that they are all Republicans born south of the Mason-Dixon line. These purported "leaders" of the "religious right" are talismans, meant to inspire fear even as the public is trained to laugh at them reflexively.

It's difficult to make a case for the Reverand Jerry Falwell as a leader of the "religious right" inasmuch as his organization, the Moral Majority, disbanded in 1989.[29] Two of Falwell's assistants at the Moral Majority—erstwhile commanders of the "easily led" Evangelicals—wrote a book in 1999 arguing that religious people should get out of politics altogether.[30] Pat Buchanan doesn't rank as religious right on the definition given by CNBC's Chris Matthews, who informed Peggy Noonan that since she was a Roman Catholic, she was not religious right.[31] (This is meant as praise from liberals.) Gary Bauer's support for campaign finance reform and John McCain led to his alienation from conservative Christians and dissociation from the Family Research Council, the organization he once led.

On close examination, the vast movement of spooky sect members infiltrating the Republican Party and threatening the nation's stability always seems to come down to just one man: Pat Robertson. Noticeably, even those who monitor the "religious right" are hard-pressed to come up with names other than Robertson's. *Church & State* magazine, a publication that issues hysterical updates on the religious right, speaks of "men such as Pat Robertson and his shock troops."[32] In National Public Radio's exposé on the religious right before the 2000 election, the Christian-watch expert referred only to Pat Robertson and "other leaders of the religious right."[33] When writer Andrew Sullivan wrote about the "religious right" for the *New York Times,* he described a single event: Pat Robertson's 70th Birthday Party.

If it's Robertson whom liberals are worried about, they scare easily.

Like Catholic schoolgirls engaging in wild promiscuity to prove they aren't fanatics about their religion, Robertson consistently takes the most pathetically moderate, establishment positions within the Republican Party. He is, after all, a Yale Law School graduate. If Robertson were from Vermont and didn't yap about God on TV, liberals would fondly refer to him as a "moderate Republican."

On the eve of the South Carolina Republican primary in 1996, Robertson dramatically threw his support to establishment choice Bob Dole. Robertson's endorsement was timed to ensure maximum damage to Dole's surging conservative rival, Pat Buchanan, who had just won the New Hampshire primary. South Carolina went for Dole, and Buchanan was effectively knocked out of the race. Dole may well have been the inevitable nominee, but whatever ends up happening always looks inevitable in retrospect.

A month after the House of Representatives impeached Clinton, Robertson declared on his television show, *The 700 Club,* that the whole impeachment business should be dropped. The Yalie advised Republicans to "dismiss this impeachment hearing and get on with something else, because it's over as far as I'm concerned."[34]

In 1999, Robertson supported Most Favored Nation status for China. In doing so he sided with "business groups" against an "unusual alliance of liberal Democrats and conservative Republicans"—as the *New York Times* described the contending sides. A year later, Robertson came out for a moratorium on the death penalty—fleetingly winning the respect of the *New York Times.* When President Bush's "faith-based" initiatives were being roundly lambasted in the press as a sop to the "religious right,"[35] Robertson publicly opposed them. A few months after that, Robertson spoke sympathetically of China's "one child" policy, which happens to include state-ordered abortions. On CNN, Robertson noted that China has 1.2 billion people, "and they don't know what to do." Expressing a startlingly un-Christian sentiment, he continued, "If every family over there was allowed to have three or four children, the population would be completely unsustainable. . . . I think that right now they're doing what they have to do."[36]

Though recovering liberal Andrew Sullivan says Attorney General John Ashcroft "makes Pat Robertson look like a bleeding-heart liberal," that's not much of a standard. William Howard Taft makes Pat Robertson look like a bleeding-heart liberal.

Demonstrating the mythological nature of the "religious right," even after Robertson publicly opposed Clinton's impeachment, the "religious right" was still being blamed for its "public and personal vindictiveness toward [Clinton] and in its unrelenting insistence that he pay for his sins with his office."[37] If liberals can invent a terrifying organization called the "religious right," they can surely invent its positions, too.

At the time of Robertson's anti-impeachment crusade, the *New York Times* predicted that Robertson's "stunning reversal" on impeachment would "carry great weight"—coming as it did from "one of the most popular and influential Christian conservatives."[38] In fact, it would be hard to argue that Robertson's instructions to his flock influenced a single human, much less a single vote in Congress. Thus, for example, Chris Cannon, a Utah Republican, was merely bemused by Robertson's "move on" advice. If there were a "religious right," Utah would be its headquarters. But Cannon dryly responded, "This is not a P.R. war—this is a matter of law."[39] Not so "easily led" after all, those Christians.

The only politicians who seemed to respond with Manchurian candidate–like obedience to Pat Robertson's call to drop the impeachment business were Democrats and the *New York Times*'s favorite Republicans— Senators John Chafee (R.I.), Susan Collins (Me.), Slade Gorton (Wash.), Jim Jeffords (Vt.), Richard Shelby (Ala.), Arlen Specter (Pa.), Olympia Snowe (Me.), Ted Stevens (Alaska), Fred Thompson (Tenn.), and John Warner (Va.).

For purposes of comparison only, how did Democrats respond to their instructions on impeachment imparted by the liberal church circular? Not one Democratic senator disobeyed the *New York Times*'s command to acquit Clinton. Atheist liberals, it seems, are "easily led." The vast influence of Pat Robertson, the lone representative of the pernicious "religious right," is strictly limited to the fervid imaginations of the nation's editorial page writers.

Considering the invective constantly being heaped on the "religious right," it is probably not surprising that few people identify themselves as members. "Religious right" is always something somebody else is, like a "son of a bitch." A LexisNexis search of the phrase "religious right" mostly turns up lots of people denying that they belong to it. This could be because there's no such thing as the "religious right."

A Virginia state senator championed a bill requiring a minute of silence in public schools by stressing that he was not from the "religious-right wing of the party."[40]

A leading opponent of legalized gambling in Missouri defended his cause by saying: "This is not the religious right. These are some of the most liberal churches in the nation."[41]

After Louisiana ranked near the top in the nation in rates of syphilis, gonorrhea, and chlamydia, the governor instituted an abstinence program. The state coordinator for the program quickly explained to the media, "We're not religious-right types. We just want to give the facts."[42]

In debate on a Fox News program about whether the characters portrayed on HBO's *Sex and the City* are sluts, the panelist staking out the slut position made a point of saying that he was citing not "the religious right" but "New York TV critics."[43]

The general manager of a Massachusetts radio station with predominently Christian broadcasting[44] told a local newspaper, "This station does not represent the religious right."[45] One erstwhile employee of the station responded to a *Boston Globe* exposé revealing that she "did in fact work for a Christian station" by insisting she was "an enemy of the 'radical right.' "[46]

Even among Evangelicals, only 39 percent claim to agree with the "religious right"[47]—a polite Southern way of saying "screw you" to Northeastern liberals. Indeed, publicly proclaiming membership in the "religious right" is generally intended only to frighten liberals. (And it *always* works.) During the 2000 presidential campaign, a cheeky nineteen-year-old Bush campaign staffer described herself on NPR as "a religious right member of the conspiracy."[48]

While conservatives deny being part of the "religious right" to the point of neurosis, liberals express affection for conservatives they like by warmly excluding them from the "religious right." Thus, an article praising William F. Buckley for supporting national education tests—a policy favored by liberals—pointedly noted that Buckley was "not religious-right."[49] And, of course, CNBC's Chris Matthews introduced a discussion of "the dangers of the religious right" by identifying frequent guest Peggy Noonan as "not from the religious right."[50]

All this prattle about who is and who isn't a member of the "religious right" refers to an organization that, strictly speaking, in the technical sense, doesn't exist.

If the "religious right" were a real organization with real power, people might not talk so tough to it. To the contrary, any mediocrity who attacks the "religious right" is guaranteed good press.

About once a year pusillanimous Republicans get spooked by the liberal obsession with the "religious right." They convene meetings and issue press releases with vague proclamations that "they, not the religious right, are the soul of the party."[51] The Republicans' ritual denunciation of the nonexistent "religious right" is invariably hailed as the party's "Sister Souljah moment." Let's look at that.

Sister Souljah is the rap singer who expressed enthusiasm for the idea of blacks taking a week to "kill white people."[52] In a taped interview with the

Washington Post she said it was "wise" for blacks rioting in Los Angeles to kill whites whom, she noted, have a "low-down dirty nature."[53] Soon after Miss Souljah praised race murder, she spoke to Jesse Jackson's Rainbow Coalition. Presidential candidate Bill Clinton spoke to the Rainbow Coalition from that same stage the very next day. Clinton's political master stroke—the act of dauntless courage about which songs will be sung for the next fifty years—consisted of his remarking that Souljah's homicidal comments were "filled with a kind of hatred that you do not honor."

That's the big rebuke to intolerance within the Democratic Party: A presidential candidate stands on a podium recently occupied by the black equivalent of David Duke and timorously takes exception to the earlier speaker's enthusiasm for mob murder. An oblique statement of opposition to racial killings is "reaching out to the middle" for a Democrat. Naturally, Jackson demanded an apology from Clinton, saying he had shown "very bad judgment" in expressing his reservations about race murder.

Adding to Clinton's heroism, many in the mainstream media were torn by Clinton's gentle reproach, questioning whether he had gone overboard. *New York Times* columnist Anthony Lewis tentatively admitted that his initial reaction was that Clinton "had done the right thing"—but Lewis then spent the rest of his column arguing Jackson's side.[54] The most Clinton had been able to muster in response to a rap singer's endorsement of racist murder was to say that such sentiments were "filled with a kind of hatred"—and that left Anthony Lewis on the fence.

Law professor and former Dukakis campaign manager Susan Estrich heaped praise on Clinton, saying he had "rebuffed Sister Souljah, refused to make deals with Jesse Jackson and reached out to the middle." By contrast, she said, the Republican had "reached out instead to the religious right."[55]

Even taking the most menacing image of the "religious right" haunting liberal nightmares—little old ladies saying the rosary beads outside abortion clinics—the "religious right" is arguably less extreme than a rap singer's endorsement of the random slaughter of white people. But Clinton's tepid rebuke of a specific racist statement by an actual person is constantly cited to prod Republican candidates into denouncing Christian conservatives simply for being Christian conservatives.

In the 2000 presidential campaign, for example, Senator John McCain was fulsomely praised by the media for his own "Sister Souljah moment." McCain had viciously attacked the "religious right" with a ferocity normally reserved for terrorists. He called Pat Robertson and Jerry Falwell "agents of intolerance" and "forces of evil." No one ever pinpointed exactly what Falwell and Robertson had done that was so justly deserving of McCain's wrath. Their only manifest offense was to believe in a Being even higher than the *New York Times.* But the establishment lemmings were in a swoon.

Politicians may have few discernible real-world skills, but one talent they have in spades is the ability to ascertain who has power. So it's interesting that while seeking the presidential nomination from the Republican Party, McCain decided it would be a good strategy to attack Christian conservatives. This would have been an extremely bizarre tactic if McCain really believed there was such a thing as the "religious right" exercising vast influence over the party—as opposed to an atheist, left-wing media that really does exercise vast influence over everything. In point of fact, so powerful were Robertson and Falwell that almost no one defended them. In a show of strength among Christian conservatives, Gary Bauer stood by McCain.

The Evil ones themselves did not join in McCain's one-sided catfight. Agent of Intolerance Robertson never responded at all. Force of Evil Falwell said nothing at first, but soon was gushing with Christian charity for McCain. "I personally think that the senator in a moment of frustration said things that he normally would not say. And it's out of character for him to be that way." For his restraint, *Time* magazine sneered that it was "the first time in the history of Christian Fundamentalism that Jerry Falwell has said 'No comment' two days running."[56]

Later that year, liberal Bill Press said on CNN, "I want to tell you, I thought that the treatment that John McCain received from Pat Robertson and those others, members of the religious right, was not only un-Christian, I thought it was un-American." CNN's conservative counterpart, Tucker Carlson, rejoined: "Bill, see, now you're making it less fun for me, because you're agreeing with me. See, you're hurting my feelings."[57] It's not surprising that most politicians would prefer knocking over lemonade stands to standing up to real bullies. But must the media keep marveling at their bravery?

For an insidious organization with unimaginable power, no one seems to hesitate before attacking and insulting the "religious right." It's no wonder liberals think conservatives are religious nuts: Only some sort of supernatural power would seem capable of allowing a person to resist the left's incessant abuse.

Postulating the existence of the ghosts of liberal imaginations and pursuing the logic of their paranoia, what is the threat posed by the "religious right" precisely? Is the nation in imminent danger of having its coarseness removed? When anal sex, oral sex, premarital sex are all gleefully laughed about on prime-time TV, the peril of religious values infecting the culture would seem to be somewhat overrated.

Liberal dogma instructs that public displays of religion are inimical to democracy, a threat to freedom as we know it. They believe religious people are self-evidently fanatical. Religious values are hateful, homophobic, sexist, racist, and the rest of the liberal catechism—unless they are kept in the closet.

It is, of course, preposterous to say religious people can't let their religion inform their views on public policy. That is more hateful and intolerant than any views attributed to the apocryphal "religious right." But that's what liberals believe, and one could have a more thoughtful debate with snake-handlers about the wisdom of fondling poisonous snakes than with liberals about the "religious right."

In a 1999 public appearance, *Today* show host Katie Couric attributed the vicious slayings of gay student Matthew Shephard in Wyoming and of James Byrd, a black man, in Texas to a climate created by "religious zealots or Christian conservatives."[58] The affable Eva Braun of morning TV authoritatively informed President George Bush (41) that the Republican National Convention had "relinquished too much time to what some term the radical religious right."[59]

On *The Early Show* during the Democratic National Convention, Bryant Gumbel interviewed *Playboy* magnate Hugh Hefner. In all seriousness, Gumbel asked Hefner, "In a macropolitical sense, do you think the Gore preoccupation with morality is a frightening turn for the party?"[60] Eternal vigilance must be maintained against the specter of morality! A guy who puts out a skin magazine is being interviewed on network television as if he were a head of state, and liberals are worried that excessive morality is wrecking the country.

A PBS radio news host stated that the image of the Republican Party as "pro-woman, pro-minorities, and pro-tolerance" was in "sharp contrast to the delegates on the floor, 60 percent of whom self-identified as conservative Christians."[61] If the reverse statement had been made—that the author of that remark is a liberal Jew and thus full of vehement angry loathing of religious Christians—you wouldn't have to wait for a book to read about it.

An op-ed piece in *USA Today* titled "Can a Deeply Religious Person Be Attorney General?" questioned John Ashcroft's qualification for the job expressly because of his "deep faith," which could make it "impossible to see other points of view." The "other points of view" included those of "casino operators, family-planning counselors and gays and lesbians."[62] In a fascinating contrast, the column specifically compared Ashcroft's "troubling" religious beliefs to "Joe Lieberman's joyful invocation of the power of God on the campaign trail"—a "joyful invocation" that included Lieberman's likening Clinton to Moses.

Interviewing independent prosecutor Ken Starr during his investigation of an adulterous felon, ABC's Diane Sawyer informed Starr that "the American people" had responded to Starr by saying, "You are the only one who is shocked. We are not shocked." (Apparently the Russians were a little bit shocked. Russian intelligence knew about Clinton's affair with Monica Lewinsky before America did.[63]) Sawyer asked Starr if he was simply pursuing "his private view of personal morality." At that point in the investigation Clinton was known to have molested subordinates, perjured himself, suborned perjury, lied to the country, smeared witnesses against him, and engaged in sodomic acts involving a cigar on Easter Sunday, among many other infractions. Eighty percent of respondents told pollsters they believed it possible that the president was a rapist. Only a religious fanatic would be troubled by any of that. Sawyer probed Starr's peculiar sectarian views with tenacity, asking Starr if he believed dancing was "wicked" and whether his religious beliefs were "fueling [his] legal work."[64]

Questions like "Do you think God is on your side?"—as Sawyer also asked Starr—have a wonderful, apostolic quality to them. All-powerful American institutions speak as one against the menace of morality in American life. Yet liberals behave as if they are under constant threat of extermination from the "religious right."

Whoever these ruthless Christian conservatives are, these snooty bullies who think "God is on their side," they are at least not influencing Diane Sawyer. Yet, like Emmanuel Goldstein, though the religious right is universally reviled, it is still, somehow, dangerously beguiling. Despite being "hated and despised by everybody, although every day, and a thousand times a day, on platforms, on the telescreen, in newspapers, in books, [Goldstein's] theories were refuted, smashed, ridiculed, held up to the general gaze for the pitiful rubbish that they were—in spite of all this, his influence never seemed to grow less."[65]

The imaginary threat of the "religious right" is important because it allows liberals to complain about their victimization by religious zealots. It is not sufficient psychic compensation to be applauded wildly on *Politically*

Incorrect and other late-night TV shows, profiled in fawning articles in the *New York Times*, photographed for *People* magazine, showered with awards, Pulitzer prizes, and other sundry tributes. Liberals insist that they also be admired for their bravery in standing up to Christians.

Never have acts of cowardice been so lavishly hailed as raw courage. In any random month, a series of no-account actresses can be found courageously advancing their careers by attacking the Catholic Church in glossy magazines. You would think it would be difficult to be taken seriously as a martyr while being favorably profiled in *Vanity Fair*. But that's the beauty of modern-day martyrdom: You never have to suffer.

In the February 2001 *Vanity Fair*, Lara Flynn Boyle announced her long-standing defiance of the Catholic Church: "I used to lie in confession all the time. I'd never tell them what I really did. Never. I don't trust the Catholic Church." Proving their point, she also said: "I got a terrible education from the nuns and the Jesuits. They kept flunking me and saying I wasn't participating. I grew up thinking I was stupid." That same month, starlet Heather Graham boldly told *Talk* magazine: "Organized religion, in my experience, has been destructive."[66] This turned out to be a smashingly newsworthy comment, as it always is. Starlet Graham continued with the script, mocking a two-thousand-year-old religion: "Why do I have to do what all these men are saying? Why is a woman's sexuality supposed to be so evil?"

In response to programmed attacks by these worthless silicone nothings leveled at a two-thousand-year-old church, the mainstream media reflexively issued their own programmed response: wild acclaim for the starlets' intrepid witticisms. A lone voice of opprobrium came from Catholic League president William Donohue. Donohue said Graham was "now free to throw off all her shackles" and accept "film roles either as a slut or a porn star." He advised her to skip therapy, saying all she needed was "counseling by a priest." *Time* magazine compared Graham's and Donohue's remarks and adjudged Graham "the winner" of the best "punch" for her tedious Catholic-bashing, despite the fact that there was nothing even remotely unique about what Graham said (right down to the unhappy adolescence). There may be some universe in which it is iconoclastic for anemic Hollywood starlets to denigrate the Catholic Church. This isn't it.

It is not particularly surprising that average people with average minds—below average, according to the Jesuits—should be eager to submit to the dictates of fashionable Catholic-bashing. But watching as cliché-spewing automatons are hailed as martyrs is more than any sane person should have to bear. Warmly received attacks on religion is not the stuff of martyrdom.

If these were truly self-generated opinions rather than popular clichés, the phraseology would not be so mind-numbingly similar. But when condemning religion, strict rules must be followed. It is never "ministers," "rabbis," "priests," "churches," "Moses," "Jesus Christ," or even just "religion" that is the problem. The proper malediction is "organized religion." Thus, other recent celebrity opponents of "organized religion" include CNN's Ted Turner ("I had no use for organized religion");[67] director Marshall Brickman ("It's the big issue, isn't it, in the last 2,000 years, whether organized religion has really been a good thing");[68] actor Rupert Everett ("I think Jesus has been completely manipulated and used by organized religion");[69] and Rachel Hunter, model and wife of singer Rod Stewart ("I'm no fan of organized religion.").[70]

Like many popular cliches, the opposition to "organized religion" is an utterly meaningless formulation. There are boatloads of religions and thousands of ways religion is organized and practiced. If absolutely none of them float your boat, it may not be a problem of organization.

One of the most ludicrous self-made martyrs of the "religious right" is Jesse Ventura, governor of Minnesota. Among many other wildly novel comments in his 1999 interview with *Playboy* magazine, Ventura attacked . . . "organized religion"! Organized religion, he said, is "a sham and a crutch for weak-minded people who need strength in numbers." This is in contradistinction to the herd of individualists condemning "organized religion."

Ventura followed the starlet script, saying religion "tells people to go out and stick their noses in other people's business. The religious right wants to tell people how to live."[71] Topping off his bigotry with a tribute to his own immense tolerance, Ventura said: "I live by the golden rule: Treat others as you'd want them to treat you. The religious right wants to tell people how to live." His only self-criticism was "I will always be honest, and I think that's my problem."[72]

For an organization whose sole raison d'être is to "tell other people how to live," it's striking that religious people can't even get celebrities, politicians, newspapers, television personalities, and magazine glossies to stop denigrating them all the time.

Almost overnight, Ventura's approval ratings plummeted nineteen points. But that was with voters. Among the cultural elites, Ventura's popularity soared. This was quite a feat since Ventura had taken the opportunity of an interview with a pornographic magazine to commit liberal heresy on the subject of sexual harassment. He said the Tailhook scandal—or, as he put it, "grabbing a woman's breast or buttock"—was "much ado about nothing."

Ventura may not be an original thinker, but he was smart enough to know how to spin his interview with the media. In short order, his spokesmen were rushing to explain that Ventura had only meant to criticize "extremists of the religious right who are often intolerant." In a priceless formulation, the spokesman said his boss—the loud-mouthed anti-Christian bigot—"cannot stand intolerance."[73] Clarifying that his attack was on the "religious right" (and the governor "cannot stand intolerance"!) was the equivalent of saying fifty Hail Marys, as far as the liberal clergy was concerned. As with Clinton, feminist hysteria can be silenced for the greater good of undermining the nation's morals.

The media responded with gushing praise for Ventura's frank honesty and daunting courage. *Newsweek* rushed out a major feature piece on the unimportant governor, calling Ventura "beguiling, blunt, a maverick." The article praised him for his "candid talk." Of his invective against religion, the magazine explained, "he had a small point; a caveat at the end of his diatribe seemed to imply that he was talking at least partly about the religious right."[74] *Newsweek* quibbled with Ventura only for his lack of subtlety— "even blunt talk has its limits, and Ventura appears bent on finding them." (Similarly, after Senator John McCain assailed Pat Robertson and Jerry Falwell as "agents of intolerance" and "forces of evil," *Time* magazine lamented that "the uproar" had "erased the nuance in his original argument."[75] One must be careful to achieve the proper "nuance" when attacking Christians.)

Time magazine followed *Newsweek* a few months later with a feature article on Ventura, explaining in the first paragraph that Ventura meant only "some" religions—you know the bad ones that have rules and things. *Time* lauded Ventura for his "authenticity": "[T]oday's political culture craves authenticity but bristles when it actually gets some."

Washington Post columnist Richard Cohen devoted an entire column to lionizing Ventura for his important insights on "reactionaries" in the religious right. Their "views are so retrograde, their thinking so inexplicable," Cohen rationally explained, "that it is simply asking too much to accord them the respect normally due religious leaders."[76]

On ABC's *20/20,* Barbara Walters referred to Ventura's explanation that he was attacking only "the conservative right" by saying, "So you made a little mistake. You went a little too far." She then asked him, "Do you think that a totally honest man can be president of the United States?"[77]

New York Times columnist Frank Rich praised Ventura for giving a "lift" to the "stultifying campaign culture."[78] Months later, Rich would be gushing that John McCain was the first major Republican candidate who was not "in hock to the religious right."[79]

Columnist Molly Ivins praised Ventura for—surprise!—his courage: "When was the last time you heard a politician take on the religious right?"[80] she demanded to know. Finally! *Someone* was willing to take on the witches of Salem. Ivins fancies herself an iconoclast, even while adopting all the appropriate prejudices and hatreds of a good Smith College/Columbia School of Journalism graduate. Her coffee mug bravely proclaims, "Well-Behaved Women Rarely Make History," and a book of her columns was titled *Molly Ivins Can't Say That, Can She?*[81] What precisely does Ivins say that everyone else is not saying? Since when is attacking the "religious right" a sign of anything but impeccably good manners? It's not as if she's doing something shocking like defending Jerry Falwell. Along with the rest of the blabocracy, she slays all the standard media whipping boys and then demands that we pretend they were dragons.

Even the conservative *Washington Times* had kind words for Ventura's "honesty" presenting "an alternative from the usual stale political fare."[82] Indeed, apart from private opinions of actual people—which were reflected in Ventura's plunging poll numbers—it was hard to find a peep of protest from any quarter for Ventura's attack on "organized religion."

Lurching beyond parody, about a year later Ventura explained that he was meeting with a group of atheists because "we have to be tolerant of different points of view."[83] The Atheist Alliance International gave Ventura an award for guess what? His "political courage."[84] In a demonstration of their hegemonic control over politics in America, religious groups in Minnesota never got a direct apology from Ventura, much less a meeting.

Though there was no shortage of journalists and pundits defending Ventura from an anticipated counterattack from Christians, the attack never materialized. A few months after his snotty, unprovoked assault on them, Ventura received three hundred long-stemmed red roses with a card from "churches, ministries and individual Christians of the Twin Cities who wish simply to bless you and extend to you their prayers for you to have a wonderful Christmas."

Notwithstanding the kind, generous, sometimes self-deprecating responses of the "weak-minded," to say nothing of the universal acclaim for Ventura, somehow he was portrayed as the victim. One columnist concluded that the whole affair demonstrated that "America is most virulently intolerant of one group: the irreligious." Ventura, she lamented, "was greeted with a torrent of criticism and a plunge in his approval ratings."[85] He got flowers. What does he want? Sex? It wasn't enough for Ventura to emit fashionable pieties of the day. He must be hailed as a martyr when he insults the powerless on behalf of the powerful.

In 1994, the Reverand Jesse Jackson blamed the Christian Coalition for the Holocaust. (Seriously: "The Christian Coalition was a strong force in Germany.")[86] While he was at it, he blamed the Christian Coalition, formed in 1989, for slavery, too. Not only that, but, Jackson said, Martin Luther King had gone to the South specifically "to fight the Christian Coalition."[87]

Jackson refused to apologize, the Clinton White House refused to comment, and David Saperstein, director of the Religious Action Center of Reform Judaism, took the occasion to criticize the "religious right." Saperstein said religious right leaders had uttered "hate-filled statements, intolerant statements, and I think the religious right needs to be held accountable."[88]

If it seems unfathomable that Heaven's Gate cult members could have really believed a spaceship riding shotgun on Comet Hale-Bopp was coming to take them to heaven, consider that half the populace believes that a vast band of religious radicals is overrunning a nation—a nation that seemingly never tires of primetime sitcoms celebrating lesbianism, rampant promiscuity, and the perennially hilarious girl-faking-orgasm routine. Half the country not only believes in the "religious right," but deeply fears and hates it.

The religious right is a totemic symbol, a permanent terrorizing influence on the brainwashed masses. Interrupting reports on advances by the indefatigable enemy, there are frequent bulletins breathlessly announcing its final defeat. As Orwell described the endless, phony war in *1984,* despite "the regrouping which occurs every few years, it is always the same war— one must realize in the first place that it is impossible for it to be decisive."[89]

The "vast shadowy army"[90] of the religious right can never be defeated. Periodic, apparently decisive victories against the "religious right" serve merely to inspire liberals in the absence of an inspiring ideology. Every few years, the religious right is defeated, but then always manages to stage a comeback with no explanation or reference to its earlier total annihilation.

You read the follow-up reports on the religious right and constantly find yourself wondering, *Didn't we beat those guys a few years ago?*

During its ten years in existence, the Moral Majority seemed to be constantly losing clout, interrupted on occasion by hysterical reports of its burgeoning influence. At its inception in 1980, a columnist in the *Washington Post* was already anticipating victory, rhetorically asking, "Will the 340,000 members of the Moral Majority have as much impact on the election, for example, as the approximately 16 million labor union members who are registered to vote?"[91]

But then one year later, the *Washington Post*'s David Broder was anxiously reporting that an "intensely religious minority was shaping "our politics and government." They were doing so because of their "penchant for activities that make them politically influential." (The infernal bloc voting and financial resources again!) Broder's information was based on a public-opinion survey, the results of which he said had "flabbergasted the people who took the survey."[92]

And then in 1983, the religious right was faltering. *Newsweek* stated religious conservatives were trying to "rebuild their influence" after being "frustrated" by a series of electoral losses at the local level.[93]

By 1984, the wily "religious right" was back! It had returned and was more powerful than ever. The *Christian Science Monitor* cited "civil-libertarians, academics, and other observers," who declared the religious right "better organized and funded than in 1980." It was a "powerful force capable of getting its conservative social agenda enacted."[94]

A few years later, in 1989, the official dispatch arrived: The Moral Majority was closing its doors. The *Boston Globe* gleefully reported that Falwell "acknowledged the Moral Majority was never a large membership organization."[95] *USA Today* reported that the "Moral Majority lost clout after the PTL and Jimmy Swaggart scandals undermined confidence in televangelism."[96] It quoted "Falwell expert" professor Robert Alley of the University of Richmond as concluding, "Closing down the Moral Majority is somewhat like closing down an abandoned house."[97] Everyone, especially "experts," agreed that the closing of the Moral Majority meant the religious right was D-E-D, dead.

But then—just a year later—the religious right had to be vanquished all over again! This time the focus was Pat Robertson, head of the Christian Coalition. Reviewing a book that told the story of this final glorious victory over the religious right, a *Los Angeles Times* headline proclaimed "Fierce in the '80s, Fallen in the '90s, the Religious Right Forgets Politics." It could finally be declared: The wicked witch was dead. There was even a book about it.

The battle against the religious right had been a nail biter. The *Los Angeles Times* reminded readers of erstwhile presidential candidate Pat Robertson's "war chest" of $17 million.[98] To put that "war chest" in perspective, labor unions alone gave $15 million to Gore in the 2000 campaign. A "Republican" operative recounted the heyday of the religious right, saying the Robertson campaign was "what a Nazi pep rally would have been like. The group was whipped into a froth, it was a real mob mentality; they were like sheep." In short, he said, it was "scary."[99]

But that was over now. Sleep peacefully, liberals. The *Times* cheerfully reported that fully 80 percent of Robertson's followers had dropped out of politics entirely. In what turned out to be one of many premature eulogies for Christian conservatives, the article concluded, "A return to politics-as-usual could have been predicted. The overarching trend in American politics is moderation. . . . Perhaps the religious right believed too strongly." This was written in 1990.

And yet, somehow, Christian Conservatives emerged again. In 1993—three years after the headline "Religious Right Forgets Politics," and four years after the Moral Majority was shut down like an "abandoned house"—the religious right had gained strength again! The "power of the religious right," according to the *Washington Post,* "shook official Washington."[100] Congressmen were quoted as calling the religious right "intimidating," saying it was "more influential than the bankers, more influential than the real estate industry and as powerful as any single labor union in America." All this despite the fact that—as was duly noted in the exact same article—the "Gospel lobby" consisted of flocks that are "largely poor, uneducated and easy to command."[101] These must have been some easily intimidated congressmen.

By July 1994, the religious right was an impotent carcass again. In *USA Today,* a columnist declared, "The influence of conservative evangelicals within the Republican Party is probably weaker today than at any point in the past 15 years."[102] Even more so, evidently, than when it was shut down like an abandoned house in 1989 and then again in 1990. Later that same summer, the *Washington Post* confirmed that the religious right had thrown in the towel. The Christian Coalition had basically morphed into Christie Todd Whitman Republicans. "[I]ts leaders in Iowa and nationally are looking to move toward the center."[103]

But by November of 1994, the religious right was back in the saddle, trying to impose its values on others again. *ABC World News Tonight* ran a show ominously titled "Christian Coalition Gaining Strength." The highlight read, "The Christian Coalition is among the most powerful and well-organized political movements in the U.S., dominating the GOP in more than a dozen states. Critics say it wants to impose its values on everyone."[104]

And then, two years later, the religious right was routed! The *New York Times* reported in 1996 that eight in ten Republican primary voters "do not think of themselves as members of the religious right political movement." Forty-nine percent of all Republican voters attacked religious conservatives as divisive.[105] The all-out public relations war portraying the "religious right" as vicious, intolerant oppressors had finally succeeded.

By 1998, they were out again, so they must have snuck back in since 1996. As explained in an article on conservative Christians titled "Coalition's Political Power Ending": "1998 might be remembered as the year that began their exile from the promised land of the Republican Party."[106]

But the religious right bounced back to exercise inordinate influence on President George W. Bush. This time they went so far as to infiltrate the Department of Justice, appointing one of their own as attorney general.

Yet and still, after Pat Robertson resigned as president of the Christian Coalition in December 2001, an op-ed column in the *New York Times* announced that victory had finally been achieved. Noting the "declining importance of the man and his movement," the column cheerfully stated, "the Christian Coalition has been losing members and financial support for years."[107]

Not only is there no meaningful definition of the "religious right," there is no coherence to its life span. It is uncanny how Orwellian it is. The "religious right" cannot be defined beyond the broadest generalities; its leaders are unknown; it exercises vast, inexplicable influence; and it is constantly being vanquished—only to rise again.

Having created a mythical enemy and trained the public to reflexively hate it, the myth can later be deployed to discredit anyone by saying he is a member of the "religious right." Thus, instinctively, the entire talking-head cabal knew just what to say about John Ashcroft, Bush's nominee for attorney general. He was religious right, Christian conservative, archconservative, far right, mean-spirited, wing nut, and divisive.

Liberals are like cats; they have a pre-programmed set of strictly limited

behaviors. They all have the same twitches, the same tropes, the same para-
noias. It is fascinating how consistent it is.

The *Los Angeles Times* described Ashcroft as "a champion of the religious right" and noted that "despite his religious beliefs," he said "his mis-
sion as attorney general will be to enforce the law."[108] According to
"observers," the article continued, the key issue with Ashcroft was "how his
strong beliefs and political ties on abortion might shape his performance as
attorney general."

NBC's Tom Brokaw referred to Ashcroft as a "Christian activist."[109]
NBC anchor Brian Williams opened the *Nightly News* on December 22,
2000, saying that Bush's selection of Ashcroft "calms the far right politically."[110] *Newsweek* assistant managing editor Evan Thomas called the
Ashcroft nomination "a sop, I assume, to buy off the wing nuts."[111] *Wall
Street Journal* executive Washington editor Al Hunt called the nominee
"mean-spirited" for voting against spending taxpayer money on government
programs supported by Al Hunt.[112]

CNN's Margaret Carlson said the Ashcroft appointment "thrills the
right, in particular the religious right" because he was "way to the right" on
issues like "Violence Against Women"[113] In fact, as a senator, Ashcroft was
a co-sponsor of the Violence Against Women Act, which was such a feminist
lunacy that it had already been struck down by the U.S. Supreme Court.

Dispensing with the pretense that "divisive" means something other than
"conservative," columnist William Raspberry called Ashcroft "highly divisive" on the grounds that Ashcroft received 100 percent ratings from both the
Christian Coalition and Phyllis Schlafly's Eagle Forum.[114] The "division is
ideological—even theological," Raspberry continued. Ashcroft's "theological" divisiveness consisted of his opposition to abortion, support for the
death penalty, and—most intriguingly—his support for school vouchers and
a flag-burning amendment.

In a particularly comical article in the witch-hunt tradition, the *New
York Times* ran a banner headline: "Religious Right Made Big Push to Put
Ashcroft in Justice Dept."[115] Taking a slightly more prominent above-the-
fold position than the other two front-page articles that day also attacking
Bush nominees, the article nervously warned of the power of the "Christian
right." As proof that Ashcroft represented the "Christian right," the *Times*
used the phrase "Christian right" approximately eighty billion times. The
Church of the New York Times was invoking its infallibility to proclaim:

"Ew, yuck, he's icky." Enumerating the policy positions that demonstrated Ashcroft's "outspoken support for the agenda of the religious right," the *Times* included his opposition to public funding of the National Endowment for the Arts. If you oppose the federal government taxing waitresses in Des Moines to subsidize the New York City Opera, you must be some sort of Jesus freak. Other positions evidencing Ashcroft's "deep religious commitment" was his support for the death penalty and opposition to gun control.

On the basis of the *Times*'s classification system, about the only Republicans who are not religious fanatics are a handful of Northeastern turncoats like Christie Todd Whitman (known as "moderate Republicans"). Probably 90 percent of all registered Republicans are with Ashcroft on those three issues. The *Times* had methodically assembled a bullet-proof case that Ashcroft was a Republican.

But the Newspaper of Record breathlessly reported that if confirmed, "Mr. Ashcroft would reach the highest office ever attained by a leading figure of the Christian right."[116] It was almost as if there were a real identifiable entity known as the "Christian right" replete with officers, membership lists, and ID cards. This was a scoop bigger than the Pentagon Papers. The *New York Times* had somehow obtained the membership list of an organization that doesn't exist! And Ashcroft was on track to get the most plum government job out of the whole lot of them.

Not to be a stickler, but doesn't the guy who appoints the attorney general hold a higher office than the attorney general? President Bush had repeatedly described the transforming effect that Christianity had had on his life. He goes to church. He even supports gun rights—which, according to the *New York Times,* is an important indicium of membership in the "religious right." In a widely publicized remark during the primary debates, Bush said the most important philosopher to him was Jesus Christ. The *Times* ought to have remembered that. An article in the *Times Magazine* section said Bush's Jesus comment marked "the time in American politics when the wall separating church and state began to collapse."[117] Times columnist Maureen Dowd had sneered that Bush's Jesus answer was evidence of either "cynicism or exhibitionism."[118]

So how did Ashcroft get to be the guy in "the highest office ever attained by a leading figure of the Christian right"? Was President Bush behind in his membership dues to "Christian Right, Inc." or something?

Further evidence that Ashcroft was the "favorite son" of the "Christian political movement" was that he had received "generous financial backing from its members." (There are no "members.") Indeed, the paper reported, Ashcroft "received more political money from religious groups and clergymen than any other Senate candidate." That news flash warranted above-the-fold, front-page coverage in the *New York Times.* You had to persevere to the flip-page to find out that the torrent of "Christian right" money being funneled to Ashcroft consisted of Pat Robertson and two other guys contributing money to a Political Action Committee founded by Ashcroft. In all, the crack investigative reporters determined that out of $8.6 million in campaign contributions to Ashcroft in the 2000 election cycle, a whopping $23,577 came from "religious groups." The largest contribution came from a personal friend of Ashcroft's and was made posthumously by the man's daughter. The *Times* actually tracked down the daughter to delve deeper into the motive behind the donation. On rigorous cross-examination by the *Times* reporters, the daughter admitted she "knew of her father's support for Mr. Ashcroft on a range of issues, among them taxes and education."

The country had just been through an administration in which the Chinese could give a campaign contribution to the president and end up with a naval base in Long Beach, California, and the *New York Times* was hyperventilating about a perfectly legal political donation from someone who agreed with Ashcroft on "taxes and education."

Also remarkably detached from recent American history, the *Times* found it newsworthy that, as governor of Missouri, Ashcroft had "pointedly" asked his prospective judicial nominees if they had been faithful to their wives. The country could have been spared a lot of trouble if the press bothered to ask that question a little more "pointedly" of a certain presidential candidate back in 1992.

But more to the point, what is the dark underbelly of such a question? Even a governor who supported the agenda of the Atheist Left might prefer judges who would not be instantly engulfed in an ugly personal scandal. Maybe the *Times* was just mad about Ashcroft's presumption that men would have wives. It's always hard to tell with that paper.

One of Ashcroft's candidates for the state bench told the *Times* that Governor Ashcroft had asked him "if he was prepared to enforce the abortion laws." As the poor sap noted blandly, it was a "fair question" and "one that you could simply answer yes to if you were pro-choice or pro-life." Still, the word "abortion" on the lips of a "member" of the Christian right sent the *Times* into an anxious reverie of speculative interpretation: "[I]t was not clear whether the question constituted what has come to be called a litmus test."

Not only that, but "[a]t the time the question was asked, Missouri had enacted some of the most restrictive laws in the nation for women seeking to have an abortion." It being a constitutional right to abort well into the third trimester, it's hard to imagine how "draconian" those laws could have been.

Several paragraphs later the article totally lost the thread of indignation about asking public officials whether they would enforce abortion laws and—with no sense of irony—began raising questions about whether Ashcroft would enforce abortions laws. A few paragraphs back, that was known as a "litmus test." You could get dizzy trying to follow the left's bizarre accusatory logic. Only through a process of mind-numbing repetition does it almost start to resemble rational thought.

Ashcroft was confirmed, but there will be future mobilizations over other nominees. The media will continue gently and subtly directing mob hatred toward conservative Christians. After relentless propaganda, the mob's instinctive rage can be "switched from one object to another like the flame of a blowlamp."[119]

The fact that liberal propaganda succeeds is not surprising. What is fairly stunning is that the left's carefully nurtured devil term—their Emmanuel Goldstein, capable of producing hate on cue—essentially comes down to accusing someone of being a Christian.

L iberals hate religion because politics is a religion substitute for liberals and they can't stand the competition. There's a reason the left's rhetoric bears such a striking resemblance to some of the nuttier religions: Abhorring real religions, liberals refuse to condemn what societies have condemned for thousands of years—e.g., promiscuity, divorce, illegitimacy, homosexuality. Consequently, the normal human instinct to condemn something bubbles up against a legion of quite modern vices, such as smoking, fur, red meat, excessive consumption, and land development.

Loathing of the religious right becomes an end in itself, a consuming passion. Liberals denounce Christian conservatives for being moralistic, for imposing their morality on others, for not separating morality from politics, and for bringing religious zeal to public life—and then work themselves into a frothing frenzy of righteous, moralistic zeal over their own moral excellence for being so rational, calm, and detached. One is reminded of the sadistic moralists from Dickens novels, who latch on to the idea that whipping is good for the child, so they can beat the hell out of him and feel good about themselves while doing it.

Consider the frenzy of indignation over George W. Bush speaking at Bob Jones University. For their religious convictions, which among other things dictate a belief in their own religion (exclusionary!) and an opposition to interracial dating (racist!), Bob Jones University has long provoked unbridled rage on the left. The media would have you think this serious religious college is overrun with slack-jawed hoodlums sporting swastikas and shaved heads, rather than gentle, earnest Christians.

Most shamelessly, liberals pretended to be deeply wounded by Bush's appearance at Bob Jones University—on behalf of Catholics. After twenty years of left-wing Catholic-bashing, this was a rather aggressive position to take. Just a few months earlier, for example, liberals had been indignantly defending a taxpayer-subsidized pornographic portrayal of the Virgin Mary on display at the Brooklyn Museum of Art. (The *New York Times* doggedly refuses to mention that the Virgin Mary artwork was decorated with close-up photos of women's vaginas from pornographic magazines, preferring instead to refer only to the cow dung also on the Virgin Mary. Christians were crazy to be upset about something that is so repellent that the *New York Times* refuses to mention it in print.)

Writing in the *Sunday Times* (London) about the ensuing brouhaha, *New York Times* columnist Andrew Sullivan had nothing but contempt for Catholics who had taken offense at the smutty Virgin Mary. He accused them of "tone-deaf self-righteousness" and sneered that they were "lining up for victim status." The proper response, Sullivan patiently instructed the flock, was a "laugh or groan." So it was interesting that just a few months later, when the issue was George Bush speaking at Bob Jones University, Sullivan decided a "laugh or groan" simply would not do. This time, writing in the *New York Times,* Sullivan bitterly remonstrated against George Bush for speaking at a private Christian school, whose past president had some rather pointed condemnations of Catholicism. Working himself into a towering frenzy of self-pity about the very existence of such a place, Sullivan indulged in painful reminiscences about the anti-Papist slights he had suffered as a child "growing up as an Irish-Catholic in England." Though he vowed never to forget that Bush had spoken at Bob Jones University, he didn't seem to have much trouble forgetting an article he had written in the London *Times* a few months earlier.

What does Bob Jones University have over taxpayer funding for a pornographic display of the Virgin Mary? More relevant, what does Bob Jones have over the Reverend Al Sharpton? In the 2000 presidential campaign, the entire Democratic Dream Team (Vice President Al Gore, former presidential contender Bill Bradley, as well as Senate candidate Hillary Clinton) all eagerly met with Al "These Are Not My Suits" Sharpton. There was not a peep about Democratic presidential candidates making the obligatory campaign stop with Sharpton.

Bob Jones never falsely accused decent men of raping and defiling Tawana Brawley and then refused ever to apologize. Bob Jones never incited ugly mob hatred toward Orthodox Jews culminating in the murder of Yankel Rosenbaum. Bob Jones didn't compare Israel to hell, and if he had, it would have been mentioned in more than one passing aside in *Newsweek*. In 1991 Sharpton replied to a Tel Aviv heckler yelling "Go to hell!" by saying "I am in hell already. I am in Israel." The incident was largely ignored by the media. Instead, reporters were probably camped outside Liberty Baptist College hoping Falwell would say something about gays.

Poor Bob Jones had insulted no one beyond the manifest requirements of his faith. Supposing, hypothetically speaking, Bob Jones were correct about his religion being the one true path to God, then all other religions are false and condemn their practitioners to eternal damnation. Catholics think Protestants are barking up the wrong tree, too. That's kind of the point of all religions. But believing Christians frighten liberals; anti-Semitic race demagogues don't.

Americans are free to believe in Sun People and Ice People, in space aliens, or in a flat earth. But if you admit to quirky beliefs based on a real religion, liberals will ritualistically denounce you. How dare George W. Bush visit the Bob Jones campus and give a speech! He must be made to apologize for failing to chastise them. (Of course, it could have been worse: Bob Jones University could have been treated like the Branch Davidians.)

If there were a modern Spanish Inquisition in America today, it wouldn't be Bob Jones rounding up Catholics. It would be liberals rounding up right-wingers and putting them on trial for hate crimes. The liberal Torquemadas would be smug and angry and self-righteous. And when they were done, they would proudly announce they had finally banished intolerance.

CONCLUSION

Part of the reason liberals prefer invective to engagement is that—as Richard Nixon said of Alger Hiss—if Americans knew what they really believed, the public would boil them in oil.

Liberals have been wrong about everything in the last half-century.

They were wrong about Stalin (praised in the *New York Times* and known as "Uncle Joe" to Franklin Roosevelt). They were wrong about Reagan (won the Cold War and now polling as the greatest president of the twentieth century). They were wrong about the Soviet Union (defeated by the twentieth century's greatest president). They were wrong even about their precious "Abraham Lincoln brigade" in the Spanish Civil War (the disgorging of Soviet archives proves that the Lincoln brigade was part of "a rigidly controlled Soviet operation").[1] They were wrong about Nicaragua (communist dictatorships in Latin America turned out not to be "inevitable revolutions," after all). They were wrong about welfare (since overhauled by Republicans to notable success). They were wrong about crime (Giuliani's achievement is evident in the number of candidates who promise to continue his policies). They were wrong about social security (now bankrupt). They were wrong about the Civil Rights Act (which was *never* going to be used as an instrument of discrimination against whites). They were wrong on the sexual revolution (witness the explosions of AIDS, herpes, chlamydia, hepatitis B, and abortion).

It is not an accident that, today, the left's single biggest cause is "global warming." This time, conservatives won't be able to prove them wrong for a thousand years.

Most devastating for the left as a cohesive political movement was the collapse of their beloved Soviet Union. For decades, the Great Issue uniting various forces on the left, from proclaimed communists to soft anti-anti-communists, was the socialist "ideal." Great Society programs have run their course—and have been a disaster. With impeached former President Clinton having proclaimed the era of big government over—even his wife, Hillary, has averred that "there are not government solutions" to most of society's problems—few people pin their dreams of a brighter tomorrow on yet one more government program.

Apart from global warming—coming in a thousand years to a planet near you!—the left's only remaining cause is abortion. For many Democrats, *Roe v. Wade* is the essence of politics. At the 2000 Democratic National Convention, presidential candidate Al Gore won the loudest, most sustained applause for his promise to protect abortion. This was in a speech that was a virtual whirligig of promises for "working families"—a euphemism for families in which no one works. Gore offered targeted tax cuts, universal health-care coverage for children, smaller class sizes, new gun and tobacco laws, and prescription-drug benefits for seniors. His speech included surefire audience pleasers, such as his pledge to pass a hate crimes law and to oppose school vouchers. He mentioned national defense and got only a lukewarm reaction. He mentioned America's role in freeing the world "from fascism and communism"—polite applause. He said he would fight for the victims of crime—sporadic clapping. But the mere mention of *Roe v. Wade* and total pandemonium broke loose.

Abortion rights would be an odd single issue for any political party. But it is nearly unbearable for a party that prides itself on moral self-righteousness. Instead of their typical smug certitude, abortion makes many Democrats queasy. This is something new: It is unusual for liberals not to conceive of themselves as Christ on the Cross and their political opponents as Nazi stormtroopers. The messy details of abortion are a bad fit with the left's preference for haughty indignation. The absurd, backward rhetoric that associates abortion rights with "women's lives" exposes the dissonance.

There is no question but that *something* gets killed in an abortion, whether one considers that thing worthy of life, like a human, or unworthy of life, like crabgrass. But the pro-killing side of the debate flips the facts upside down to claim that they are protecting women's "lives"—as opposed to women's convenience. At best, some women's "lives" would be saved by abortion if one presupposes women will make good on their threat to: (1) refuse to use birth control and (2) when they get pregnant, engage in unsafe and illegal abortion procedures. Which is kind of a stretch if you think about it.

Since abortion is not the left's proudest moment, liberals prefer to keep reminiscing about the last time they were giddily self-righteous. Like a senile old man who keeps telling you the same story over and over again, liberals babble on and on about the "heady" days of civil rights marches. Between 1995 and 2001, the *New York Times* alone ran more than one hundred articles on "Selma" alone. I believe we may have revisited this triumph of theirs sufficiently by now. For anyone under fifty, the "heady" days of civil rights marches are something out of a history book. The march on Selma was thirty-five years ago.

To put this in perspective, almost thirty-five years before *that* was the beginning of the Great Depression, also a newsworthy event. In 1965, were newspapers jammed with biweekly "Great Depression Updates"? Indeed, the country is as different a place today compared to 1965, as it was in 1965 compared to 1930. What civil rights do people lack now? What bus is anyone not allowed to ride on?

Where there is a vacuum of ideas, paranoia slips in. Much of the left's hate speech bears greater similarity to a psychological disorder than to standard political discourse. The hatred is blinding, producing logical contradictions that would be impossible to sustain were it not for the central element faith plays in the left's new religion. The basic tenet of their faith is this: Maybe they were wrong on facts and policies, but they are good and conservatives are evil. You almost want to give it to them. It's all they have left.

But the personal invective is getting a teensy bit wearying. It always takes an enormous exertion just to ascertain what liberals are so damn upset about. Once you finally figure out what has propelled the tolerant crowd into frenzies of demonic rage, it invariably turns out to be a perfectly ordinary view held by many good-hearted Americans.

A classic of the genre was a *New York Times* editorial on Newt Gingrich—about whom liberals were also wrong. When Republicans won the House of Representatives for the first time in fifty years, the *Times* ran a welcoming editorial to mark the occasion titled "Newt Gingrich, Authoritarian"[2] Among other utterly pointless criticisms, the *Times* accused Gingrich for being "in the throes of post-election gloating." Despite the length of the

Times's diatribe, what made Gingrich an "authoritarian" remained murky. The only point that came through clearly was that the *New York Times* really disliked Gingrich. I mean—really. "Mr. Gingrich wants to be obeyed," the *Times* psychoanalyzed, "both within a Republican majority that exists mainly to rubber stamp his legislative menu and within a country where behavior would be regulated by a society that is emphatic about right and wrong." The *Times* was clearly indignant about the idea of a society that is "emphatic about right and wrong." But apart from Gingrich opposing the *Times*'s evident preference for a society that is ambivalent about right and wrong, it wasn't manifest why the editors were frightened of this man.

In only one of eight vituperative paragraphs did the *Times* allude to any of the positions demonstrating Gingrich's latent fascism. Even these rare substantive points were nearly buried in the hysterical bile:

> The authoritarian undergirdings of Mr. Gingrich's politics show not only in the conventional ways, such as his outlining of a nation of plentiful executions where juries and judges cannot exercise their independent judgment about probation and sentencing. It is even more tellingly revealed by the areas of individual social behavior Mr. Gingrich wants to bring under control. Schoolchildren will be required by law to seek their education in classrooms where prayer is imposed by the will of the majority. As soon as he gets the votes, medical decisions on abortion will be taken from the hands of women and physicians and the treatment itself proscribed by the state.

Four policy positions can be gleaned from that paragraph: Gingrich apparently differs with the editorial position of the *Times* on the death penalty, sentencing guidelines, prayer in schools, and abortion. This is a peculiar collection of policies on which to base a charge of "moral authoritarianism." Vast majorities of Americans agree with Newt Gingrich on at least three of the issues—school prayer, the death penalty, and sentencing guidelines.

It's a little difficult to gauge the public's feelings about the fourth—abortion—on account of abortion's preposterous status as a "constitutional right." But evidently liberals don't think a majority of Americans supports abortion—otherwise they would welcome the overturning of *Roe v. Wade,* which would do nothing more than put abortion to a vote. As their theatrics on *Roe* demonstrate, the last thing they want is a vote. Once Americans were allowed to vote on abortion. Then *Roe* came along and overturned the democratically enacted laws of forty-eight states.

But however the vote would go if abortion were ever returned to the democratic process, it is sheer lunacy to attack any House member for his views on abortion, anyway. No mere congressman can have the slightest, tertiary effect on the legal status of abortion. Only the Supreme Court can do that, and House members don't even vote on Supreme Court nominees.

That leaves sentencing guidelines, the death penalty, and school prayer.

Federal sentencing guidelines were once championed by liberal Democrats. (Their idea was that uniform sentences would prevent racist judges from imposing longer sentences on minorities.) Senator Ted Kennedy joined Strom Thurmond as one of the original co-sponsors of the bill that created the guidelines.[3] Michael Dukakis supported federal sentencing guidelines in his 1988 campaign.[4] The Guidelines Commission was headed by former Kennedy staffer Stephen Breyer, who was later appointed to the Supreme Court by Clinton. So Gingrich was an authoritarian who wanted to be obeyed because he supported a policy also supported by Teddy Kennedy, Michael Dukakis, and Stephen Breyer.

Unlike sentencing guidelines, liberals have always opposed the death penalty and school prayer. But vast majorities of Americans have consistently supported both.

So it's not really that surprising that the editors of the *New York Times* might not want to highlight their precise points of disagreement with Gingrich. A forthright statement of their outrage would make clear that the official editorial position of the *Times* is that the American people are "authoritarians." The *New York Times* has every right to call Americans authoritarian race baiters. That's indubitably what the editors believe. But that's not what they say. That is why the *Times* must attack politicians who share the views of large majorities of Americans by obscuring the point beneath vicious personal tirades.

Most amusingly, the *Times* denounced Gingrich for—of all things—his "implicit" belief that "intellectual dissent is unpatriotic and infuriating." At least the *Times* doesn't bother with being "implicit." Gingrich's dissent from the positions of the *New York Times* editorial page constitutes, as the *Times* calmly put it, "a threat to civil liberties, racial justice and religious freedom."

Bereft of winning issues, persuasive arguments, or real ideas, liberals are bitter. The one impulse that consistently unites them is hate. It is an arresting fact that an impeached, disgraced, disbarred Democratic president successfully rallied liberals to his cause merely by calling his opponents "right-wing Republicans."

The hate-mongering and name-calling on the left might be a droll irrelevancy, except that it has a debilitating effect on real issues. It is often absurdly said that scandals such as Gary Hart's affair with Donna Rice will discourage young idealists from going into politics. This is mainly said by Gary Hart. Of course, another possible response to adultery scandals involving politicians is not good people avoiding politics, but politicians avoiding adultery.

By contrast, it is surely true that if holding political opinions can itself be scandalous, fewer people are going to want to have any of those opinion things. Lies and personal attacks are deeply corrosive of public debate and democratic compromises. Of necessity, therefore, almost all serious political debate takes place exclusively among conservatives—out of earshot of the children so as not to upset them. Not coincidentally, for about twenty years now, all new ideas have bubbled up from the right wing. (It's amazing how productive debate can be when one is not constantly being called a racist.) Almost by definition all new ideas are "right-wing"—whether dubbed "conservative" or "libertarian." Where are the great liberal thinkers?

Some of the new public policy ideas to bubble up from the right wing are School Vouchers, Welfare Reform, the Flat Tax, Quality of Life Crimes, Privatizing Social Security, Videotaping Criminal Confessions, the Strategic Defense Initiative, Pollution Tax Credits, Enterprise Zones, and Winning the Cold War. These ideas were once ridiculed by liberals. ("Shut up," they explained.)[5] But, despite liberals' infernal squawking, these ideas are changing the world.

To take one example, when President Clinton "triangulated" on welfare reform, the left denounced him for capitulating to Newt Gingrich and the Republican Congress. This was true. Despite Clinton's campaign pledge to "end welfare as we know it," somehow it took a Republican Congress coming in two years later to enact welfare reform. Clinton's complex-sounding "triangulation" was nothing more than capitulation on the installment plan. By 2001, one of the Democratic officials who had resigned from the Clinton administration to protest the Republicans' welfare reform made this startling and welcome admission: "In many ways welfare reform is working better than I thought it would. . . . The sky isn't falling anymore. Whatever we have been doing over the last five years, we ought to keep going."[6]

Another example of Republican progress in the face of liberal carping is Mayor Rudolph Giuliani. Throughout his wildly successful mayoralty, Giuliani was regularly protested as "Adolf Giuliani" and portrayed with a Hitler mustache.[7] By the end of his term—even before September 11—he had cleaned up the city so spectacularly that his prospective successors were tripping over one another in their rush to promise to continue his policies. And after September 11, Giuliani's heroic status was so daunting he could have gotten a table at Elaine's. It was not surprising that Giuliani performed magnificently when New York came under a savage terrorist attack. What was surprising—stunning, in fact—is how liberals began saying novenas to Giuliani's immortal soul.

In a break from their otherwise fiendish cleverness, the hijackers' one grievous miscalculation had been to attack Manhattan, the stronghold of domestic liberalism. The only thing the terrorists could have done to instill greater fear in Manhattanites would have been to release a list of rent-controlled apartments. The city was in a panic: After September 11, the average New Yorker faced a risk of death or bodily harm not seen since David Dinkins was mayor.

Thus, Liberal Manhattan began worshipping Giuliani both out of terror and also to detract from President Bush's spectacular performance. There was no question, for example, but that *Time* magazine would make Giuliani Man of the Year. It might have been the mastermind of the attack, Osama bin Laden, but it sure wasn't going to be Bush. The characterization of Giuliani as a heartless brute vanished into thin air like the blather it always was.

Most of the time, liberals do not imagine the world is real. Their contribution to political debate is worthless, since even they do not believe the things they say. The more shocking and iconoclastic they are, the more fashion points they accrue. Liberal Manhattanites believe in redistribution of their own wealth and ceaseless police brutality like they believe in Martians. It is very possible that Giuliani's critics never seriously considered the consequences of a single thing they said. September 11 was real. It took a terrorist attack for liberals to suspend their usual hateful palaver.

In a fascinating case study of liberal hate and paranoia, Andrew Sullivan, former editor of the *New Republic* and contributing writer for the *New York Times Magazine*, actually sought the company of conservatives. And not just any conservatives. He went to the belly of the beast—or the "enemy," as he put it—attending a Christian Coalition gala in honor of Pat

Robertson's seventieth birthday.[8] When Sullivan breathlessly reported back to liberals the breaking news that Christian Coalition members are people, too ("They seemed neither fanatics nor bigots"), the left was forced to come to terms with its own bigotry.

Just kidding. Sullivan's own small step forward turned out not to be a giant leap for liberalkind. The precise reaction he received from his liberal friends was redoubled hatred and loathing. As Sullivan reported, they "viscerally compared the event to a Nazi rally, and said that I might have met many personally charming advocates of bigotry there as well." After an agonizing exegesis on his own soul searching ("Most human goods are alloyed with most human failings"), Sullivan cheerfully resolved that Robertson was "intolerant" but "not evil."

Having himself ventured onto enemy territory, Sullivan concluded by proposing that Christian conservatives meet and spend time with "some of the radicals they claim to be fighting against." Then they "might see that the bogeymen of the cultural left are not quite as terrifying as they thought," but "are human beings, too." This might not change their minds, he said, but "it might change their tone."

In point of fact, conservatives do spend time with the radicals they oppose—and lots of it. It can't be avoided. Liberals are forever leaping out at us from our TV screens, newspapers, magazines, movies, and college lecterns. We know liberals and we know what they think. Unlike Sullivan's exotic incursion into a right-wing gathering, any conservative can already attach names and faces to entire colonies of liberals. Ironically, regular church-going, middle-class Americans are far more cosmopolitan than the self-styled sophisticates of the left.

This isn't merely to say that liberals have near-exclusive control over all major sources of information in this country, though that is true. Nor is the point that liberals are narrow-minded and parochial, incapable of seeing the other fellow's point of view, though that is also true. And it's not that, as a consequence, liberals impute inhumanity to their political opponents and are unfathomably hateful and vicious. That's true, too.

The point is that conservatives in America are the most tolerant (and long-suffering) people in the world. They already have "met and spent time with" liberals. They do it every day, day in, day out, their entire lives.

Andrew Sullivan spends a few hours at a conservative gathering and it's a milestone. Conservatives are bludgeoned with opposing views their every waking moment, and merely for refusing to join the cult, they are denounced as "intolerant." By contrast, liberals have absolutely no contact with the society they decry from their Park Avenue redoubts.

The day after seven-time NASCAR Winston Cup champion Dale Earnhardt died in a race at the Daytona 500, almost every newspaper in America carried the story on the front page. Stock-car racing had been the nation's fastest-growing sport for a decade, and NASCAR the second-most-watched sport behind the NFL. More Americans recognize the name Dale Earnhardt than, say, Maureen Dowd. (Manhattan liberals are dumbly blinking at that last sentence.) It took the *New York Times* two days to deem Earnhardt's death sufficiently important to mention it on the front page. Demonstrating the left's renowned populist touch, the article began, "His death brought a silence to the Wal-Mart."[9] The *Times* went on to report that in vast swaths of the country people watch stock-car racing. Tacky people were mourning Dale Earnhardt all over the South!

Except for occasional exotic safaris to the Wal-Mart or forays into enemy territory at a Christian Coalition dinner, liberals do not know any conservatives. It makes it easier to demonize them that way. It's well and good for Andrew Sullivan to talk about a "truce." But conservatives aren't the ones who need to be jolted into the discovery that the "bogeymen" of their imaginations are "not quite as terrifying as they thought." Conservatives already know that people they disagree with politically can be "charming." Also savagely cruel bigots who hate ordinary Americans and lie for sport.

NOTES

ONE. LIBERALS UNHINGED

1. Peter Perl, "Absolute Truth; Tom DeLay Is Certain That Christian Family Values Will Solve America's Problems. But He's Uncertain How to Face His Own Family," *Washington Post Magazine*, May 13, 2001, p. W12.

2. "Dangerous Delay," *News and Observer* (Raleigh, N.C.), March 26, 1997, p. A18.

3. Peter Perl, "Absolute Truth," p. W12.

4. Passim. This refers to the fact that DeLay built a half-million-dollar Houston pest control company before entering politics.

5. Maureen Dowd, "Liberties; The God Squad," *New York Times*, June 20, 1999, Sec. 4, p. 15.

6. Ibid.

7. Katie Couric, *Today*, March 6, 2001. Couric interviewed Senator Arlen Specter just weeks after Specter had warned darkly that the ex-president could be impeached, even though he was out of office, for selling presidential pardons. Couric asked him if he had any regrets. Specter had, after all, voted to acquit Clinton two years earlier. But those weren't the regrets she was asking about. She said: "You know you, you angered a lot of feminists when you accused Anita Hill. . . . And you accused her publicly of, quote, 'Flat out perjury.' Any regrets?"

8. Katie Couric, *Today*, June 8, 2000. Couric asked Heston if there were not "any other position the NRA could take in terms of trying to decrease the number of school shootings." Heston cited the millions of dollars the NRA spends on arms safety education (including the runaway hit *Eddie Eagle* video). When Couric dismissed education, Heston asked her what she would suggest. She replied: "I don't know, perhaps greater restrictions."

9. Matt Lauer, *Today*, June 12, 2000. The cherubic, earnest Lauer casually observed: "I feel strange saying, I never stopped to think about the fact there is no official U.S. policy on vacation time."

10. *New York Times*, April 11, 2000.

11. *Salon*, April 30, 2000. Ehrenreich noted that "its message is a timeless one that bears repeating every century or so: The meek shall triumph and the mighty shall fall; the hungry and exhausted will get restless and someday—someday!—rise up against their oppressors. The prophet Isaiah said something like this, and so, a little more recently, did Jesus."

12. Dan Rather, *CBS Evening News*, August 17, 2000. Rather attributed rumors of an impending indictment of Bill Clinton to a "carefully orchestrated," "Republican-backed" leak, one day before a Carter-appointed judge admitted that he had been the source.

13. Lewinsky 8/26/98 Deposition, at 18-20, cited in the Starr Report, "The Findings of Independent Counsel Kenneth W. Starr on President Clinton and the Lewinsky Affair," with analysis by the staff of the *Washington Post* (1998) at 329.

14. Bryant Gumbel, "Hugh Hefner and Christie Hefner Discuss the Controversy Surrounding the Democratic Convention's Fund-raiser, Which Was to Have Taken Place at the Playboy Mansion," *The Early Show*, August 15, 2000.

15. Director Robert Altman quoted in the *New York Post* (from the *London Times*):

"When I see an American flag flying, it's a joke. This present government in America I just find disgusting, the idea that George Bush could run a baseball team successfully—he can't even speak! I just find him an embarrassment."

16. Michele Kayal, "Flag Flying Causes Stir at Palace in Honolulu," *New York Times,* November 25, 2001. (Quoting Dan Boylan, a political analyst at the University of Hawaii-West Oahu: "This is when people start acting very, very dumb in their patriotism and flag waving.")

17. Felicia R. Lee, "Flag-Waving: Reading Between the Stripes," *New York Times,* September 30, 2001. (Quoting David Nasaw, a historian at the City University of New York Graduate Center: "New York has just been too much of a cosmopolitan town for flag-waving.")

18. Clyde Haberman, "60's Lessons on How Not to Wave Flag," *New York Times,* September 19, 2001.

19. Barbara Walters and Jami Floyd, "Abortion Clinics in U.S. Targeted by Religious Terrorists," ABC's *20/20,* November 28, 2001.

20. Frank Rich, "How to Lose a War," *New York Times,* October 27, 2001.

21. Ibid. Though Rich claimed that abortion clinics had plenty of experience with "home grown Talibans" and, thus, Planned Parenthood could have provided leads on "the convergence of international and domestic terrorism," no anthrax had ever been sent to an abortion clinic, though a white powder had been. The mailer of the harmless white powder was a bank robber–cum–anti-abortionist who was already on the FBI's most wanted list. Among the critical advice Rich said Planned Parenthood could have imparted to Ashcroft was that offering a reward for the capture of terrorists would never work: "The sight of Mr. Ashcroft and other federal Keystone Kops offering a $1 million reward for anthrax terrorists [was] a laughable indication of how little grasp they have of the enemy." The mailer of the white powder was captured by the FBI about one month later—in response to widely circulated wanted posters offering a $50,000 reward.

22. Bruce Ackerman, "On the Home Front, a Winnable War," *New York Times,* November 6, 2001.

23. Former senator Dale Bumpers of Arkansas in his defense of Clinton during the impeachment trial in the U.S. Senate. The *New York Times* called it "a speech of rare eloquence." R. W. Apple, "The Trial of the President: The Defense—In the Chamber," *New York Times,* January 22, 1999.

24. James Carville and Paul Begala, "A Battle Plan for the Democrats," *New York Times,* May 27, 2001.

25. Statement of Senator James Jeffords, "Declaration of Independence," May 24, 2001, Burlington, Vermont, at www.senate.gov/~jeffords/524statement.html.

26. Keith Olbermann, *The Big Show,* MSNBC, August 18, 1998. (Quoted in editorial "And the Winner Is . . . ," *Union Leader* [Manchester, N.H.], December 31, 1998.)

27. William Tuohy, "Jesse Jackson Competes with Queen on TV; Britain: As She Hails N. Ireland Progress on BBC, American Assails Tories on Another Channel," *Los Angeles Times,* December 26, 1994, p. A4.

28. LexisNexis search of *New York Times* archives from December 1994 through January 1995 for "Jesse Jackson and Germany and fascism and South Africa" produces no documents.

29. Michele Parente with William Douglas, "Promoters of GOP Pact 'Worse Than Hitler,' " *Newsday,* February 19, 1995, p. A20.

30. Paul Richter and Edwin Chen, "Biden Vows to Oppose Foster, Then Flip-Flops," *Los Angeles Times,* February 11, 1995, p. A4.

31. Fred W. Lindecke, "Schroeder Lambastes Limbaugh; Coloradan Urges Shows to Offset 'Rush' Radio," *St. Louis Post-Dispatch,* March 7, 1995, p. 2B.

32. Chris Matthews, "Attorney Alan Dershowitz and Former Democratic Pollster Patrick Caddell Discuss Election Reform," CNBC's *Hardball with Chris Matthews,* July 31, 2001.

33. Kenneth J. Cooper, "Plan to Curb Caucuses Draws Plenty of Heat; House Democrats Say Advocacy Would Suffer," *Washington Post,* December 8, 1994, p. A7.

34. Joe Hallett, "Gore Hits Hard in Michigan," *Columbus Dispatch,* November 6, 2000, p. 1A.

35. Rob Morse, "Those Other F-Words," *San Francisco Examiner,* February 14, 1999.

36. Marla Romash, Eric Hauser, Steve McMahon, Peter Fenn, Dick Morris, Sean Hannity, and Alan Colmes, "Race for the Democratic Presidential Nomination," Fox News Network, January 5, 2000, Transcript #010501cb.253. ("But I think the point that Donna is trying to make and has been trying to make is to be inclusive rather than exclusive, to bring in people from all walks of life, from all colors. And that's what makes a good campaign.")

37. See, e.g., James Gerztenzang, "Powell Warns Gore Not to Play the 'Race Card,' " *Los Angeles Times,* January 7, 2000.

38. L. Brent Bozell III, "Pooh-poohing Election Results," *Washington Times,* November 26, 1994, p. D1.

39. "Interview with Joycelyn Elders," *Playboy,* June 1995 and passim.

40. Joseph Lowery, at a Southern Christian Leadership Conference meeting, quoted in the *New Yorker,* May 6, 1996.

41. Ibid.

42. Julianne Malveaux, "To the Contrary," November 6, 1994.

43. Editorial, "Newt Gingrich, Authoritarian," *New York Times,* November 13, 1994.

44. Quoted in Editorial, "And the Winner Is," *Union Leader* (Manchester, N.H.) December 31, 1998.

45. Lonnae O'Neal Parker, "White Girl?; Cousin Kim Is Passing. But Cousin Lonnae Doesn't Want to Let Her Go," *Washington Post,* August 8, 1999.

46. Alison Mitchell, "Centrist Senator Found Middle Ground," *New York Times,* April 7, 2001, p. A11.

47. "Mr. Bush's Fumble," *New York Times,* May 25, 2001, p. A22.

48. Ceci Connolly, "Gore Runs into Flak on Foray into N.H.; DLC Raps Tradition-Based Campaign; GOP Hits Plans for 'Official' Events," *Washington Post,* November 20, 1999; R. H. Melton and Jamie Stockwell, "Allen Starts Senate Race by Attacking Robb's Record," *Washington Post,* March 14, 2000; Spencer S. Hsu, "Area Legislators Shed Light on Their Impeachment Votes," *Washington Post,* February 28, 1999.

49. In 1999, Kerry won a 95 percent liberal voting record from Americans for Democratic Action and a 5 percent score from the American Conservative Union. Robb got a 100 from the ADA and an 8 from the ACU. That same year, the Republicans' ADA/ACU ratings were Trent Lott (R-Miss.), 0 / 96; Bob Smith (R-N.H.), 15 / 96; Connie Mack (R-Fla.), 0 / 91; and Don Nickles (R-Okla.), 0 / 96. Reported by the Center for International Policy's Columbia Project, at www.ciponline.org/columbia/senvotes.htm.

50. CNN's *The Capital Gang,* July 24, 1999.

51. Richard Cohen, "The '50s Are Back," *Washington Post,* June 22, 1999.

52. Howell Raines, *Fly Fishing Through the Midlife Crisis,* New York: Anchor, 1994.

53. U.S. Newswire, transcript of press briefing by Vice President Gore, October 28, 1994.

54. Michael Weisskopf, "Energized by Pulpit or Passion, the Public Is Calling; 'Gospel Grapevine' Displays Strength in Controversy over Military Gay Ban," *Washington Post,* February 1, 1993, p. A1.

55. Syl Jones, "Imagine What Betty Currie Must Be Thinking Now," Minneapolis *Star Tribune,* January 29, 1999.

56. Greta Van Susteren and Wolf Blitzer, "House Judiciary Committee Releases New Batch of Starr Evidence," CNN's *Burden of Proof,* October 2, 1998.

57. Julianne Malveaux, "Special Vast, Right-Wing Conspiracy: Bon Mot from Malveaux," *Weekly Standard,* 1998.

58. Michael Musto, "La Dolce Musto," *Village Voice,* March 2, 1999.

59. Heather Mallick, "The Reconstitution of Monica Lewinsky: Kenneth Starr Violated Every Civil Right She Ever Had. But Finally, the Most Publicly Humiliated Woman on Earth Has Found a Defender in Andrew Morton," *Ottawa Sun,* March 14, 1999.

60. Quoted in "With Interview and Book, Monica Lewinsky Returns to the Media Spotlight," CNN's *Crossfire,* March 4, 1999.

61. Liz Langley, "Clinton vs. the Uglies: There Is Going to Be a Backlash Against All This Prudery, an Era of Uninhibited, '70s-Type Sexuality," *Toronto Sun,* January 10, 1999.

62. "Tripp: Says Scandal Made Her Aware of 'How Ugly' She Was," *People,* January 12, 2001.

63. Geraldo Rivera, "Paula Jones and Writer Joe Conason Discuss Jones' Penthouse Photos and Her Involvement in the Clinton Impeachment," *Rivera Live,* CNBC, October 25, 2000.

64. Belinda Luscombe, "People," *Time,* August 24, 1998.

65. Robin Givhans, "The Eyelashes Have It," *Washington Post,* November 18, 2000, p. C1.

66. Ibid.

67. Hayley Kaufman, "Go! Thursday; Fashion Victim," *Boston Globe,* November 16, 2000, p. D2.

68. Kevin Sack, "The 43rd President: After the Vote—A Special Report," *New York Times,* December 15, 2000, p. A1.

69. Bob Herbert, "In America: The Mean Strategy Backfires," *New York Times,* May 28, 2001.

70. Said to rape victim Jan License after her victims'-rights speech to the 1996 Republican Convention. Quoted by Media Research Council.

71. Fox News/Opinion Dynamics Poll, February 24–25, 1999. N = 924 registered voters nationwide.

72. Discussing CBS's skittishness on the Broaddrick story on Fox News Channel's *O'Reilly Factor,* Rather said, "When the charge has something to do with somebody's private sex life, I would prefer not to run any of it." "Personal Stories," *The O'Reilly Factor,* May 15, 2001, Transcript # 051503cb.256.

73. Editorial, "Newt's Natterings Backfiring on Him," *Tacoma News Tribune,* November 25, 1995, p. A11.

74. Rob Morse, "No Newt Is Good Newt," *San Francisco Examiner,* January 12, 1996, p. A20.

75. Richard L. Berke, "In a G.O.P. Stronghold, Support, but Little Passion," *New York Times,* December 14, 1995, p. B16.

76. Carl Rowan, "Poor Bob Dole a Hostage of GOP Zealots," *Buffalo News,* January 13, 1996, p. 3C.

77. President Bill Clinton, February 24, 1995.

78. Nancy Benac, "Mrs. Clinton Lunches with Kids, Defends Federal Lunches," Associated Press, March 1, 1995.

79. Representative Patricia Schroeder, March 21, 1995.

80. Jennifer Dixon, "Showdown in the House over GOP's Sweeping Welfare Bill," Associated Press, March 21, 1995.

81. Matt Lauer, "Interview with President George W. Bush," *Today,* April 25, 2001.

82. Matt Lauer, "Hillary Rodham Clinton Discusses Allegations Against Her Husband, Child Care, and State of the Union Address," *Today,* January 27, 1998.

83. John Roberts, *CBS Evening News,* April 29, 2001.

84. Tim Russert, *Meet the Press,* April 29, 2001.

85. John Herndon, "Campaigns Against Distorted Talk Radio Continue," *Austin American-Statesman,* January 25, 1996, p. 25.

86. Michelle Quinn, "Money Pouring in for Cub—Not Kids; Town Shocked over Skewed Priorities," *Houston Chronicle,* May 29, 1994.

87. Kathy O'Malley and Dorothy Collin, *Chicago Tribune,* January 6, 1992, p. 12.

Two. The Gucci Position on Domestic Policy

1. Michiko Kakutani, "The Strange Case of the Writer and the Criminal," *New York Times,* September 20, 1981.

2. Glenn Kessler, "The Very Rich Pay Growing Tax Share," *Washington Post,* March 15, 2001, p. E1.

3. Editorial, *Las Vegas Review-Journal,* January 14, 2002.

4. "Twilight of the ERA Era; With Time Running Out, Women Rally Round the Amendment," *Time,* July 13, 1981.

5. See, e.g., Associated Press, "Disney Executives Top Donors for Mrs. Clinton," *New York Times,* February 25, 2000 (reporting that the top donors to Hillary Clinton's Senate campaign were from the legal profession and the entertainment industry).

6. Don Van Natta Jr., "The 2000 Campaign: The Fund-Raising," *New York Times,* April 25, 2000 (" 'The Republicans' average donation is $55,' officials said. Jenny Backus, the Democrats' spokeswoman, said the party did not reveal its average donation because it viewed the information as proprietary.") See also Margaret Warner, "Political Jousting," The NewsHour, PBS online MacNeil/Lehrer Productions, April 24, 1997, http://www.pbs.org/newshour/bb/congress/april97/leaders_4-24.html (Democratic National Committee chairman Governor Roy Romer refusing to respond to GOP chair Jim Nicholson's claim that the average donation to the Democrats is a great deal higher than the average donation to the Republicans.)

7. Amy Keller, "The Roll Call 50 Richest," Roll Call, January 15, 2001.

8. Ibid. Sen. John Kerry (D-Mass., $620 million); Sen. Jon Corzine (D-N.J., $400 million); Sen. Herb Kohl (D-Wis., $300 million); Sen. Jay Rockefeller (D-W. Va., $200 million); Sen. Lincoln Chafee (R-R.I., $63 million); Sen. Dianne Feinstein (D-Calif., $50 million); Sen. Maria Cantwell (D-Wash., $40 million, later bankrupt); Sen. Peter Fitzgerald (R-Ill., $40 million); Sen. Bob Bennett (R-Utah, $30 million); Sen. John Edwards (D-N.C., $25 million); Sen. Edward Kennedy (D-Mass., $25 million.)

9. Compare Republican Senator Bob Bennett ("Utah's junior Senator is still reaping the benefits of his days as a CEO of Franklin International Institute . . . Under Bennett's direction the firm went from four employees to 800 and revenues skyrocketed from almost zero to more than $80 million annually.") to Democratic Senator John Kerry ("Kerry still boasts a massive fortune thanks to his ketchup heiress wife's wealth. Teresa Heinz was booted off Forbes' list of the 400 wealthiest Americans in 1999 when the magazine estimated her ketchup riches at $620 million, narrowly missing that year's cutoff of $625 million."). Amy Keller, "The Roll Call 50 Richest."

10. Doron P. Levin, "Maker of Documentary That Attacks G.M. Alienates His Allies," *New York Times,* January 19, 1990. (Quoting Pauline Kael in the January 8 issue of the *New Yorker* magazine.)

11. Jacques Ellul, *Propaganda: The Formation of Men's Attitudes,* New York: Vintage Books, 1965, p. 166.

12. Ibid.

13. Ibid., p. 74.

14. Denise Hamilton, "The People's Pornographer; *Hustler's* Larry Flynt Is Flying High with a Purified Publishing Empire and a New Movie About His First Amendment Fights," *New Times Los Angeles,* October 24, 1996.

15. Crispian Balmer, "Porn King Flynt Seeks Dirt on President Bush," *Yahoo News,* copyright © 2001 Reuters, May 16, 2001.

16. Alan Johnson, "Hollywood Should Clean Up Its Act, Says Actor Sheen: 'West Wing' Star Rallies Democrats on Dayton Visit," *Columbus Dispatch,* September 24, 2000.

17. Denise Hamilton, "The People's Pornographer."

18. Dan Horn, " 'Larry Flynt's Return Is an Attempt to Return Cincinnati to the Past. He Came Back with the Intent of Lowering our Community Standards,' " *Cincinnati Enquirer,* May 2, 1999.

19. Denise Hamilton, "The People's Pornographer."

20. Ibid.

21. Carol Felsenthal, *Phyllis Schlafly: The Sweetheart of the Silent Majority,* Washington, D.C.: Regnery, 1982, pp. 63–64. At the time, it was technically Radcliffe, of course, but no one knows what that is anymore, and she was in class with Harvard boys.

22. Ibid., p. 56.

23. Ibid., p. 65.

24. See George Gilder, *Men and Marriage,* New Orleans, La.: Pelican Publishing Co., 1987, pp. 101–103.

25. Carol Felsenthal, *Phyllis Schlafly*, pp. 114–16.

26. John Updike, "Is Sex Necessary?: A History of the Revolution," *New Yorker*, February 21, 2000 (reviewing *Make Love Not War: The Sexual Revolution: An Unfettered History*, Boston: Little, Brown, 2000).

27. "Onward, Women!," *Time*, December 4, 1989. ("The superwoman is weary, the young are complacent, but feminism is not dead. And, baby, there's still a long way to go.")

28. "After the Storm; Free from Silence: Ms. Steinem," *Primetime Live*, ABC News, January 23, 1992.

29. Liz Smith, "A Contretemps over Mort," *Newsday*, December 17, 1991.

30. "After the Storm" *Primetime Live.*

31. "1936–1986 Year by Year; An Almanac of Victories, Disasters, Heroes and Hurrahs," *Time*, Fall 1986, Special Issue.

32. "After the Storm," *Primetime Live.*

33. Jim Salter, "Conservative Matriarch Schlafly Tries to Remain Relevant on the Right," *Chicago Tribune*, August 1, 1996, p. 2.

34. "The Attack Machine," *New York Times Magazine*, November 12, 1995.

35. Scot Haller, "Picks & Pans; The Muppets Take Manhattan," *People*, July 16, 1984.

36. Kristin McMurran, "Harlan Ellison: Scarred by the Insults of Childhood, a Manic Fantasist Slashes Back at the World," *People*, December 2, 1985, p. 97.

37. Maria Wilhelm, "People San Francisco's No. 1 Nun in Drag, Sister Boom Boom, Tries Out a New Habit: Marriage to (Gasp) a Woman," *Time*, October 7, 1985.

38. Scot Haller, "If Papa Won't Preach It, Young Ron Reagan Will, with a TV Pitch Promoting Safe Sex," *People*, July 13, 1987.

39. Howard Fineman, "Among the Believers," *Newsweek*, July 26, 1999. (" 'The perception at the grass roots is that the fix is in,' fumed Phyllis Schlafly, a founding mother of the New Right.")

40. Jerrold K. Footlick with Martin Kasindorf, Diane Camper, Susan Argrest, Pamela Ellis Simons, "Legal Battle of the Sexes," *Newsweek*, April 30, 1979. (" 'We now have a whole new class of impoverished women not equipped to go into the work force,' snaps Schlafly." [sic])

41. Jane O'Reilly, "And Ladies of the Club; Women in Dallas Showed Signs of Comfort, and Discomfort," *Time*, September 3, 1984.

42. Diane Roberts, "For a Good Time, Call the Democrats," *St. Petersburg Times*, August 20, 2000. (People for the American Way gala at the Beverly Hills Hilton including "feminists like Gloria Steinem," where guests were "handed a party favor they could use: Right to Choose condoms printed with the relevant Web address.")

43. Larry King prediction quoted in "Yearenders, Predictions: A Sampler," *The Hotline*, January 4, 1993.

44. Phil McCombs (whom Limbaugh ridiculed in 1994) "Review of *Saturday Night Live* writer Al Franken's book *Rush Limbaugh Is a Big Fat Idiot and Other Observations*," *Washington Post*, January 19 Style section, December 16, 1996.

45. Gerald W. Bracey, "The Sixth Bracey Report on the Condition of Public Education," *Phi Delta Kappan*, October 1996.

46. Raymond Edel, "Imus Is Dropping Old Routine," *Bergen County Record*, May 30, 1997.

47. Editorial by Lewis H. Lapham, "Hide-and-Go-Seek: The Shame of the Bill Clinton Scandal and the Kenneth Starr Investigation," *Harper's Magazine*, November 1998, p. 11; Lewis H. Lapham, "Notebook: Punch and Judy; Fact and Fiction in the News Media," *Harper's Magazine*, September 1998, p. 11; Lewis H. Lapham, "Notebook: Painted Fire; Satire;" *Harper's Magazine*, November 1996, p. 11; Gerald W. Bracey, "The Sixth Bracey Report on the Condition of Public Education," *Phi Delta Kappan*, October 1996, p. 127; Editorial by Lewis H. Lapham, "Joint Venture. *Harper's Magazine's* Relationship with Its Readers," *Harper's Magazine*, June 1996, p. 8; Lewis H. Lapham, "Notebook: Old-Time Religion; Paralysis in Government and the U.S. Constitution, *Harper's Magazine*, March 1996, p. 8; Lewis H. Lapham, "The Frozen Republic: How the Constitution Is Paralyzing Democracy,"

Harper's Magazine, March 1996, p. 8; Lewis H. Lapham, "Seen but Not Heard: The Message of the Oklahoma Bombing," *Harper's Magazine,* July 1995, p. 29; Lewis H. Lapham, "Notebook: Jefferson on Toast; Mock Movie Concept," *Harper's Magazine,* June 1995, p. 7; Lewis H. Lapham, "Reactionary Chic: How the Nineties Right Recycles the Bombast of the Sixties Left," *Harper's Magazine,* March 1995, p. 31; Editorial by Lewis H. Lapham, "Thunder on the Right; Republican Party Wins Control of Congress," *Harper's Magazine,* January 1995, p. 6; Editorial by Lewis H. Lapham, "Gospel Singing; Politics and Morality," *Harper's Magazine,* November 1994, p. 8; Editorial by Lewis H. Lapham, "Trial by Klieg Light; Whitewater Inquisition," *Harper's Magazine,* June 1994, p. 9; Editorial by Lewis H. Lapham, "Answering the Call; Crisis of Leadership in U.S.," *Harper's Magazine,* May 1994, p. 10; Editorial by Lewis H. Lapham, "Spring List; List of Accepted Ideas," *Harper's Magazine,* March 1994, p. 11; Editorial by Lewis H. Lapham, "Music Man; Ross Perot," *Harper's Magazine,* July 1993, p. 4; Editorial by Lewis H. Lapham, "Tower of Babel; Expansion of Cable Television Capacity," *Harper's Magazine,* March 1993, p. 9.

48. See Jim Rutenberg, "Koppel's 'Nightline' Caught in Cross-Fire," *New York Times,* March 4, 2002; "Business Digest," *New York Times,* March 4, 2002.

49. David E. Sanger, "The 2000 Campaign: World Views," *New York Times,* October 30, 2000. ("But beyond those trips Mr. Bush, now 54, has left America's shores only three times in his adult life.")

50. Jonathan Alter, "The Lessons of Oprahland 'Between The Lines,' " *Newsweek,* October 2, 2000.

51. Matt Lauer and Katie Couric "Jonathan Alter of Newsweek Magazine Gives His Final Thoughts on the Upcoming Presidential Debate," *Today* show, October 11, 2000.

52. Lester Holt and Jonathan Alter, "Effects of Mideast Violence on U.S. Presidential Campaigns," *Saturday Today,* October 14, 2000.

53. Jonathan Alter, "What Presidents Are," *Newsweek,* October 23, 2000.

54. "A Yank at Oxford," Sunday *Times* (London), October 25, 1992.

55. "A Low Blow on Clinton's Russia Trip?" *Nightline,* ABC News, October 8, 1992. See also Andrew Rosenthal, "The 1992 Campaign: The Republicans; Bush Escalates Attack on Clinton for His Anti-Vietnam War Protests," *New York Times,* October 9, 1992; Douglas Jehl, "Bush Raises Issue of Foe's Patriotism," *Los Angeles Times,* October 8, 1992; Ron Fournier, "Clinton: Bush Statements on War Protest 'Sad, Desperate'," Associated Press, October 8, 1992; Ann Devroy, "Bush Camp Apparently Planned Attack; Aides, Rep. Dornan and 3 Others Urged President to Push Antiwar Issue," *Washington Post,* October 9, 1992.

56. Mike Allen, "Fund-Raising in N.Y. Sets Record Pace," *Washington Post,* March 31, 2000.

THREE. HOW TO GO FROM BEING A "JUT-JAWED MAVERICK" TO A "CLUELESS NEANDERTHAL" IN ONE EASY STEP

1. "The Packwood Case; Excerpts from Senator Packwood's Diaries and Depositions by Accusers," *New York Times,* September 8, 1995.

2. See, e.g., interview by Vicki Kemper, "The Reporter Who Knew Too Much; How Florence George Graves Developed the Packwood Story," *Common Cause Magazine,* Fall 1995.

3. Evan Thomas and Thomas Rosenstiel with Michael Isikoff, "Decline and Fall," *Newsweek,* September 18, 1995.

4. See, e.g., Mark Shields and Robert Novak, "The Expulsion and Resignation of Senator Packwood," CNN's *The Capital Gang,* September 9, 1995.

> KATE O'BEIRNE: I just want to say one thing—
> MARK SHIELDS: Yes?
> KATE O'BEIRNE: —about the feminist treatment of Bob Packwood and disagree with you a bit. I submit a lot of this would have been public years ago if Bob

Packwood weren't "good on women's issues" and I think there was probably pressure to have people who experienced these things with Bob Packwood say, "Oh but he's so good on our issues."

ROBERT NOVAK: You mean [crosstalk]

MARK SHIELDS: Kate O'Beirne is absolutely right. In 1992 when he was running against Les AuCoin, the Democratic Congressman who had been a pro-choice leader in the House, NARAL, the National Abortion Rights Action League, publicly, in spite of all the stories about Bob Packwood, endorsed and backed Packwood.

ROBERT NOVAK: Right.

MARK SHIELDS: Which may have been the difference in a very, very close race.

5. Special to the *New York Times,* "Man in the News; Iconoclastic G.O.P. Senator," *New York Times,* March 15, 1982.

6. Ibid.

7. Martin Tolchin, "Packwood Apologizes to Reagan for Saying He Is Harming G.O.P.," *New York Times,* March 3, 1982.

8. Special to the *New York Times,* "Man in the News."

9. Steven V. Roberts, "Packwood Loses Party Job in Senate," *New York Times,* December 3, 1982.

10. Donald M. Rothberg, "Packwood Says GOP Losing Support Among Women, Minorities," Associated Press, March 2, 1982.

11. Special to the *New York Times,* "Man in the News."

12. See, e.g., interview by Vicki Kemper, "The Reporter Who Knew Too Much."

13. Florence Graves and Charles E. Shepard, "Packwood Accused of Sexual Advances; Alleged Behavior Pattern Counters Image," *Washington Post,* November 22, 1992.

14. Ibid.

15. Jean Marbella, "The Senator Who Mistook His Errands for History," *Baltimore Sun,* September 25, 1995.

16. Special to the *New York Times,* "Man in the News."

17. Evan Thomas and Thomas Rosenstiel with Michael Isikoff, "Decline and Fall."

18. Special to the *New York Times,* "Man in the News."

19. Evan Thomas and Thomas Rosenstiel with Michael Isikoff, "Decline and Fall."

20. Judy Bachrach, "Sen. Bob Packwood Is the Republican Gadfly Who Keeps Stinging the President," *People,* March 22, 1982.

21. Evan Thomas and Thomas Rosenstiel with Michael Isikoff, "Decline and Fall."

22. Judy Bachrach, "Sen. Bob Packwood Is the Republican Gadfly Who Keeps Stinging the President."

23. Evan Thomas and Thomas Rosenstiel with Michael Isikoff, "Decline and Fall."

24. Judy Bachrach, "Sen. Bob Packwood Is the Republican Gadfly Who Keeps Stinging the President."

25. Jean Marbella, "The Senator Who Mistook His Errands for History."

26. Francis X. Clines, "Got It; The Senate, Embarrassed and Proud of It," *New York Times,* September 10, 1995.

27. Helen Dewar, "Senate Urged to Weigh Packwood's Expulsion; Buchanan at Odds with Presidential Rivals," *Washington Post,* August 11, 1995.

28. Editorial, " 'Senator No' Says Goodbye," *New York Times,* August 23, 2001, p. 18.

29. Lizette Alvarez, "Man in the News—James Merrill Jeffords; A Longtime Maverick," *New York Times,* May 25, 2001.

30. "Topics of the Times; Profiles in Opportunism," *New York Times,* November 11, 1994.

31. CNN Live Event/Special, February 10, 1999.

32. Iver Peterson, "The 1994 Campaign: Whitman; Move Over, Rockefeller, G.O.P.'s Got a New Idol," *New York Times,* October 4, 1994.

33. David M. Halbfinger, "A Telling Silence Greets Whitman Frisking Photo," *New York Times,* July 16, 2000.

34. Among other genius rulings, the Whitman court overturned a law requiring parents to be notified before a doctor can perform an abortion on their teenage daughters—though parental consent and notification laws have been upheld in thirty-two other states and by the U.S. Supreme Court (*Planned Parenthood v. Farmer,* 2000); held that when you are accused of a hate crime, the judge can withdraw the issue of hate motivation from the jury and enhance your sentence himself, even if the jury would not find you guilty of bigotry (*State v. Apprendi,* 1999, rev'd by U.S. S. Ct. *Apprendi v. New Jersey,* 2000); ruled that the Boy Scouts are a "public accommodation," like a hotel, and therefore could be required to take openly gay men as scout leaders (*Dale v. Boy Scouts,* 1999, rev'd by U.S. S. Ct. *Boy Scouts v. Dale,* 2001); found that a single joking use of the phrase "jungle bunny" creates a hostile environment (*Taylor v. Metzger,* 1998); ruled that shopping malls must be forced to accommodate any protester who wishes to demonstrate, free of charge, and to waive any insurance requirement to insulate itself against fights caused by the protester's provocative speech (*New Jersey Coalition Against War in the Middle East et al. v. JMB Realty Corp.,* 1994). Before Whitman left her own unmistakable imprint on the court, it had made the rather stunning ruling that consent does not constitute a defense to a charge of rape (In the Interest of M.T.S., 129 N.J. 422, 1992). Whitman later signed into law a rule of evidence that expressly approved the "consent is no defense" rape rule in legislative findings.

35. Cokie Roberts, Sam Donaldson, George Will, "The Senate Trial, Sen. Robert Byrd," *ABC News, This Week,* February 7, 1999.

FOUR. CREATING THE PSYCHOLOGICAL CLIMATE

1. Roper poll. Another study conducted by Stanley Rothman and S. Robert Lichter in 1979 through 1980 surveyed the views of journalists from the *Washington Post,* the *New York Times,* the *Wall Street Journal, Time, Newsweek, U.S. News & World Report,* the three commercial television networks and public television (PBS), among others. The study concluded that journalists were skeptical of "traditional American institutions" and "well to the left of business elites."

2. Howard Kurtz, "Buchanan's Supporters Bristle with Ire for News Media," *Washington Post,* February 26, 1996.

3. "Rush Limbaugh" (television show), May 7, 1996.

4. Ibid.

5. Bruce Nussbaum, "The Myth of the Liberal Media," *Business Week,* November 11, 1996, p. 34.

6. Joseph P. Kahn, "Talk Radio's Mr. Right; Limbaugh Rules the Airwaves—But His Local Fans Aren't Flocking to Restaurant 'Rush Rooms,' " *Boston Globe,* April 14, 1993, p. 65.

7. Dan Radmacher, "Media's Liberal Bias Real, but Conservative Bias Much More Blatant," *Charleston Gazette,* November 17, 2000.

8. *Larry King Live,* May 15, 2001.

9. "Media Bias: The 2001 Awards," *New York Post,* December 31, 2001 (quoting an exchange on CNN's *Inside Politics*).

10. "Pundit 101 with Lawrence O'Donnell," *Shuttle Sheet,* June 2001.

11. "Dan Rather Talks About His New Book," *The O'Reilly Factor,* May 18, 2001, Transcript #051805cb.256. See also Dan Rather and Paula Zahn, "Is the Media Biased?" *Fox the Edge with Paula Zahn,* May 22, 2001. Transcript #052203cb.260. ("There's also a blood sport on the other side of, you know, accusing you of being a tool of corporate America and therefore a reactionary.")

12. "Rush Limbaugh," May 7, 1996.

13. Quoted in John Carmody, "The TV Column," *Washington Post,* February 19, 1997.

14. Howard Kurtz, "Colleague Punches CBS in the Eye; Correspondent's Essay Riles Network Newsroom," *Washington Post,* February 15, 1996, p. C1.

15. Bernard Goldberg writing in the *Wall Street Journal,* quoted in Greg Pierce, "Bad Day for Contrarians," *Washington Times,* May 25, 2001.

16. C-SPAN's *Washington Journal,* May 24, 2001.

17. Ibid.

18. Tom Shales, "Ex-Newsman's Case Full of Holes," Electronic Media Online, www.emonline.com/shales/010702shales.html.

19. Chuck Raasch, "Revolving Door Blurs Line Between Journalism," Gannett News Service, March 9, 1994.

20. William Safire, "The Voting Trigger," *New York Times,* October 29, 1992. ("Mr. Clinton's reluctance to stand foursquare against unnecessary secrecy is troubling, but Mr. Bush's embrace yesterday of a document that may figure in a criminal conspiracy is far worse: his encouragement of Barr's stonewalling places the Iraqgate scandal in the Oval Office.

("New York Times columnists traditionally do not endorse any candidate, and I'm for traditional values. But any reader who cannot figure out against whom this lifelong Republican is voting this year isn't trying.")

21. CNN's *NewsNight,* December 18, 2001.

22. Walter Goodman, "Television; They Let the Talking Heads Talk, but They Set the Tone," *New York Times,* April 19, 1998.

23. There are hundreds of such sites. This one is titled "Liberal Media? Yeah, Right!" at www.radio4all.org/anarchy/crock2.html. The conservative journalists are Pat Buchanan (TV, P), Robert Novak (TV, P), William Buckley (TV, P), Cal Thomas (P), Paul Gigot (TV, P), Pat Robertson (TV), Arianna Huffington (P), Charles Krauthammer (P), John Leo (P), James J. Kilpatrick (P), Ben Wattenberg (TV, P), Armstrong Williams (TV, R, P), Thomas Sowell (P), Fred Barnes (TV), G. Gordon Liddy (R), Michael Reagan (R), James Dobson (R), James Pinkerton (P), Suzanne Fields (P), Bob Grant (R), George Will (TV, P), Rush Limbaugh (R), William Safire (P), William Kristol (TV), Bay Buchanan (TV), John McLaughlin (TV), Oliver North (R), Kate O'Beirne (TV), Linda Chavez (P), Tony Snow (TV, P), James Glassman (TV, P), Robert Bartley (P), Mona Charen (P), Laura Ingraham (TV), John Stossel (TV), Ken Hamblin (R), Michael Barone (P), Maggie Gallagher (P), Sean Hannity (TV, R), and R. Emmett Tyrrell (P). Those listed as "Centrist or Right-of-Center 'Moderates'" are Sam Donaldson, Cokie Roberts, George Stephanopoulos, Bill Press, Michael Kinsley, Bob Beckel, Margaret Carlson, Al Hunt, Mark Shields, David Broder, Juan Williams, and Susan Estrich.

24. Diane Sawyer, *Good Morning America,* July 24, 2001.

25. See, e.g., Kausfiles.com: 01.07.00. Jeffrey Toobin, Hypocrite; 01.23.00. Jeffrey Toobin, Hypocrite, Part III!; 05.11.00. Toobin's Cave-in; 02.19.00. Jeffrey Toobin, Chicken!; 05.26.00. The Toobin Crisis, Day 141.

26. *Penguin Books and Jeffrey R. Toobin v. Lawrence E. Walsh, Office of Independent Counsel,* 929 F.2d 69 (2d Cir. 1991). Giving Walsh one of his rare legal victories, Judge Irving Kaufman refused to affirm the lower court ruling and found the case moot—because of Toobin's manipulation of procedure by publishing the book before a ruling.

27. Since that was in violation of the motto requiring that the news "fit," the *Times* poked around and a month later finally produced a second reviewer who was sufficiently unfamiliar with the facts of the Clinton investigation to praise Toobin's book fulsomely. The make-up review complained only that Toobin might not have gone far enough in saying Clinton was "the good guy in this struggle."

28. "Pundit 101 with Lawrence O'Donnell," *The Shuttle Sheet.*

29. "CNBC, *Vanity Fair* Hire Dee Dee Myers," Associated Press, May 3, 1995.

30. See, e.g., Monica Yant, "Myers Doesn't Regret Late-Night Decision," *St. Petersburg Times,* July 12, 1995. ("Myers, who was arrested for driving under the influence of alcohol in Washington, D.C., on June 27 . . . had been scheduled to appear on Leno's show Monday along with Grant, who was charged with lewd conduct with a prostitute, also on June 27.")

31. "James Carville Interviews Sam Donaldson and Others," *Larry King Live,* March 30, 1995.

32. Dean E. Murphy and Michael Cooper, "What's Next for Green? Politics (and a Beard) May Be Out," *New York Times,* December 3, 2001.

33. Inderfurth worked for Senators George McGovern and Gary Hart, the Carter administration, and the Democratic Senate Foreign Relations Committee.

34. Elizabeth Brackett was a candidate for the Democratic National Committee and the 43rd Ward Democratic Committeeman.

35. Editorial, "The Lindsay Legacy," *New York Times,* December 21, 2000, p. A38.

36. Al Kamen, "The Federal Page; In the Loop," *Washington Post,* November 26, 1997, p. A17.

37. Melinda Henneberger, "Naomi Wolf, Feminist Consultant to Gore, Clarifies Her Campaign Role," *New York Times,* November 5, 1999, p. A26.

38. Lewis W. Wolfson, "The Beltway Allure: Switch-Hitting Journalists, Government Spokesmen May Damage Press Credibility; Campaign '92" *Quill,* March 1992, p. 24; and Eleanor Randolph, "Crossing Over: From Politics to Journalism; Old Taboo on Image-Makers Switching to News Media Careers Seems to Be Disappearing," *Washington Post,* May 3, 1988, p. A11, final edition.

39. John Carmody, "The TV Column," *Washington Post,* April 13, 1987, p. B8, final edition.

40. Daniel Williams, "Coping with Shortcomings at State; Talbott's Selection Made with Two Weaknesses of Secretary in Mind," *Washington Post,* December 29, 1993, p. A4, final edition.

41. Jane Hall, "CNN Readies Jesse Jackson Talk Show," *Los Angeles Times,* July 30, 1991, p. F10.

42. Editorial, "Bad; Jesse Jackson's Candidacy," *New Republic,* April 18, 1988, p. 7.

43. Howard Rosenberg, "Jackson's New CNN Talk Show Widens Spectrum of Thought," *Los Angeles Times,* January 20, 1992, p. F1.

44. Phil Rosenthal, "Air Jackson; Congressman to Host Show in Early 2000," *Chicago Sun-Times,* November 11, 1999, p. 45.

45. Howard Kurtz, "Susan Molinari Pulled from CBS Anchor Slot," *Washington Post,* June 24, 1998, p. D1.

46. Adam Nagourney, "A New Job Requirement for Molinari: Nonpartisanship," *New York Times,* May 29, 1997. ("Yes, Ms. Molinari said, she would be offering analysis of the news, but not, Mr. Heyward hastened to add, any commentary.") See also Sandy Grady, "Molinari Joins List of Pols Becoming Quasi-Journalists," *Fresno Bee,* June 1, 1997. (" 'She'll be doing commentary, not analysis,' said the CBS man.")

47. Sandy Grady, "Molinari Joins List of Pols Becoming Quasi-Journalists."

48. Lawrie Mifflin, "CBS's Remake Now Includes Molinari," *New York Times,* May 29, 1997, p. B3.

49. The quote was made on May 31, 1997, on CBS's *Inside Washington* (source: Media Research Council). See also Simon Beck, "The News Is It's Politics as Usual," *South China Morning Post,* June 5, 1997.

50. Frazier Moore, "CBS Adds Molinari, Loses Credibility," *Chicago Tribune,* June 11, 1997, p. 6.

51. Editorial by Lee Coppola, "Hiring Susan Molinari, A Ratings-Hungry CBS Gave TV Journalism a Setback," *Buffalo News,* June 9, 1997, p. 2B.

52. Marianne Means, "Molinari Move to CBS Blurs Journalistic, Political Lines," *Chattanooga Times,* June 5, 1997, p. A11.

53. Lewis Wolfson, "Government-Media Revolving Door a Threat to Press," *Houston Chronicle,* June 3, 1997, p. 21.

54. Sandy Grady, "Is It News, or Is It Propaganda?" *Buffalo News,* May 31, 1997, p. 3C.

55. Bradley F. Norpell, "The Faces Are New, the Biases Aren't," *Plain Dealer,* June 11, 1997, p. 10B.

56. Eric Mink, "Susan Molinari's Signing with CBS News Causing Quite a Stir," *Florida Times-Union* (Jacksonville, Fla.), June 6, 1997, p. E2.

57. Editorial, "Susan Molinari Is Not Walter Cronkite," *Hartford Courant,* June 2, 1997, p. A8, Statewide correction appended.

58. This is not one freakish search result. Both Molinari and Bradley were hired by CBS in 1997, and no matter how the search is formulated, the indignation was about Molinari alone. A LexisNexis search of "all newspapers" in 1997 for "susan molinari and cbs and partisan or protest or complaint" produces 117 documents. A LexisNexis search of "all newspapers" in 1997 for "bill bradley and cbs and partisan or protest or complaint" produces 25 documents. A LexisNexis search of "all newspapers" in 1997 for "susan molinari w/s cbs and revolving door" = 29 docs. Adding to that search "and bill bradley" yields 7 docs. A LexisNexis search of "all news" in 1997 for "susan molinari w/s cbs and revolving door" = 50 documents. Adding to that search "and bill bradley" yields 12 docs. A LexisNexis search of "all newspapers" in 1997 for "bill bradley w/s cbs and revolving door" = 17 docs. Adding to that search "and susan molinari" yields 17 docs. A LexisNexis search of "all news" in 1997 for "bill bradley w/s cbs and revolving door" = 10 documents. Adding to that search "and susan molinari" yields 10 documents.

59. Jacqueline Sharkey, "Prime-Time Pete; Is the Pentagon's Truth-Blocking Spokesman Fit for Network Journalism?" *Washington Post,* May 2, 1993.

60. Ibid.

61. Editorial by Bonnie Erbe, "Gay Socialist Gets Journalism in a Tizzy," *Denver Rocky Mountain News,* August 24, 1996, p. 56A.

62. Jacqueline Sharkey, "Prime-Time Pete."

63. Piper Fogg, "People for May 5, 2001," *National Journal,* May 5, 2001.

64. Tony Schwartz, "From Nixon Aide to Kuralt's Co-Anchor," *New York Times,* September 30, 1981, p. C23.

65. Richard Zoglin, Melissa August, Mary Cronin, and William Tynan, "Star Power; Diane Sawyer, with a New Prime-Time Show and a $1.6 Million Contract, Is Hot. But Are Celebrity Anchors Like Her Upstaging the News?" *Time,* August 7, 1989, p. 46.

66. After Nixon resigned, Sawyer joined her boyfriend Frank Gannon in San Clemente, where he was helping Nixon write his autobiography. See, e.g., Richard Zoglin, "Star Power."

67. John Carlin, "Dying Rabbi 'Names' Watergate's Deep Throat," *Independent* (London), June 28, 1995, p. 12.

68. Harry F. Waters with George Hackett and Mary Lord, "CBS's New Morning Star," *Newsweek,* March 14, 1983, p. 74.

69. Tony Schwartz, "From Nixon Aide."

70. Richard Zoglin, "Star Power."

71. "Nixon Chastises 'Ladies of the Press'," UPI, June 2, 1982.

72. Harry F. Waters, "CBS's New Morning Star."

73. Ibid.

74. Kenneth R. Clark, "Journalist of the Hour Lesley Stahl's Impossible Dream Comes True on '60 Minutes'," *Chicago Tribune,* December 1, 1991, p. 4.

75. All years, all news LexisNexis search for items on John Lindsay, including the words "Lesley Stahl" or articles about Lesley Stahl, including the words "john lindsay" yield eight documents. Same searches for diane sawyer and (richard w/2 nixon) = 748 docs.

76. Kenneth R. Clark, "Journalist of the Hour."

77. Eric Boehlert, "Fox Guarding the Henhouse," *Salon.com,* November 15, 2000.

78. Todd Gitlin, "How TV Killed Democracy on Nov. 7," *Los Angeles Times,* February 14, 2001.

FIVE. ADVANCE AS IF UNDER THREAT OF ATTACK: FOX NEWS CHANNEL AND THE ELECTION

1. FAIR Special Report, "The Most Biased Name in News: Fox News Channel's Extraordinary Right-Wing Tilt," FAIR Press Release (Fairness & Accuracy in Reporting), 130 West 25th Street, New York, NY 10001, July 2, 2001.

2. Joan Konner, "Eye on the Media: Media's Patriotism Provides a Shield for Bush," Newsday.com, January 9, 2002.

3. Sean Hannity and Alan Colmes, "Is the Media Too Conservative?" *Fox Hannity & Colmes,* April 6, 2001 (interview with Cheryl Guttman).

4. Mark Jurkowitz, "Exit-Poll Flap Keeps Flapping," *Boston Globe,* December 16, 2000.

5. hotlinescoop.com, "Media: Murdoch Defends Ellis, Fnc to Drop VNS?" The National Journal Group, Inc., November 16, 2000.

6. Eric Boehlert, "Fox Guarding the Henhouse," Salon.com, November 15, 2000. ("By hiring George Bush's cousin to run a crucial part of its election coverage, the right-wing Fox Network hits a new low in conflict of interest.")

7. Jake Tapper, Bill Sammon, Bill Press, and Robert Novak, "Revisiting Election 2000: Who Should Have Won?" CNN *Crossfire,* May 28, 2001.

8. Howard Kurtz, "Bush Cousin Made Florida Vote Call for Fox News," *Washington Post,* November 14, 2000.

9. Michiko Kakutani, "Critic's Notebook: Books That Make a Case for Shades of Gray," *New York Times,* June 18, 1993, p. C1. ("Of the Clinton adviser Paul Begala, Mr. Rosenstiel writes that he 'believed the teachings of Republican strategist Roger Ailes that the press was mostly interested only in conflict, scandal, polls, process and gaffes.' Mr. Rosenstiel adds: 'So to get coverage of a speech, he usually included attack lines, making his speeches more malicious than they would otherwise be.' ")

10. Diane Sawyer, Charles Gibson, Antonio Mora, George Stephanopoulos, "Highlights from Presidential Debate; How Al Gore and George W. Bush Feel They Did on Last Night's Debate; Post-Debate Analysis," *Good Morning America,* October 18, 2000.

11. Minneapolis, Minn., *Star Tribune,* November 14, 2000, p. 6A.

12. "Notebook; Fox News Says Bush Cousin Had Role in Projecting He'd Won," hotlinescoop.com, "Media Monitor," February 15, 2001.

13. Roger Ebert, "GOP Won by Planting Seeds of Deception," *Chicago Sun-Times,* December 14, 2000, p. 7.

14. David Barstow and Don Van Natta Jr., "Examining the Vote; How Bush Took Florida: Mining the Overseas Absentee Vote," *New York Times,* July 15, 2001. ("The *Times* asked Gary King, a Harvard expert on voting patterns and statistical models, what would have happened had the [unpostmarked absentee] ballots been discarded. He concluded that there was no way to declare a winner with mathematical certainty under those circumstances. His best estimate, he said, was that Mr. Bush's margin would have been reduced to 245 votes. Dr. King estimated that there was only a slight chance that discarding the questionable ballots would have made Mr. Gore the winner.")

15. Howard Kurtz, "Bush Cousin Made Florida Vote Call for Fox News."

16. John R. Lott, Jr., "Documenting Unusual Declines in Republican Voting Rates in Florida's Western Panhandle Counties in 2000," December 10, 2000, revised May 8, 2001.

17. Ibid.

18. Lott was later falsely accused by *Newsweek* of having been "hired by one partisan group" to perform the research. Since liberals treat "studies" as weapons in an ideological war, it is impossible for them to grasp the concept of a disinterested researcher performing a serious study. See Matt Bai, "The Gun Crowd's Guru: John Lott Has a High Profile and a Target on His Back," *Newsweek,* March 12, 2001.

19. See, e.g., Bill Sammon, *At Any Cost: How Al Gore Tried to Steal the Election,* Washington, D.C.: Regnery, 2001, p. 20; Bill Sammon, "Insight, Elections Concern Noted," *Florida Times-Union* (Jacksonville, Fla.), May 13, 2001; "Networks' Early Call Kept Many from Polls; Florida Section Affected by TV," *Washington Times,* May 7, 2001.

20. Tom Rosenstiel, "Bush Cousin's Role Further Tarnishes Journalism," *Houston Chronicle,* November 17, 2000. ("Rosenstiel is vice chairman of the Committee of Concerned Journalists, based in Washington, D.C.")

21. Alicia C. Shepard, "How They Blew It," *American Journalism Review,* January 2001/February 2001.

22. John Ellis, "A Hard Day's Night: John Ellis' Firsthand Account of Election Night," *Inside Magazine,* December 11, 2000.

23. See, e.g., Alicia C. Shepard, "How They Blew It."

24. Incorrect calls for Gore: 7:49 P.M., NBC; 7:50 P.M., CBS; 7:52 P.M., Fox News Channel; 7:55 P.M., CNN (over five minutes); 8:02 P.M., ABC (over 12 minutes). Even at 8:02, three ABC analysts were warning against calling Florida for Gore. Correct calls for Bush: 2:16 A.M., Fox (2:16:46 A.M.); 2:17 A.M., NBC and CBS; 2:18 A.M., CNN; 2:20 A.M., ABC (3 minutes, 41 seconds later).

25. Bill Carter, "Counting the Vote: The Fox Executive; Calling the Presidential Race, and Cousin George W.," *New York Times,* November 14, 2000.

26. Jacques Ellul, *Propaganda: The Formation of Men's Attitudes,"* New York: Vintage Books, 1965, p. 18.

27. For example, George Bush had talked to the governors of various states about their absentee ballot numbers, and Jeb Bush could tell Ellis how outstanding precincts had voted in his elections. John Ellis, "A Hard Day's Night."

28. Bill Carter, "Counting the Vote."

29. Paul Krugman, "Reckonings: The Two Larrys," *New York Times,* November 19, 2000.

30. Jacques Ellul, *Propaganda,* p. 18.

31. Terry Jackson, "Media Struggled with Election Night Meltdown," *Miami Herald,* November 9, 2000.

32. Martha T. Moore, "TV, Newspapers Get Big One Wrong; Vote Projections Err One Way, Then the Other," *USA Today,* November 9, 2000.

33. Alicia C. Shepard, "How They Blew It."

34. Ibid. The only difference between the AP and VNS numbers was the extent of Bush's lead. At 2:16 A.M., with 99 percent of Florida precincts reporting, both VNS and AP showed Bush winning—AP had Bush winning by about thirty thousand votes, whereas VNS had Bush ahead by about fifty thousand votes. Though both its internal numbers and the VNS numbers showed Bush with an insuperable lead, AP stubbornly refused to call Florida for Bush.

35. Megan Garvey, "Studies Blame TV Networks for Election 'Debacle,' " *Los Angeles Times,* February 3, 2001. The *Times* lauded the AP for refraining from calling Florida for Bush when its "independent reports showed Florida tallies different from those of VNS." That statement would seem to suggest that the AP's "independent reports" showed Gore ahead in Florida, in contrast to the VNS tallies, which showed Bush ahead. In fact, the only difference between the AP and VNS numbers was the extent of Bush's lead. By contrast, when AP had projected Gore as the winner in Florida earlier in the evening, its own internal numbers really did contradict the VNS numbers. But that time, AP disregarded its own "independent reports" showing Bush the winner of Florida and called Florida for Gore at 7:52. Alicia C. Shepard, "How They Blew It."

36. Steve McClellan, Paige Albiniak, and John M. Higgins, "Networks on the Defensive," *Broadcasting and Cable,* November 20, 2000.

37. Jim Abrams, "House GOP Miffed at Networks." AP Online, Associated Press, November 16, 2000. Twenty-six states and the District of Columbia were awarded to a candidate immediately after polls closed.

38. Ibid.

39. Dan Rather, "Florida Secretary of State Katherine Harris Certifies the Florida Votes," *CBS News Special Report,* November 26, 2000 (Burrelle's Information Services, CBS News Transcripts).

40. Diane Sawyer, "Interview with Florida Secretary of State Katherine Harris," ABC's *Primetime Thursday,* January 11, 2001.

41. Congressman Jesse Jackson, Jr., quoted on *ABC World News Now,* December 14, 2000, and passim.

42. New York Congressman Charles Rangel quoted on *ABC World News Now,* December 14, 2000, and passim.

43. Diane Sawyer and Charles Gibson, "Law Professors Alan Dershowitz of Harvard Law School and William Lash of George Mason University Debate U.S. Supreme Court Ruling on Florida Election," *Good Morning America,* December 13, 2000.

44. Jules Witcover, "Not a Banana Republic, but One Divided," *Baltimore Sun,* December 17, 2000.

45. Jane Clayson, "Presidential Historian Douglas Brinkley Discusses the Decision Last Night by the U.S. Supreme Court and How the Court Will Be Viewed in a Historical Context," *Early Show,* CBS News, December 13, 2000.

46. Robert Kuttner, "Forget Nice Talk: New Administration Deserves to Be Questioned," *Boston Globe,* December 17, 2000. (Kuttner is coeditor of the *American Prospect.*)

47. Robert Reno, "It's Theft Fair and Square—So Get Over It," New York *Newsday,* December 14, 2000.

48. Jules Witcover, "Not a Banana Republic."

Six. Samizdat Media

1. Couric hosting a 92nd Street Y appearance in New York City on March 3 shown by C-SPAN on April 3, 1999.

2. Harry Smith, "Questioning Mario Cuomo," *CBS This Morning,* December 30, 1994.

3. Cass Sunstein, *Republic.com,* Princeton: Princeton University Press, 2001.

4. Bill Clinton, in an address to the American Association of Community Colleges, April 24, 1995.

5. Dan Rather and Rita Braver, "Clinton Urges Americans to Stand Against Violent Behavior and Speech," *CBS Evening News,* April 24, 1995.

6. Bryant Gumbel, *Today,* April 25, 1995.

7. Peter S. Fosl, "Conservatives Should Own Up to Their Share of the Blame," *Roanoke Times & World News,* May 6, 1995.

8. hotlinescoop.com, "National Briefing: Oklahoma City: The Politics of Bombing quoting, 'Equal Time,' " CNBC, April 26, 1995.

9. He did not name Limbaugh specifically, but the implication was missed by no one. See e.g., Charles Krauthammer, "Talk Radio, Ghoul Politics," *Washington Post,* April 28, 1995, p. A27. ("[Clinton] refused, however, to admit the point openly. Indeed, his aides denied that the president was even referring to talk radio, though the implication was so obvious that practically every major news broadcast went directly from Clinton's 'purveyors of hate' speech to reports on talk show hosts like Rush Limbaugh and Oliver North.")

10. Terry Kelleher, "Talking About Talk: The Author of 'Inside Talk Radio' Has Something to Say, Too," *Newsday,* May 3, 1995, p. B69.

11. David Hinckley, "Vanity Reflects New & Old Radio Stars," *Daily News* (New York), November 26, 1996, p. 68.

12. Judy Woodruff, "Former Politicos Hart and Weicker to Enter Radio Fray," CNN's *Inside Politics,* February 3, 1995, Transcript # 758-3.

13. Judy Woodruff, "Former Politicos Hart and Weicker to Enter Radio Fray." ("Earlier this afternoon I talked with two prominent politicians who are out of office and about to be on the air, spending some of their time hosting talk radio programs.")

14. Harry Smith, "Smith Questioning Mario Cuomo."

15. Howard Kurtz, "Mario Cuomo, The Limbaugh of the Left?; Democrats Hitch Their Hopes to Newest Talk-Radio Host," *Washington Post,* June 20, 1995, p. E1.

16. "On the Prowl," *American Spectator,* September 1996.

17. Editorial, "Pump Up the Volume: Michael Moore, Jim Hightower," *The Nation,* August 8, 1994, p. 145.

18. Editorial by John Nichols, "Hightower—Making a Progressive Difference," Madison, Wis. *Capital Times,* December 5, 1997.

19. Richard Reynolds, "Take Back the Airwaves! Progressive Talk Radio Programs," *Mother Jones,* January 1995, p. 18.

20. Evan Smith, "Jim Hightower: A Hellraising Texas Radio Personality Fights to Stay on the Dial; Interview," *Mother Jones,* November 1995, p. 58.

21. Richard Reynolds, "Take Back the Airwaves!"

22. Evan Smith, "Jim Hightower."

23. Top talk radio audiences by size (weekly cume low-end estimates 12-plus in millions rounded off to the nearest .25 million based upon *Talkers* magazine analysis of a national sampling of Arbitron reports supported by other reliable indicators in rated and non-rated markets for Fall 2000):

1. **Rush Limbaugh**	**15.00+**		7. Mike Gallagher	2.25+
2. **Dr. Laura Schlessinger**	**14.00+**		7. **Michael Savage**	**2.25+**
3. Howard Stern	8.50+		8. Tom Joyner	1.75+
4. Dr. Joy Browne	5.75+		8. Kim Komando	1.75+
5. Jim Bohannon	4.50+		8. **Tom Leykis**	**1.75+**
5. Don Imus	4.50+		8. Jim Rome	1.75+
5. Bruce Williams	4.50+		8. Doug Stephan	1.75+
6. Ken & Daria Dolan	2.50+		9. Bob Brinker	1.25+
6. Clark Howard	2.50+		9. **Matt Drudge**	**1.25+**
6. **G. Gordon Liddy**	**2.50+**		10. Phil Hendrie	1.00+
6. Mike Siegel	2.50+		10. Motley Fool	1.00+
7. **Neal Boortz**	**2.25+**		10. Dave Ramsey	1.00+
7. Dr. Dean Edell	2.25+		10. **Michael Reagan**	**1.00+**

24. "Chronicles: Wzzzzzzzz . . . ," *Time,* July 3, 1995.

25. Newswatch . . . People, "Station Is Not Amused, Pulls Plug on Limbaugh," *Baltimore Sun,* February 9, 1995. At one point in 1996, the press gleefully announced Limbaugh's ratings were faltering. *(Victory over Eastasia is near.)* But then, sadly, it turned out this reflected nothing more than the general dip experienced by all radio stations not covering the O. J. trial. Al Brumley, "Conservatively Speaking; In Talk Radio's Battle for the Nation's Ears, It's All Over but the Shouting," *Dallas Morning News,* April 7, 1996. ("Several reports have cropped up in recent weeks noting a slide in Mr. Limbaugh's ratings.")

26. NPR was given $250 million in taxpayer funds in 1998, and was budgeted to receive $300 million in fiscal year 2000, and $340 million in fiscal year 2001.

27. PBS Annual Report for fiscal year 1998 claims public broadcasting overall received 36.4 percent of its funding from government sources. This includes state government funding (18.9 percent) as well as subsidies from the federal government (17.5 percent)—from not only the Corporation for Public Broadcasting, but also the Department of Commerce and the Department of Education.

28. Thomas L. Friedman, "Low-Tech Democracy," *New York Times,* May 1, 2001.

29. Jeff Guinn, " 'Bestseller' May Not Mean What You Think It Means," *Fort Worth Star-Telegram,* May 10, 2000, Life & Arts p. 1.

30. Jean Savage, "The Marketplace of Ideas; Forty Years of Best-Selling Conservative Books" (The Heritage Foundation), *Policy Review,* Fall 1984, p. 62.

31. Stephen Goode and Eli Lehrer, "Keeping Books," *Insight,* August 31, 1998.

32. David Streitfeld, "Writers of the Right; Conservatives Have Taken the Capitol; Now They're On to the Bestseller List," *Washington Post,* December 20, 1994, p. B1.

33. David Streitfeld, "Book Report," *Washington Post,* September 25, 1988, p. X15.

34. Katha Pollitt, "This Just In: We're Not as Wise as Plato," *New York Times,* August 8, 1993, sec. 7, p. 9.

35. Robert Kuttner, "Books & Business; Primers for Presidents," *New York Times,* October 23, 1988, p. 1.

36. Malcolm Jones, "Odd Outing," *Newsweek,* February 7, 2000, p. 69.

37. Steve Sailer, "Commentary: Bush-Gore Marks Return of American Dynasties," United Press International, October 12, 2000.

38. Kevin M. Grace, "The Bad Boy of Academe: His Publisher Has Caved In to Threats, but Psychologist Philippe Rushton Will Not Be Silenced," *Report Newsmagazine,* February 28, 2000, pp. 50–51.

39. Howard Fineman, "The No Bull Campaign," *Newsweek,* October 14, 1991. See also Jocelyn Mcclurg, "The Least Returned Gift of Holidays: Best-Sellers; Fiction or Non, Works

That Make Novel Gifts," *Hartford Courant,* December 1, 1991. (*"Parliament of Whores* has been a surprise best-seller"); and Bill Virgin, "O'Rourke Finds Evil's New Face," *Seattle Post-Intelligencer,* April 13, 1992. ("O'Rourke's last book, *Parliament of Whores,* a surprise best-seller.")

40. David Landis, "Best Bets for the Weekend," *USA Today,* July 8, 1994. See also "Storybook Pokes Fun at Political Correctness," *Charleston Daily Mail,* August 2, 1994. ("James Finn Garner's updated version of 13 fairy tale classics, *Politically Correct Bedtime Stories,* has become a surprise bestseller.")

41. Thom Geier, "Eye on the '90s," *U.S. News & World Report,* May 29, 1995, p. 21.

42. Susan Ferraro, "Author, a Hot Political Commodity, Hints at How He'd Repair the System," *New York Times,* April 7, 1995, p. 33.

43. Kevin Phillips, "Alleged Clinton Scandals Should Receive Closer Scrutiny," NPR's *Morning Edition,* July 22, 1996, Transcript # 1916-11.

44. James Warren, "Bork Blames Yale for Decline of Western Civilization," *Chicago Tribune,* December 8, 1996, p. 2.

45. Ed Bark, " 'Adventures from the Book of Virtues' Is a Gosh-Darned, Lofty 'Toon," *Buffalo News,* September 3, 1996, p. 5C.

46. "Undaunted History," *Newsweek,* November 1996, p. 80.

47. "Washington Whispers," *U.S. News & World Report,* October 5, 1998, p. 9.

48. David J. Lynch, "Major Best Seller," *USA Today,* November 8, 1999, p. 11A.

49. Martin Arnold, "Making Books; Run It Up, See Who Salutes," *New York Times,* May 18, 2000, p. E3.

50. Bruce Fretts, "Talking Tall; TV Journalists Ted Koppel, Bill O'Reilly, and Larry King Share Their Innermost Thoughts. But Are They Fit to Print?" *Entertainment Weekly,* November 17, 2000, p. 115.

51. Richard Zoglin, "A Vast Left-Wing Conspiracy?" *Time,* January 28, 2002, p. 12.

52. Richard Bernstein, "A Publisher of Conservative Books Complains," *New York Times,* July 19, 1993.

53. Ibid.

54. Anthony Lewis, "Abroad at Home: Sleaze with Footnotes," *New York Times,* May 21, 1993, p. A27.

55. Deirdre English, *"The Real Anita Hill:* The Untold Story," *The Nation,* June 28, 1993, p. 910.

56. David Streitfeld, "Writers of the Right." ("If *Strange Justice* is lucky and sells 70 percent of its print-run, the net sale will be about 80,000 copies—significantly under the 115,000 achieved by *The Real Anita Hill.* ")

57. Matthew Flamm, "Right Makes Might; Books by Political Conservatives Are the New York Publishing Establishment's Hottest Ticket," *Newsday,* January 30, 1995, p. B3.

58. Edwin McDowell, "As Book Companies Grow, They Seem to Become Timid," *New York Times,* August 7, 1989, p. D8.

59. Free speech-loving liberals such as Michael Harrington called Buckley's book "fascist," and Arthur Schlesinger Jr. called it "totalitarian."

60. Martin Arnold, "Making Books; Run It Up, See Who Salutes."

61. Walter Goodman, "He's No. 1," *New York Times,* February 21, 1993.

62. Martin Arnold, "Making Books; Best-Seller Lists Get a New Job," *New York Times,* January 10, 2002.

63. See, e.g., Matthew Grimm "Corridor Talk," *Brandweek,* October 21, 1991 ("The publisher gave Naomi Wolf a $600,000 advance for a follow-up to her *The Beauty Myth* [*Fire with Fire*], reports *Variety.* Wolf's book blasted the continued stereotyping of post-feminist women."); Chauncey Mabe, "Pulling No Punches Author Naomi Wolf Takes On the Hard-Core Leftists Who Alienate Those Feminism Should Embrace," *Sun-Sentinel,* January 2, 1994 ("And Wolf's defense of sex—in her case, the good old, politically suspect heterosexual variety—is so strong that her next book [*Promiscuities*] is due to be a combination of sexual memoir and theoretical discussion of adolescent sexuality. She is reported to have received a $500,000 advance."); Cokie Roberts and Sam Donaldson, "Naomi Wolf Talks About Her Role in the

Gore Campaign," *ABC News This Week,* November 7, 1999 (Wolf said she "took a cut in pay to work for Al Gore" at $180,000 per year, referring to a book advance for *Misconceptions* of between $400,000 and $600,000.).

64. Naomi Wolf, *Promiscuities,* New York: Random House, 1997.

65. "You Ask the Questions: Naomi Wolf," *The Independent* (London), September 12, 2001. ("She shot to fame in 1990 with the publication of *The Beauty Myth,* a scorching attack on the exploitation of women by the beauty industry, which was described by the *New York Times* as 'one of the most important books of the 20th century' . . ."); Femail.com, www.femail.com.au/misconceptions.html, *"Misconceptions,* a new book by Naomi Wolf." ("Naomi Wolf's first book, *The Beauty Myth,* was named one of the most significant works of the twentieth century by the *New York Times.* Published in more than fourteen countries, it was an international bestseller.")

66. "And Bear in Mind," *New York Times,* May 26, 1991. (*"The Beauty Myth:* How Images of Beauty Are Used Against Women, by Naomi Wolf. [Morrow.] A sweeping, vigorous book about the ways women enslave themselves—and their bank accounts—to an industry that promises physical perfection.")

67. Nancy S. Dye, "What Color Is Your Reading List?" *New York Times,* March 31, 1991.

68. Cited in Michiko Kakutani, "Books of the Times; Helpful Hints for an Era of Practical Feminism," *New York Times,* December 3, 1993.

69. "Notable Books of the Year 1993," *New York Times,* December 5, 1993, p. 42. (*"Fire with Fire: The New Female Power and How It Will Change the 21st Century.* By Naomi Wolf. [Random House.] A rambunctious book calling for women to lay siege to America's crumbling male-centered, male-controlled social structure, to claim the victory they have already won.")

70. Laurel Graeber, "New & Noteworthy Paperbacks," *New York Times,* September 18, 1994.

71. Geraldine Fabrikant, "The Media Business; Random House's Evans: Big Spender, Big Sales," *New York Times,* March 8, 1993, p. D1.

72. Franklin Foer, "Book Publishing," *Slate Magazine,* December 6, 1997.

73. Martin Arnold, "Making Books; Run It Up, See Who Salutes."

74. See, e.g., Paul D. Colford, "A Voluminous Publishing Merger / Random House Valued at $1.3B in Planned Sale to Bertelsmann," *Newsday,* March 24, 1998, p. A43. In short, for every *Primary Colors* and *Midnight in the Garden of Good and Evil,* both Random House runaway best-sellers, there is a costly disappointment, such as Kelly Flinn's memoir *(Proud to Be),* which earned the former Air Force flier $1 million but barely registered on the sales meter. Elisabeth Bumiller, "Public Lives; Random House Editor Ready to Talk Books," *New York Times,* April 3, 1998, p. B2. ("One of her biggest flops is *Proud to Be* by Kelly Flinn, the bomber pilot forced out of the Air Force.")

75. Martin Arnold, "Making Books; Celebrity Books Lose Panache," *New York Times,* December 10, 1997.

76. "Art Hoppe; Almost the Last of a Generation of American Humorous Columnists," *The Guardian* (London), February 10, 2000, p. 24.

77. "Best Sellers: September 8, 1991," *New York Times,* September 8, 1991, sec. 7, p. 36. ("And Bear in Mind [editors' choices of other recent books of particular interest], *Make No Law: The Sullivan Case and the First Amendment,* by Anthony Lewis. [Random House, $25.] A *New York Times* columnist's splendid account of a libel suit against the *Times* that resulted in one of the most significant of all press-freedom cases.")

78. Frank Rich, "Journal: David Brock's Women," *New York Times,* January 6, 1994, p. A21.

79. Alter is coauthor of *Selecting a President,* New York: Farrar, Strauss & Giroux, and the coeditor of *Inside the System,* Englewood Cliffs, N.J.: Prentice Hall. Neither book ever made any best-seller list.

80. Jonathan Alter, "Between the Lines Online: Back to the Battlefield," *Newsweek,* May 24, 2001. Referring to Ted Olson and "his relentless wife Barbara (the author of a hatchet book on Hillary Clinton)."

81. Bernard Weinraub, "Guatemala Exiles Assail Junta," *New York Times,* June 3, 1982.

82. Larry Rohter, "Tarnished Laureate: A Special Report: Nobel Winner Finds Her Story Challenged," *New York Times,* December 15, 1998, p. A1.

83. See, e.g., Larry Rohter, "Tarnished Laureate."

84. Ibid.

85. Anthony Ramirez, "The Nation: The Lock and Load Myth; A Disarming Heritage," *New York Times,* April 23, 2000, sec. 4; p. 3.

86. Garry Wills, "Spiking the Gun Myth," *New York Times,* September 10, 2000, sec. 7, p. 5.

87. "Arming America," *New York Times,* October 1, 2000, sec. 7, p. 4.

88. Scott Veale, "New & Noteworthy Paperbacks," *New York Times,* September 16, 2001, sec. 7, p. 32.

89. Lawrence Van Gelder, "Footlights," *New York Times,* April 12, 2001, sec. E, p. 1.

90. Robert F. Worth, "Historian's Prizewinning Book on Guns Is Embroiled in a Scandal," *New York Times,* December 8, 2001.

91. Kathy Sawyer, "Unfortunate Son: The Burglary, the Embezzlement, the Conspiracy to Murder?" *Washington Post,* March 19, 2000.

92. Ibid.

93. Jenny Lyn Bader, "Publishing, the Moral Mirror of Politics," *New York Times,* October 24, 1999, sec. 4, p. 2.

94. Hatfield's next publisher responded to questions about the author's credibility by noting that Bush had spoken at Bob Jones University—"a place that's basically, like, really really scary, Nazi-type Christians." Bush spoke at Bob Jones so—as the *Times* had already concluded—it was his fault. Kathy Sawyer, "Unfortunate Son."

95. Kathy Sawyer, "Unfortunate Son."

96. Anthony Summers, *The Arrogance of Power: The Secret World of Richard Nixon,* New York: Viking Press, 2000.

97. Ralph de Toledano, "Insight: 'Gay' Edgar Hoover and Other Smears," *Insight on the News,* March 26, 2001, p. 19. (Reviewing Anthony Summers, *Official and Confidential: The Secret Life of J. Edgar Hoover:* "The New York Post, when it was owned by socialist Dorothy Schiff, spent close to $1 million in the 1950s attempting to find even the most trifling evidence of [Hoover's alleged homosexuality] and then gave up. . . . According to Summers' fevered imagination, the FBI director showed up in drag at Mafia parties not once but twice. The 'source' was the disgruntled ex-wife of a man who allegedly had given the parties. The FBI director, Summers asks readers to believe, was mad enough to appear among his most vicious enemies dressed as a woman and seeking homosexual entertainment. And the Mafia, having caught Hoover so to speak in flagrante, didn't whoop with joy and give the Hoover story to enemy Drew Pearson to be plastered all over the left-wing press.")

98. John Greenya, "A Capital Book Town," *Washington Post,* March 6, 1988.

99. George F. Will, "Arid Lives, Lurid Falsehoods," *Washington Post,* April 14, 1991, p. B7.

100. Maureen Dowd, "All That Glitters Is Not Real, Book on Nancy Reagan Says," *New York Times,* April 7, 1991, sec. 1, p. 1.

101. Maureen Dowd, "Liberties; Legacy of Lust," *New York Times,* September 23, 1998, sec. A, p. 29.

102. Connie Chung and Bernard Goldberg, "Just the Facts, Ma'am; Christina Hoff Summers, Author, 'Who Stole Feminism: How Women Have Betrayed Women,' Discusses False Statistics That Are Released About Women and Men," *Eye to Eye with Connie Chung,* August 11, 1994.

103. See, e.g., Dan Ackman, "Air Travel Is Scary but Safe," Forbes.com, November 13, 2001. "The number of auto crash fatalities was nonetheless 41,821 [including 4,739 pedestrians] in 2000, according to the National Highway Transportation Safety Administration.")

104. Martin Arnold, "Making Books; Best-Seller Lists Get a New Job."

105. Even if Christopher Ruddy's *The Strange Death of Vince Foster* was considered a conservative hoax book, it was also conservatives who discredited it. The *New York Post* fired him

over the Vince Foster business. The *American Spectator*'s Byron York took apart Ruddy's book in a series of articles and TV appearances. Regnery Publishing paid a liberal journalist, Dan Modea, an atypically large advance of $100,000 to write a book discrediting the conspiracy theories surrounding Foster's death, resulting in *A Washington Tragedy: How the Death of Vincent Foster Ignited a Political Firestorm.* See, e.g., Philip Weiss, "The Clinton Haters; Clinton Crazy," *New York Times,* February 23, 1997.

106. As a former FBI agent, Aldrich had been required to submit his manuscript to the FBI for pre-publication review. Howard Shapiro, the FBI general counsel, immediately turned it over to the White House.

107. www.top9.com/news_media/politics_new_media.html, citing data from PC Data Online for March 2001. ("Sites appearing on the "Top9" listings are based on objective rankings; rankings cannot be purchased or influenced by outside factors or opinions.") Other months listed have similar results.

108. top9.com/organizations_government/think_tanks.html, citing data from PC Data Online.

109. The Top 9 organizations and government Think Tanks as of December 2000: (1) **heritage.org** (The Heritage Foundation—conservative); (2) **ncpa.org** (Pete Dupont's National Center for Policy Analysis—conservative); (3) **cato.org** (CATO Institute—libertarian); (4) **aei.org** (American Enterprise Institute—conservative); (5) **rand.org** (the RAND Corporation—politics unclear, but really, really boring: "RAND Classics: N. Dalkey, B. Brown, S. Cochran, "The Delphi Method, III: Use of Self Ratings to Improve Group Estimates," RAND); (6) **brook.edu** (The Brookings Institution—liberal); (7) **kci.org** (Koch Crime Institute); (8) **frc.org** (Gary Bauer's Family Research Council—conservative); and (9) **nas.edu** (National Academy of Sciences—nonpolitical).

110. www.top9.com/01_2001/organizations_government/think_tanks.html. Top9>Organizations & Government January 2001

111. Paul Berman, "The Wrong Passions," *New York Times,* July 9, 2000, sec. 7, p. 6.

112. Paul Elie, "John Paul's Jewish Dilemma," *New York Times,* April 26, 1998, sec. 6, p. 34.

113. Emily Eakin, "New Accusations of a Vatican Role in Anti-Semitism; Battle Lines Were Drawn After Beatification of Pope Pius IX," *New York Times,* September 1, 2001, p. B9.

114. Joe Sharkey, "Word for Word/The Case Against the Nazis; How Hitler's Forces Planned to Destroy German Christianity," *New York Times,* January 13, 2002, sec. 4, p. 7.

115. John R. Lott, Jr., "The Missing Gun," NYPOST.com, January 25, 2002.

116. Results of a Google search of the web for **"Appalachian Law School gun"**: NYPOST.COM Post Opinion: www.nypost.com/postopinion/opedcolumnists/38115.htm; Media Ignore Fact That **Gun** Owners Stopped **School** Shooter: www.newsmax.com/archives/articles/2002/1/25/153427.shtml; CNSNews.com, News This Hour: www.cnsnews.com/ThisHour.asp; Media reports sting Grundy residents: www.roanoke.com/roatimes/news/story124656.html; Legallinks: www.patriots4the2ndamendment.com/Legallinks.htm and www.net2one.com/annuaire/newsbox.asp; PsycPORT Handhelds: www.psycport.com/stories/csmonitor_2002_01_18_eng-csmonitor_eng-csmonitor_080751_6143423279999214515.xml.html; 13 News Archives: wvec.com/news/archive.htm; and POE News Page—Archived Evil News: www.poenews.com/default.htm.

117. Paul Krugman, "A Fiscal Fantasy," *New York Times,* January 22, 2002.

118. Paul Krugman, "The Ascent of E-Man; R.I.P.: *The Man in the Gray Flannel Suit,*" *Fortune,* May 24, 1999, p. 42.

119. Paul Krugman, "Reckonings: Enron Goes Overboard," *New York Times,* August 17, 2001, sec. A, p. 19.

120. David Barstow and Don Van Natta Jr., "Examining the Vote: How Bush Took Florida: Mining the Overseas Absentee Vote," *New York Times,* July 15, 2001. Admittedly, the *Washington Post* did give the missile defense test major front-page coverage. Vernon Loeb, "Interceptor Scores a Direct Hit on Missile; Successful Test a Boost to Bush's Shield Plan," *Washington Post,* July 15, 2001.

121. James Dao, "Pentagon Officials Report Hit in Latest Missile Defense Test," *New York Times,* July 15, 2001, Sec. 1, p. 12.

122. Editorial, "Nude Dancing and Free Expression," *New York Times,* March 30, 2000.

123. Editorial, "The Mayor as Art Censor," *New York Times,* September 24, 1999, p. A26.

124. Editorial, "Censoring Cyberspace," *New York Times,* November 26, 1998, p. A38.

125. Stephen Labaton, "Click Here for Democracy," *New York Times,* May 13, 2001.

126. Brent Bozell and Brent Baker, *And That's the Way It Isn't,* Washington, D.C.: Media Research Center, 1990, p. 213.

127. Ibid., p. 74–75.

128. John Noble Wilford, "Ages-Old Icecap at North Pole Is Now Liquid, Scientists Find," *New York Times,* August 19, 2000.

129. Keith J. Kelly, "No President, but Election Books Are Coming," *New York Post,* December 5, 2000.

130. Dan Keating and Dan Balz, "Florida Recounts Would Have Favored Bush; But Study Finds Gore Might Have Won Statewide Tally of All Uncounted Ballots," *Washington Post,* November 12, 2001. ("The study showed that if the two limited recounts had not been short-circuited—the first by Florida county and state election officials and the second by the U.S. Supreme Court—Bush would have held his lead over Gore, with margins ranging from 225 to 493 votes, depending on the standard.") *USA Today* led another group of newspapers, which also found that Bush won.

131. Bill Schneider, CNN's *Inside Politics,* August 16, 2001.

132. FreeRepublic.com, "Why We Should Celebrate Paying Taxes," (Cass R. Sunstein, *republic.com,* Princeton University Press, 2001). Posted on 4/08/2001 by Benoit Baldwin.

133. Richard Zoglin, "The News Wars," *Time,* October 21, 1996. *Time's* explanation for why Americans are becoming "inattentive" to the mainstream media: "The news is less interesting today."

134. Transcript of the First Lady's Press Briefing on Millennium Project Part 5 of 5, U.S. Newswire, February 11, 1998.

135. In 1996, Abrams defended an ABC program on the grounds that it was not "substantially false" and "they thought was true." Noreen Marcus, "Attacking '20/20' Vision," *Palm Beach Daily Business Review,* November 11, 1996.

136. Abrams defended NBC for making false statements about singer Wayne Newton in three separate broadcasts, on the grounds that the stories were not the product of "ill will." Henry Weinstein, "Court Urged to Overturn Libel Award to Singer," *Los Angeles Times,* April 14, 1990.

137. Abrams defended the right of *Fortune* magazine to publish vicious attacks on public figures, "so long as the materials published were not knowingly false." "Court Throws Out $550,000 Libel Verdict," Associated Press, August 6, 1992.

138. Abrams defended a Consumer Reports advisory on the grounds that is was not "deliberately false." Denise Gellene, "Suzuki Sues Magazine for Critical Samurai Review," *Los Angeles Times,* April 12, 1996.

139. Abrams defended a politician's false statements about an opponent, saying candidates "frequently make statements which are true on a rather broad level but are arguably false when viewed more narrowly." Karl Vick, "Brock Cleared of Slandering Aron in Race; Jurors Blame Both Parties for Nasty Senate Contest," *Washington Post,* March 13, 1996.

140. See, e.g., *Hustler Magazine v. Jerry Falwell,* 485 U.S. 46, February 24, 1988.

141. We have that on the authority not only of the courts, but of the *New York Times:* "the $1.8 million judgment won by Carol Burnett, the actress, in her suit against the *National Enquirer,* and a jury's $26.5 million award . . . in a suit by a former Miss Wyoming against *Penthouse* magazine, . . . has touched off worrying *among journalists* that it may be growing more hazardous to publish criticism of rich and powerful people." Stuart Taylor Jr., "Post Libel Verdict Worries the Press," *New York Times,* August 1, 1982.

142. Tom Goldstein, "Journalist or Kangaroo?" *Columbia Journalism Review,* January 2001/February 2001.

143. Janet Wiscombe, "What Hath the Web Wrought?" *Los Angeles Times,* August 16, 1998.

144. See, e.g., Anthony Lewis, "Abroad at Home: Bork on Free Speech," *New York Times,* September 3, 1987. Lewis denounced Judge Robert Bork for saying speech that advocates the "forcible overthrow of the Government" or a "violation of law" was not necessarily protected by the First Amendment. Lewis pompously—and irrelevantly—quoted Powell's no false idea point. Advocating law-breaking or the violent overthrow of the government, of course, is not a "false" idea, any more than the statement "your money or your life" is a "false" idea. Falsity is also not the reason such speech might be banned.

145. *Gertz v. Robert Welch, Inc.,* 418 U.S. 323, 339 (1974).

SEVEN. THE JOY OF ARGUING WITH LIBERALS: *YOU'RE STUPID!*

1. Bob Cohn, "Dirt Trail; The Press Coverage of the Clarence Thomas—Anita Hill Episode," *New Republic,* January 6, 1992, p. 16.

2. Ruth Richman, "Where Are They Now? The Key Players Find Their Lives Will Never Be the Same," *Chicago Tribune,* September 27, 1992.

3. See, e.g., Ishmael Reed, "Feminists v. Thomas; The Anita Hill Crusaders' Double Standard," *Washington Post,* October 18, 1992.

4. L. Brent Bozell III, "Turner's 'Century' of Liberal Women," *Washington Times,* June 19, 1994, p. B3.

5. Gloria Borger, Ted Gest, and Jeannye Thornton, "The Untold Story," *U.S. News & World Report,* October 12, 1992.

6. Jacques Ellul, *Propaganda,* New York: Vintage Books, 1965, p. 25.

7. Kevin Merida, "Shades of Gray Matter; The Question Dogs George W. Bush: Is He Smart Enough? There's No Simple Answer," *Washington Post,* January 19, 2000, p. C1.

8. Jonathan Alter, "Spiro Agnew with Brains," *Newsweek,* November 28, 1994, p. 34.

9. Bill Maher, ABC, *Politically Incorrect,* February 6, 2001.

10. Robert Wright, "Against Dumb," *Slate Magazine,* November 3, 2000.

11. Howell Raines, *Fly Fishing Through the Midlife Crisis,* New York: Anchor, 1994.

12. Michael Kinsley, "Acquired Plumage," *Time,* August 29, 1988.

13. "Today's Best," *Calgary Herald,* July 16, 1992, p. C1.

14. Michael Finnegan, "Campaign 2000; Bush, Gore Sprint as the Race Comes Down to the Wire," *Los Angeles Times,* November 6, 2000, p. 1; Katharine Q. Seelye and Kevin Sack, "The 2000 Campaign: The Vice President; Focus Is on Crucial States in Campaign's Final Hours," *New York Times,* November 6, 2000, p. A1.

15. Cintra Wilson, "Cintra Wilson Feels Your Pain: Florida 2000: It's Conspiracy Theory Time," *San Francisco Examiner,* November 17, 2000, p. C19.

16. James Gill, "A Long Way from Thomas Jefferson," *Times Picayune* (New Orleans), November 5, 2000, p. 7.

17. Burt Constable, "Fear Not, Liberals; There's a Method to Our Madness," *Chicago Daily Herald,* November 7, 2000, p. 12.

18. John P. Sears, who twice managed Ronald Reagan's presidential campaigns, quoted in Lynn Rosellini, "Former Reagan Insider Perceives Signs of Drift," *New York Times,* October 26, 1981.

19. Ronald Brownstein, "Replaying 1980?" *National Journal,* September 15, 1984.

20. Ibid.

21. Editorial, "Weak, Dumb or Afraid?" *New York Times,* October 23, 1984.

22. Lloyd Grove, "Politicking for Mom & Pop; The Candidates' Sons & Daughters Take to the Trail," *Washington Post,* October 31, 1984, p. C1.

23. Ann L. Trebbe, "Personalities," *Washington Post,* May 19, 1982.

24. Andrew Ferguson, "Voice of America: Reagan on the Radio," *Weekly Standard,* February 5, 2001.

25. Mike Royko, *Chicago Sun-Times,* July 22, 1982.

26. Pete Hamill, *Village Voice,* April 29, 1986, cited in John Sieler, "Ten Years of Sound and Fury," *Policy Review,* Summer 1987. ("Qaddafi has founded terrorism beyond his own borders, perhaps planned it, possibly ordered specific acts, all in the name of a fuzzyheaded political ideology. But so has Reagan. . . . Muammar reduces most political thinking to dumb slogans; Reagan grins and says, 'I'm a contra too.' ")

27. Laurence Chollet, "Pulling No Punches," *Bergen County Record,* November 22, 1985, p. A22.

28. Richard Cohen, "The Knee-Jerk Conservative," *Washington Post,* February 15, 1986, p. A27.

29. Michael Solot, "Reaganism's Strange Logic," *Manchester Guardian Weekly,* December 28, 1986, p. 2.

30. Walt Harrington, "Revenge of the Dupes." *Washington Post Magazine,* December 27, 1987, p. W17. (Attributed to "satirist Mort Sahl," though AFL-CIO President Lane Kirkland used it in an address to a union regional conference in March, 1994. U.P.I., March 13, 1984, General News.)

31. Michael Kinsley, "The Real Dirt Is Yet to Be Slung," *Los Angeles Times,* October 10, 1987, pt. 2, p. 8.

32. Welton Jones, "Theater Review: Trudeau's Darts Blunted by His Own Reagan Character," *San Diego Union-Tribune,* September 28, 1985. ("But something went wrong between the drawing board and the Rep stage. In this show, Ronald Reagan seems almost lovable!")

33. "Texas Congressman Says Reagan May Be Senile," U.P.I., December 9, 1983. Overwhelmed with the force of his own argument, Gonzalez prattled on, saying, "One of the aspects of senility is they get hard-headed and unable to modify their opinions and decisions."

34. David Espo, "Civil Rights Bill Dominates Presidential Politics," Associated Press, March 22, 1988.

35. "Giving Railroads Away," *Bergen County Record,* December 19, 1986, p. A34.

36. Clyde Haberman, "Mayor Calls Reagan's Plan to Cut Transit Aid 'Dumb,' " *New York Times,* February 24, 1981.

37. Mike Royko, "High Employment Is in the Stars," *Chicago Tribune,* November 3, 1986, p. 3.

38. Hobart Rowen, "Downright Dumb," *Washington Post,* December 13, 1984.

39. James Reston, "Washington: A Week to Remember," *New York Times,* May 30, 1984, p. A23.

40. Maureen Dowd, "Liberties; Mexico Likes Us!" *New York Times,* May 6, 2001, p. 15.

41. Lou Cannon with David S. Broder and Cristine Russell, "Age Emerges as New Issue in Campaign," *Washington Post,* October 10, 1984, p. A1.

42. Linda Greenhouse, "Taking the Supreme Court's Pulse," *New York Times,* January 28, 1984, p. 8.

43. George W. Ball, "A President at 74 (77) Is a Considerable Risk," *New York Times,* June 24, 1984, p. 23.

44. Editorial, "On Being 73," *Washington Post,* October 24, 1984, p. A17.

45. Matt Clark, "The Doctors Examine Age," *Newsweek,* October 22, 1984; Evan Thomas, "Questions of Age and Competence; The President Seems Fit—But Is He Too Detached?" *Time,* October 22, 1984; Emma Elliot, "My Name Is Mrs. Simon," *Ladies Home Journal,* August 1984. (" 'Senile old people can hurt themselves with those false teeth,' a nurse's aide explained."); "Today's Senior Citizens: 'Pioneers of New Golden Era,' Interview with Dr. Robert Butler, Geriatric Specialist," *U.S. News & World Report,* July 2, 1984.

46. "How to Have a Longer Life and Enjoy It More, Interview with Dr. Robert N. Butler, Director, National Institute on Aging," *U.S. News & World Report,* July 12, 1976, p. 29.

47. The identical LexisNexis search for the same time period in 1988 (first ten months) produces only a few obscure legal publications, e.g., "Permitting the Destruction of Unworthy Life: Its Extent and Form," *Issues in Law & Medicine,* September 22, 1992 (first published in 1920 by Verlag von Felix Meiner in Leipzig, Germany).

48. The same search for 1996 produces only one large-circulation magazine article on

senility (Jill Smolowe, "Older, Longer; Researchers Are Finding More Ways to Keep Senility at Bay, but How Long Should We Aim to Live?" *Time,* Fall 1996) amid even more obscure publications, including *Vegetarian Times* and three issues of *Townsend Letter for Doctors & Patients*—both unavailable on LexisNexis in 1984, and also one article in *Psychology Today,* which had recently begun to republish and had a low circulation.

49. Barbara Wickens, "Brain Detectives," *Maclean's,* March 13, 2000, p. 32.

50. This is excluding small-circulation magazines, many of which are not in the Lexis-Nexis database for 1984.

51. Katie Couric, Ann Curry, and Sara James, *Today,* September 27, 1999.

52. Matt Lauer, Katie Couric, and Ann Curry, *Today,* September 28, 1999.

53. Katie Couric, "Edmund Morris Discusses His Book, *Dutch: A Memoir of Ronald Reagan,*" *Today,* September 29, 1999.

54. Ibid.

55. Kevin Merida, "Shades of Gray Matter."

56. Herbert Mitgang, "Books of the Times: Recounting the Lowlights of the Reagan Years," *New York Times,* March 20, 1991, p. C15.

57. John Kenneth Galbraith, "Sleepwalking Through History: America in the Reagan Years," *Atlanta Journal and Constitution,* March 3, 1991.

58. John Dillin, "Iran-Contra Crisis May Have Peaked," *Christian Science Monitor,* January 7, 1987. ("Gage says poll results must be properly analyzed. For example, in last month's Gallup poll, Reagan's approval rating fell from 63 percent to 47 percent. But Reagan's personal popularity fell only from 80 percent to 75 percent. 'The first figure represents public reaction to the headlines,' Gage says. 'The second reflects the public's actual feelings toward the President.' ")

59. James Gerstenzang, "Barbs Feared Eroding President's Ability to Govern," *Los Angeles Times,* January 24, 1987; David Lamb, "The Times Poll: Many Doubt President's Ability to Lead," *Los Angeles Times,* February 25, 1987. ("However, Reagan remains well-liked: 55% of Americans approve of the President's job performance, up from 50% in December, and a whopping 79%—including 90% of Republicans and 67% of Democrats—said they like Reagan personally.")

60. Robert Sherrill, "*Reagan's America* Innocents at Home, by Garry Wills" *Washington Post Book World,* January 11, 1987.

61. Jonathan Schell, "Shock over Latest Scandal May Finally Wake Up Americans," *Bergen County Record,* April 22, 1991, p. B9.

62. Sam Howe Verhovek, "The 2000 Campaign: The Electorate: Missing Their Man, Devotees of McCain Wonder Which Way to Turn," *New York Times,* March 12, 2000 (citing voters who describe Bush as "an airhead," "out of his depth," and "unqualified"); Nicholas D. Kristof, "The 2000 Campaign: The Texas Governor, Ally of an Older Generation Amid the Tumult of the 60's," *New York Times,* June 19, 2000. ("[Some of Bush's Yale classmates saw] seeing him as an airhead party boy, tended to think of him as affable and unusually helpful to his friends.")

63. Kevin Merida, "Shades of Gray Matter."

64. Nancy Gibbs, "Primary Questions; As the Dust Settles in a Two Man Race, the Question Now Is: Does Bush Have the Brains, McCain the Temperament to Preside in the Oval Office?" *Time,* November 15, 1999.

65. Matthew Mosk, "Bottom's Up for Midshipman: Classmates Tip Hats to Dead-Last Grad," *Washington Post,* May 25, 2000, p. B1.

66. Nancy Gibbs, "Primary Questions."

67. Roger Simon, "Is It Wrong to Call Him George Dumbya Bush?" *U.S. News & World Report,* July 19, 1999.

68. Mary Leonard, "Real Smarts, Grades in College Are Not the Best Indicators of How Good a President a Candidate Might Be," *Boston Globe,* November 26, 1999, p. A1.

69. Bill Turque, "What Mr. Smooth Is Teaching Mr. Stiff," *Newsweek,* September 2, 1996. Republicans are often described as having a lack of "intellectual curiosity," which is noteworthy for being such an utterly meaningless formulation. See, e.g., Jonathan Chait, "Presumed Igno-

rant," *New Republic,* April 30, 2001. This said Bush was "dumb" in the sense of having "a persistent incuriosity that has kept him in a state of childlike ignorance."

70. Nicholas D. Kristof, "The 2000 Campaign: The Texas Governor."

71. James Carney, "Why Bush Doesn't Like Homework," *Time,* November 15, 1999.

72. Kevin Merida, "Shades of Gray Matter."

73. Nicholas D. Kristof, "The 2000 Campaign: The Texas Governor."

74. Frank Bruni, "Political Memo; Bush's Odd Pitch: Ignorance Is Bliss," *New York Times,* June 4, 2000.

75. "George W. Wins the 'Phony War,' " *Newsweek,* November 20, 2000, p. 62.

76. This included Johnson's claim that he and Bush "high-fived" about not knowing what conference speakers were talking about and his praising Bush for making it "really evident" that he didn't know a lot.

77. The Hotline, "White House 2000, Bush: Stumbles in Interview Game of Name That Leader" (citing headlines), November 5, 1999.

78. Charles Gibson, "How Damaging Was Presidential Hopeful George W. Bush's Poor Performance in Foreign Policy Pop Quiz to His Campaign," Interview with George Stephanopoulos, *Good Morning America,* November 5, 1999.

79. Brian Williams, "Interview with Paul Begala," *The News with Brian Williams,* MSNBC, November 4, 1999, FDCH Political Transcripts.

80. *ABC This Week,* November 7, 1999.

81. Howard Fineman, "The Outside Shooter . . . and the Fighting Pilot," *Newsweek,* November 15, 1999.

82. Terry M. Neal, "Gore Blasts Quiz Answer," *Washington Post,* November 6, 1999, p. A9.

83. Editorial, "A Pop Quiz for Mr. Bush," *New York Times,* November 6, 1999, p. A16.

84. Steve Kraske, "Garbage: It Tips Politics Differently," *Kansas City Star,* November 7, 1999.

85. Maureen Dowd, "Liberties: Name That General!" *New York Times,* November 7, 1999, sec. 4, p. 15.

86. Thomas L. Friedman, "George W.'s Makeup Exam," *New York Times,* November 7, 1999. In his capacity as a *New York Times* columnist, Friedman also advised the Democrats to "run commercials over and over again just showing that look on his face." He even suggested an appropriate voice-over for the commercial.

87. Adam Nagourney, "We Must Go Forward Together: Clinton Team Capitalizes on the Limelight," *USA Today,* January 18, 1993, p. 1A.

88. Caroline Schaefer, "A Case Study: *Later Today*'s Asha Blake Suffered from a Sluggish Metabolism Until a Pro Showed Her How to Get Up and Go," *In Style,* Summer 2000, p. 175.

89. David Bloom, Jodi Applegate, Asha Blake, and Florence Henderson, "George W. Bush Ambushed with Foreign Policy Questions," *Later Today,* November 5, 1999.

90. Richard L. Berke with Rick Lyman, "Training for a Presidential Race," *New York Times,* March 15, 1999, p. A16, appended.

91. Ibid.

92. "Ex-Museum Chief's History Is Impeachable," *New York Post,* July 18, 2001.

93. Dan Rather and Bob Schieffer, "Performance of Candidates in the Presidential Debate," *CBS News,* October 3, 2000.

94. Matt Lauer, Katie Couric, and Tom Brokaw, "Governor George W. Bush Discusses the Debate," *Today,* October 4, 2000.

95. Mike Allen, "Bush's Gaffes Are Back as Debates Near," *Washington Post,* October 1, 2000, p. A8.

96. See, e.g., Curtis Wilkie, "Clinton Urges Program to Aid Industry," *Boston Globe,* September 9, 1992.

97. "Current Quotes from the 1992 Presidential Campaign Trail," *Associated Press,* September 9, 1992. (Vice President Dan Quayle on Bill Clinton referring to the anti-missile Patriot missiles as flying down chimneys and through doors.)

98. "National Editorial Sampler: What Newspapers Are Saying," United Press International, September 16, 1992. (Quoting *Los Angeles Times.*)

99. Janice Castro, "Moments from Last Week Bush, Clinton and Quayle Would Like to Forget," *Time,* September 21, 1992.

100. Frederick Allen, "Winner and Loser of the Week? It's Harry Truman," *CNN Prime News,* September 12, 1992, Transcript #158-8.

101. Both the cruise missile and smart bombs have amazing targeting technology—accurate to about three feet, not accounting for wind and other natural conditions. The cruise missile hits targets guided by laser, satellite, or pre-programmed destination. The "smart bombs" guide themselves on the way down, as the fins on the back move back and forth to hit the exact target, also guided by laser or satellite.

102. Bill Tammeus, "A Few Quotes to Enliven These Sluggish Times," *Plain Dealer,* December 29, 1992, p. 5B. Clinton said this in a speech at the University of Florida in Gainesville on October 8, 1992.

103. Matt Pommer, "Pols Speak, Find a Place for Foot," *Capital Times* (Madison, Wis.), June 28, 1999, p. 3A. State Sen. Carol Roessler, R-Oshkosh, has borrowed an idea from Art Linkletter, a TV personality of yesteryear who wrote the popular book *Kids Say the Darndest Things.* Roessler is out with a new book, *Politicians Say the Dumbest Things.* The book is kind—it doesn't credit the Wisconsin legislators who let their tongues run ahead of their brains.

104. Greg Freeman, "Brother-Sister Team Compiles Officials' Most Inane Utterances," *St. Louis Post-Dispatch,* September 30, 1999, p. B1.

105. Michelle Mittelstadt, "Attorney General Says Verdict Shows Government Acted Properly," Associated Press, February 26, 1994.

106. "Overlooked," The Hotline, September 27, 1991. ("Al Gore, on the Senate floor this week, used the simile 'like a zebra changing its spots.' [Noting: 'Of course, the Congressional Record will show otherwise.']")

107. Trevor Kavanagh, "Prepare to Fight," *Sun,* October 11, 2001.

108. "Mrs. Clinton Slips from Script on Aspiration," *New York Times,* July 19, 2001.

109. "Speech by Vice President Albert Gore, Jr., at the Emily's List Majority Council Conference Breakfast, Washington Hilton Hotel, Washington, D.C.," Federal News Service, June 11, 1999.

110. Hilary Bowker, "Text of Hillary Clinton Whitewater Press Conference," CNN *Prime News,* April 22, 1994, Transcript #389-1.

111. Steve Kroft, "Governor and Mrs. Bill Clinton Discuss Adultery Accusations," *60 Minutes,* January 26, 1992.

112. Ross Petras and Kathryn Petras, *The 776 Stupidest Things Ever Said,* New York: Doubleday, 1993; Paul Kirchner, *Oops! A Stupefying Survey of Goofs, Blunders and Blotches, Great and Small,* General Publishing Group, 1995; David Olive, *Political Babble,* New York: John Wiley and Sons, 1995; David Wallechinsky and Amy Wallace, *The Book of Lists,* Boston: Little, Brown.

113. Eric Nash, "Endpaper: The Annotated Calvin and Hobbes," *New York Times,* January 9, 1994, p. 50.

114. Paula LaRocque, "For Politicians of the World, Words Have Always Had Leanings," *Dallas Morning News,* May 18, 1998.

115. Jack Smith, "Even Short Quotations Leave a Mark," *Los Angeles Times,* March 7, 1994.

116. Bob Herbert, "In America: Leading America Beyond Fear," *New York Times,* September 24, 2001.

117. Richard L. Berke, "A Nation Challenged: The Democrats: Bush Winning Gore Backers' High Praises," *New York Times,* October 20, 2001.

118. Ibid.

119. Ibid.

120. Ibid.

121. Ibid.

122. Jena Heath, "A Look at Bush's Approach to Intellect," Cox News Service, November 27, 1999. (Reprinted in the *Atlanta Journal and Constitution, Austin American-Statesman,* and the *Times-Picayune.*)

123. Thomas L. Friedman, "Foreign Affairs: George W.'s Makeup Exam," *New York Times,* November 7, 1999.

124. Dan Balz and Bob Woodward, "America's Chaotic Road to War; Bush's Global Strategy Began to Take Shape in First Frantic Hours After Attack," *Washington Post,* January 27, 2002.

125. Bill Nichols, "Followers and Foes Anticipate Bush's Foreign Policy Speech," *USA Today,* November 19, 1999.

126. Ibid.

127. Thomas L. Friedman, "Foreign Affairs: George W.'s Makeup Exam."

128. Maureen Dowd, "Liberties: Name That General!"

129. Nancy Gibbs, "Primary Questions."

130. Jonathan Alter, "National Affairs: Between the Lines," *Newsweek,* November 22, 1999, p. 47.

131. The Hotline, "People: Cher: If Dubya Wins, She'll Try to Turn Back Time," *National Journal,* November 3, 2000.

132. David E. Sanger and Don Van Natta Jr., "In Four Days, a National Crisis Changes Bush's Presidency," *New York Times,* September 16, 2001.

133. R. W. Apple Jr., "After the Attacks: Assessment; President Seems to Gain Legitimacy," *New York Times,* September 16, 2001.

134. Ibid.

135. Richard Cohen, "Taking Command," *Washington Post,* September 22, 2001. Cohen also reminded readers that Bush had been "a middling student," "incurious and intellectually inert," and had "back-slapped his way into the presidency." Only among graduates of the Columbia School of Journalism is the Columbia Graduate School considered more impressive than Harvard Business School.

136. R. W. Apple Jr., "A Nation Challenged: A Clear Message: 'I Will Not Relent'," *New York Times,* September 21, 2001.

137. R. W. Apple Jr., "After The Attacks: Assessment; President Seems to Gain Legitimacy."

138. Ibid.

139. Ibid.

140. Bob Herbert, "In America; Leading America Beyond Fear."

141. Maureen Dowd, "Liberties: Rip Van Rummy Awakes," *New York Times,* August 22, 2001.

Eight. Clever Is as Clever Does: The Liberal Dilemma

1. Ross G. Brown, "Voting: Beating Up Smarty Pants," *Los Angeles Times,* October 28, 2000.

2. Michael Beschloss, "How Well-Read Should a President Be?" *New York Times,* June 11, 2000. In the entire LexisNexis archives, this fact has been repeated by only one other person: columnist George Will.

3. Roger Simon, "Is It Wrong to Call Him George Dumbya Bush?" *U.S. News & World Report,* July 19, 1999, p. 26.

4. Eric Pooley, "New York State of Mine; Hillary Clinton Opens Her Undeclared Candidacy for the U.S. Senate by Making a Show of Listening—and Sidling Away from Bill," *Time,* July 19, 1999, p. 26.

5. Ibid.

6. See generally Jean O. Pasco, "Kitty Dukakis Tells Students of Her Diet-Pill Addiction," *Orange County Register,* October 5, 1988, p. B6.

7. Bob Drogin, "But Inner Resolve Serves Him Well; Dukakis' Determination: Both Strength, Weakness," *Los Angeles Times,* July 20, 1988, pt. 1, p. 1, home edition.

8. " 'Off Night' or Advancing Years, Reagan's Age Is Emerging Issue," *San Diego Union-Tribune,* from News Services, October 12, 1984. ("Democrats are saying President Reagan's performance in the presidential debate may be a sign of advancing age, but Republicans are shrugging it off as an 'off night.' ")

9. See, e.g., "The Banzai Bunny," *Newsweek,* September 10, 1979 ("As Jimmy Carter tells it, he had escaped for a spot of solitary fishing on a Georgia pond last April when suddenly he found himself eye to eye with a vicious rabbit swimming, like a torpedo, toward the Commander in Chief's canoe."); Editorial, "Standard Summer," *New York Times,* August 28, 1980 ("Is it that there's something about politics that brings out the animal in people: Jimmy Carter flogging away at that killer rabbit . . .").

10. See, e.g., Robert A. Jordan, "They're Boring Toward 2000 but Steering Clear of Trouble," *Boston Globe,* April 18, 1999.

11. Editorial, "Gore Gets a Little Competition," *San Francisco Chronicle,* December 8, 1998.

12. Jo Mannies, "Bradley Touts New Book, Ideologies; Public Trust Tops Priorities in New Appeal," *St. Louis Post-Dispatch,* February 9, 1996, p. 1C.

13. Brian C. Mooney, "Gore 'Policy Speech' Says Volumes About His Ailing Campaign," *Boston Globe,* July 14, 1999.

14. "Al Gore Gets Labor Day Endorsement in Iowa; Bush Enjoys Star Status in South Carolina; Lesser-Known Republicans Continue Fight for Attention," CNN's *Inside Politics,* September 6, 1999.

15. Michael Winerip, "A Moderate's Moment," *New York Times,* July 20, 1997, p. 18.

16. "McCain, Bush Vie for Spotlight in South Carolina; Bill Bradley Discusses His Uphill Battle; Al Gore Makes Play for Latino Support," CNN's *Inside Politics,* June 21, 1999.

17. Marc Lacey and Mark Z. Barabak, "National Perspective; Politics; In Upstart Campaign, Bradley Flexes His Fund-Raising Muscles," *Los Angeles Times,* July 20, 1999.

18. Geoff Kabaservice, "Bill Bradley's SAT Scores," *Slate Magazine,* January 26, 2000.

19. See, e.g., Carol Innerst, "SAT Scores Edge Up, Thanks to Math Rise; Verbal Average Same as Last Year," *Washington Times,* August 27, 1997. ("The scores released yesterday reflect the first year in which all student scores were based upon a 'recentered' scale that was phased in starting in 1995."); Geoff Kabaservice, "Bill Bradley's SAT Scores." ("The SAT has been 'recentered' in recent years, boosting overall scores by up to a hundred points.")

20. Joseph Berger, "You Can't Judge a Leader by His Scores in the SATs," *New York Times,* March 22, 2000; Roger Simon, "Who's the Dimmest Dim Bulb?" *U.S. News & World Report,* April 3, 2000; Gene Weingarten, "The Lowest Scoring in Bill Bradley's Career," *Washington Post,* January 31, 2000.

21. James Dao, "McCain Joins Bradley in War on Soft Money," *New York Times,* December 17, 1999.

22. "Transcript of Foreign Policy Speech by Vice President Gore in Milwaukee Jan. 6, White House Office of the Press Secretary," U.S. Newswire, January 6, 1994.

23. Mike Allen, "Bush's Gaffes Are Back as Debates Near," *Washington Post,* October 1, 2000, p. A8.

24. Bill Nichols, "The Heir Apparent Has Solid Record and Stolid Image," *USA Today,* August 29, 1996.

25. Richard L. Berke and Janet Elder, "The 2000 Campaign: The Poll; In Final Days, Voters Still Wrestle with Doubts on Bush and Gore," *New York Times,* October 23, 2000, p. A1.

26. Roger Simon, "Is It Wrong to Call Him George Dumbya Bush?" (Quoting Jim Hightower, a radio commentator and former Democratic official from Texas.)

27. Editorial, "Show Time for Al Gore," *New York Times,* August 13, 2000. ("Voters understand that Mr. Gore is smart.")

28. Richard Benedetto, "Poll: Bush More Honest, Likable Gore Losing Ground After First Debate," *USA Today,* October 10, 2000. (". . . likely voters rated Gore smarter . . .")

29. James Q. Wilson, "Campaign 2000; Photo Finish; Why the Economy's Success Hasn't Been a Decisive Factor," *Los Angeles Times,* November 5, 2000. ("Voters have told pollsters they think Gore is smart.")

30. Charlie Cook, "Buyer's Remorse, Fate, and Close Calls," *National Journal*, October 28, 2000. ("[Swing voters] like Gore's smarts, knowledge of the issues.") See also Dan Robrish and Ann Mcfeatters, "Give Him 60 Seconds and He'll Tell Your Life Story; Gore's Long March," *Pittsburgh Post-Gazette*, October 3, 1999. ("Gore is smart.")

31. Maureen Dowd "Liberties: Gore's Gawky Phase," *New York Times*, October 10, 1999.

32. Paul Reid (quoting David Gergen), Cox News Service, "Campaign 2000: Albert Gore Jr.; A Passion for the Nation's Top Position," *Atlanta Journal and Constitution*, May 2, 1999.

33. Bill Turque, "What Mr. Smooth Is Teaching Mr. Stiff," *Newsweek*, September 2, 1996.

34. Jonathan Capehart, "Next Gore-Bush Debate Might Turn Nasty Again," Bloomberg News, October 9, 2000.

35. See, e.g., among many, many others: Jonathan Capehart, "Next Gore-Bush Debate Might Turn Nasty Again." ("He is the most intelligent kid in the class."); Ross G. Brown, "Voting: Beating Up Smarty Pants," *Los Angeles Times*, October 28, 2000. (Gore is "the smartest kid in [his] class."); Susan Page, "The Male Vote Stands as Gore's Achilles' Heel," *USA Today*, April 26, 2000. ("Gore reminds some people of the smartest kid in the class," quoting Andrew Kohut, director of the independent Pew Research Center.)

36. Richard L. Berke, "The 2000 Campaign: News Analysis—The Context; Debates Put in Focus Images and Reality," *New York Times*, October 19, 2000. (Quoting Don Hewitt, the creator of *60 Minutes*.)

37. David Maraniss and Ellen Nakashima, "Gore's Grades Belie Image of Studiousness; His School Transcripts Are a Lot Like Bush's," *Washington Post*, March 19, 2000, p. A1.

38. Ibid.

39. "Today's Gore Campaign News," *Bulletin's Frontrunner*, June 15, 2000 (citing Gore's comments on Fox News's *Special Report*, June 14, 2000).

40. Charles Gibson and Diane Sawyer, "Second Presidential Debate a More Subdued Face-Off; Al Gore and George W. Bush Discuss How They Feel They Did on the Second Presidential Debate; Debate Analyzed," *Good Morning America*, October 12, 2000. (Burrelle's Information Services)

41. Ibid.

42. Based on various LexisNexis searches including: "good morning america and gore and (invent! w/s internet).

43. Juju Chang, "New Republican Ad Attacking Al Gore; Pentagon Monitoring Growing Iraqi Threats Against Kurds; Former Los Alamos Scientist Wen Ho Lee Could Be Out of Prison Today," *Good Morning America*, September 1, 2000.

44. Hedrick Smith, "No Clear Winner Apparent; Scene Is Simple and Stark," *New York Times*, October 29, 1980, p. 1.

45. Lou Cannon, "Reagan; President, GOP Standard-Bearer Crisscross Nation in Stump Finale; Reagan: Declaring U.S. the 'Last Best Hope'; Affirmation of U.S. as Man's 'Last Best Hope'," *Washington Post*, November 4, 1980, p. A1.

46. Martin Schram, "Nation's Longest Campaign Comes to an End; Long Campaign Ends, and It Often Was Anything but Presidential," *Washington Post*, November 4, 1980, p. A1.

47. Dave Anderson, "Sports of the Times; Roger Staubach's Political Football," *New York Times*, November 9, 1980, sec. 5, p. 7; UPI, "Staubach Out of Bounds?" *New York Times*, November 4, 1980, p. B14.

48. UPI, "Staubach Out of Bounds?" *New York Times*.

49. Maureen Dowd, "The 1992 Campaign: News Analysis; A No-Nonsense Sort of Talk Show," *New York Times*, October 16, 1992, p. A1. (Bush "seemed uncomfortable and sometimes grew testy. By 9:50 P.M., he was checking his watch.")

50. Jeffrey Schmalz, "The 1992 Campaign: The Voters; Americans Sign Up in Record Numbers to Cast a Ballot," *New York Times*, October 19, 1992, p. A1. (" 'Bush doesn't care,' Ms. Jojola, 38, agreed. She had once been registered Republican but could not remember when she last voted. She registered two weeks ago as a Democrat. 'Bush doesn't care about things here,' she said. 'He kept looking at his watch in the debate. He was bored.' ") R. W. Apple Jr., "The 1992 Campaign: News Analysis; A Late-Round Flurry for Bush but Shape of Race Appears Unaltered," *New York Times*, October 20, 1992, p. A1. ("He changed his ways for the better. There

was no looking at his watch in last night's encounter in East Lansing, Mich., as there had been last week, and no suggestion of languor. His message was clear. He did his best to make voters think about character and trust, rather than blaming him for costing them their jobs, even invoking Horace Greeley to the effect that character counts most.") Maureen Dowd, "The 1992 Campaign: The Surrounding Scene; Bush Wins One Contest with a Sharp, Red Tie," *New York Times,* October 20, 1992, p. A19. ("The President cheered up his debate coaches immensely this morning, in a practice in the Old Executive Office Building, when, halfway through, he pointedly raised his wrist and looked at his watch. Everyone laughed at Mr. Bush's ability to make fun of the fuss that ensued when he looked at his watch three times during the second debate in Richmond—a repetitive stress syndrome that was widely interpreted as a sign that the President was dispirited.")

51. The *Times*'s accuracy-meter supported Bush's claim that Gore's spending plan was three times what Clinton had proposed. The *Times* complained, however, that the ten-second description of Bush's tax plan was not a half-hour infomercial, and therefore described only the effect of the Bush tax plan on a family with two children.

52. Dan Rather and John Roberts, "Life and Careers of Vice President Al Gore," CBS News Transcripts, Campaign 2000: Democratic National Convention, August 17, 2000. (John Roberts: "What the public has come to know about Al Gore has been. He's claimed to have invented the Internet, and, of course, his storied woodenness.")

53. John Cochran and Anderson Cooper, "New Republican Ad Campaign Attacking Al Gore's Character," *World News Now,* September 1, 2000.

54. Matt Lauer and Ann Curry, *Today,* October 31, 2000; Dan Rather, "Late-Night Programs Poke Fun at Presidential Candidates," *CBS Evening News,* November 3, 2000; Dan Rather and Eric Engberg, "Game Plan for Bush and Gore in Tonight's Debate," *CBS Evening News,* October 3, 2000; Dan Rather, "Late Night Television Presidential Candidate Humor," *CBS Evening News,* September 15, 2000.

55. Carole Simpson and Ron Claiborne, "Behind the Scenes of Campaign Politics," *ABC World News Tonight,* September 17, 2000.

56. Scott Shepard, "Gore More Victimized Than Guilty of Falsehoods, Press Critics Say," Cox News Service, April 6, 2000.

57. Ibid.

58. Ibid.

59. Robert Parry, "He's No Pinocchio; Media Coverage of Al Gore Misrepresents Him," *Washington Monthly,* April 1, 2000.

60. Cokie Roberts, Sam Donaldson, and George Will, "Roundtable Talk on Presidential Campaign and WTO Talks," *ABC News' This Week,* December 5, 1999.

61. Chris Matthews, "Lois Gibbs and Douglas Brinkley Discuss the Love Canal Toxic Waste Site in Upstate New York," *Hardball with Chris Matthews,* December 1, 1999.

62. Paul Krugman, "Reckonings: Unsound Bytes?" *New York Times,* October 22, 2000, sec. 4, p. 15.

NINE. SHADOWBOXING THE APOCRYPHAL "RELIGIOUS RIGHT"

1. Jacques Ellul, *Propaganda,* New York: Vintage Books, 1965, p. 31.

2. In a one-year period (roughly corresponding to calendar year 2000) the *New York Times* found occasion to mention either "Christian conservatives" or the "religious right" 187 times. Not once did the paper refer to "atheist liberals" or "the atheist left."

3. George Orwell, *1984,* (New York: Signet, 1950), p. 14.

4. Douglas Jehl, "A Nation Challenged: Saudi Arabia; Holy War Lured Saudis as Rulers Looked Away," *New York Times,* December 21, 2001.

5. See, e.g., "Are the Religious Right's Political Tactics Nasty?" CNN's *Inside Politics,* June 21, 1994, transcript #607-4.

6. See, e.g., "Washington Dateline," Associated Press, December 9, 1994.

7. Susan Saulny, "A Night Out With: The Rev. Jesse Jackson; The Moviegoer," *New York Times,* January 7, 2001, sec. 9, p. 3.

8. Editorial, "The Religion Wars," *New York Times,* March 2, 2000.

9. A. M. Rosenthal, "On My Mind; With Friends Like These," *New York Times,* August 13, 1996.

10. Michael Weisskopf, "Energized by Pulpit or Passion, the Public Is Calling; 'Gospel Grapevine' Displays Strength in Controversy over Military Gay Ban," *Washington Post,* February 1, 1993. Correction issued February 2, 1993: "CORRECTION: An article yesterday characterized followers of television evangelists Jerry Falwell and Pat Robertson as 'largely poor, uneducated and easy to command.' There is no factual basis for that statement."

11. Dudley Clendinen, "The Electoral Evangelism of Pat Robertson," *New York Times,* September 21, 1986. (Quoting Samuel S. Hill, a professor of religion at the University of Florida and the author of *The New Religious Political Right in America,* published by the Methodist Press.)

12. Arthur Hoppe, "Is There Life Before Death?" *San Francisco Chronicle,* February 14, 1996.

13. Timothy Gorski, Margaret Downey, David Silverman, and Lynn Neary, "Atheism," NPR's *Talk of the Nation,* October 5, 1998.

14. "King Lear; Witty and Brave, Norman Lear Toppled Taboos by Getting Us to Laugh at Our Foibles," *People Special,* March 15, 1999/March 22, 1999.

15. T. Christian Miller and Ronald Brownstein, "McCain Delivers Hard Left to Christian Right," *Los Angeles Times,* February 29, 2000.

16. "The Lonely Charge of John McCain," *The Economist,* March 04, 2000. ("They [the religious right] account for around a fifth of all party members and a third in many states' primary electorates.")

17. Laurie Goodstein, "Coalition's Woes May Hinder Goals of Christian Right," *New York Times,* August 2, 1999, p. A1.

18. Source: Center for Responsive Politics, tracking donations from January 1, 1999, through June 30, 2000 (quoted in Robert T. Garrett, "Big Money Politics: How Bush, Gore Might Change the Rules," *Press-Enterprise* [Riverside, Calif.], October 15, 2000).

19. Ibid.

20. According to the tracking report of the Center for Responsive Politics, from January 1, 1999 through June 30, 2000, lawyers contributed over $11 million to the presidential campaign. When soft money and other political donations are included, the legal profession spent over $100 million on the 2000 election—70 percent to Democrats and 30 percent to Republicans.

21. George Lardner Jr., "Lawyers Gave Bulk of Money in Election," *Washington Post,* March 4, 2001.

22. Bennett Roth, "Quest for Soft Money Goes Unabated; Tight Races for President, Congress Could Double 1996 Election Funding," *Houston Chronicle,* September 18, 2000.

23. Editorial, "The Religion Wars," *New York Times,* March 2, 2000.

24. This was conducted by Voter News Service for CNN. Twenty-nine percent of the respondents identified themselves as conservatives, and 20 percent of respondents identified themselves as liberals.

25. Ronald Sider, "Evangelicals Don't Fit Political Stereotype," *Dallas Morning News,* March 6, 2001. ("One recent national survey discovered that 28 percent of white evangelicals were registered Democrats and that another 29 percent were independents. [Forty-one percent were Republicans.]")

26. See, e.g., Tom Mashberg, "Vote Reflects Culture Clash," *Boston Herald,* November 26, 2000.

27. Steven Waldman, "Doubts Among the Faithful," *New York Times,* March 7, 2001. ("Many Christians, even some conservative Protestants, embrace a limited form of pluralism ... But the president's statements about his new initiative suggest that he really belongs to a different group of Americans, those who approve of religion generally and are tolerant of all ...")

28. David Johnston and Neil A. Lewis, "Religious Right Made Big Push to Put Ashcroft in Justice Dept.," *New York Times,* January 7, 2001. See also Laurie Goodstein, "Religious Right, Frustrated, Trying New Tactic on G.O.P.," *New York Times,* March 23, 1998. ("Christian conservatives" seek "elimination of financial support for the National Endowment for the Arts.")

29. Even in its heyday, the Moral Majority was not particularly frightening, except as an imaginary enemy. In the ten years of its existence, the Moral Majority raised $69 million. To put this in perspective, in the 2000 election, labor unions contributed more than $15 million to Al Gore's campaign alone. (Robert T. Garrett, "Big Money Politics," *Press-Enterprise* [Riverside, Ca.], October 15, 2000.) Foreshadowing the "compassionate conservatism" of George Bush (who, according to the *New York Times,* "really belongs to a different group of Americans than the religious right) back in 1980 Falwell worried "that the public sees them as 'hard right' wingers rather than compassionate moralists." Indeed, twenty years ago, Falwell was saying he believed Christianity had flourished in this country "because America has been totally free and open to any and all religious faiths. I would literally fight to the death for the right of a Madalyn O'Hair to say what she believes, for the Mormon church to preach what it preaches." (Megan Rosenfeld, "The New Moral America and the War of the Religicos; Born Again Political Forces Not Singing the Same Hymn," *Washington Post,* August 24, 1980.)

30. Cal Thomas and Ed Dobson, *Blinded by Might,* Grand Rapids, Mich.: Zondervan, 1999.

31. Chris Matthews, "Upcoming Election Campaigns," *Hardball with Chris Matthews,* March 9, 2000.

32. "Freedom from Religion: The First Amendment Protects Non-Belief, Too," *Church & State,* October 1, 2000, p. 13.

33. Mr. John Green, political scientist, University of Akron (introduced: "no one in the country tracks the opinions and activities of the religious right more closely than John Green") in Robert Siegel and David Molpus, "Religious Right Lines Up in Support of George Bush," National Public Radio's *All Things Considered,* November 2, 2000. See also John Zogby, "Campaign 2000, John Zogby Delivers Remarks at a Foreign Press Center Briefing," FDCH Political Transcripts, October 27, 2000. (Referring to the political views of the religious right, Pollster John Zogby cites simply "one of their leaders, Pat Robertson." Dana Milbank, "Key Goals Face Early Obstacles," *Washington Post,* February 27, 2001, p. A1. Calls Robertson a "lion of the religious right.")

34. Richard L. Berke, "State of the Union: The Politics; Robertson, Praising Speech, Sees Trial as a Peril to G.O.P.," *New York Times,* January 21, 1999.

35. "He comes out with faith-based programs as a sop to the religious right." Bill Press on *CNN Crossfire,* "The Bush Tax Cut Plan: Is the Honeymoon Over?," February 5, 2001; "Bush is giving a vast payback to the religious right for help in his election." Barry Lynn, executive director of Americans United for Separation of Church and State, quoted in Mary Leonard, "Bush Boosts Faith's Role in Charity, Sets Initiatives on Social Needs," *Boston Globe,* January 28, 2001; "Jewish leaders" remained "guarded" with Bush's faith-based plan, because Bush "has courted the religious right." Marc Dollinger, "Bush's Faith-Based Plan Borrows a Page from FDR," *Los Angeles Times,* February 18, 2001; Bush's faith-based initiative "reaches out to Christian conservatives." Bedard, *U.S. News & World Report,* February 5, 2001.

36. "United States and China Prepare to Fight over Flights," CNN *Wolf Blitzer Reports,* April 16, 2001. Robertson later "clarified" that he opposes forced abortion.

37. Cary McMullen, "Coalition's Political Power Ending," *The Ledger* (Lakeland, Fla.), November 14, 1998.

38. Richard L. Berke, "State of the Union: The Politics; Robertson, Praising Speech, Sees Trial as a Peril to G.O.P."

39. Representative Christopher Cannon (R-Utah) quoted in Richard L. Berke, "State of the Union: The Politics; Robertson, Praising Speech, Sees Trial as a Peril to G.O.P."

40. Stephen Dinan, "Senate Panel OKs School Minute of Silence," *Washington Times,* January 28, 2000.

41. Phil Linsalata, "Going for the Jackpot; Will November's Vote on Legalizing Slot Machines Determine the Future of Casinos in Missouri? Both Sides Hope So," *St. Louis Post-Dispatch,* October 2, 1994.

42. Alisa Stingley, "Statewide Campaign Takes Aim at STDs," Associated Press, June 12, 2000.

43. "Sex and Violence on TV," *Fox News Network the Edge with Paula Zahn,* September 13, 2000, Transcript #091304cb.260.

44. Radio station WEZE-AM out of Quincy, Massachusetts, runs Christian programming twenty-four hours a day with many well-known Christians, including attorney Jay Sekulow, described in the *New York Times* as attorney for "a conservative religious rights group"; James Dobson, identified in the *Times* as "a leading religious conservative"; and radio personality Janet Parshall, described in the *Times* as a conservative and Christian radio talk show host. See Gustav Niebuhr, "Number of Religious Broadcasters Continues to Grow," *New York Times,* February 12, 1996; Dirk Johnson, "Schools Seeking to Skirt Rules That Bar Ten Commandments," *New York Times,* February 27, 2000.

45. Lane Lambert, "Tuning Into Religion; From Marina Bay in Quincy, a Station for 'Missionary Land,' " *Patriot Ledger* (Quincy, Mass.), April 8, 2000, p. 24, ROP edition.

46. Clea Simon, "Graf Must Be Accountable, Too," *Boston Globe,* June 1, 2000.

47. Ronald Sider, "Evangelicals Don't Fit Political Stereotype," *Dallas Morning News,* March 6, 2001.

48. Robert Siegel and David Molpus, "Religious Right Lines Up."

49. Kerry Crist, "National Testing Can Offer Useful Guideposts," *St. Louis Post-Dispatch,* December 10, 1997.

50. Chris Matthews, "Upcoming Election Campaigns," *Hardball with Chris Matthews,* March 9, 2000.

51. Mary Jacoby, "Centrist Image Sought for GOP," *St. Petersburg Times,* April 5, 1999.

52. Thomas B. Edsall, "Clinton Stuns Rainbow Coalition; Candidate Criticizes Rap Singer's Message," *Washington Post,* June 14, 1992.

53. Gwen Ifill, "The 1992 Campaign: Democrats; Clinton at Jackson Meeting: Warmth, and Some Friction," *New York Times,* June 14, 1992.

54. Anthony Lewis, "Abroad at Home; Black and White," *New York Times,* June 18, 1992.

55. Susan Estrich, "The Changing Face of the GOP; Practicing Politics of Exclusion," *Los Angeles Times,* August 23, 1992.

56. Nancy Gibbs, reported by James Carney with Bush and John F. Dickerson and Priscilla Painton with McCain, "Campaign 2000: Fire and Brimstone; How McCain and Bush Waged a Holy War Over the Power of the Religious Right and Turned God into a Campaign Issue," *Time,* March 13, 2000, p. 30.

57. Bill Press and Tucker Carlson, "Is George W. Bush Making the 'Right' Choices," CNN's *The Spin Room,* December 22, 2000.

58. "Let's talk a little bit more about the right wing because I know that's something you feel very strongly about. But this is actually not necessarily about the right wing, but perhaps a climate that some say has been established by religious zealots or Christian conservatives. There have been two recent incidents in the news, I think, that upset most people in this country, that is the dragging death of James Byrd Junior and the beating death of Matthew Shepard. I just would like you to reflect on whether you feel people in this country are increasingly intolerant, mean-spirited, et cetera, and what, if anything, can be done about that because a lot of people get very discouraged when they hear and see this kind of brutality taking place."—Katie Couric to former Texas Governor Ann Richards as she hosted a 92nd Street Y appearance in New York City on March 3 shown by C-SPAN on April 3, 1999.

59. *Today,* October 30, 1992.

60. *The Early Show,* August 15, 2000.

61. Bonnie Erbe, NBC Radio News/Westwood One reporter, hosting *To the Contrary on PBS,* August 16, 1996.

62. Tony Mauro, "Can a Deeply Religious Person Be Attorney General?" *USA Today,* January 16, 2001.

63. Richard Sale, "Russians Knew About Lewinsky Before Public," United Press International, March 13, 2001. ("Former Russian President Boris Yeltsin knew about President Clinton's affair with Monica Lewinsky as early as 1996, according to former U.S. intelligence officials who said that they believe that the Russians obtained the knowledge by compromising secure White House communications.")

64. Diane Sawyer, "Ken Starr," *20/20,* November 25, 1998, Transcript #98112501-j11.

65. George Orwell, *1984,* p. 15.

66. Chris Connelly, "Heather Heats Up," *Talk,* February 2001.

67. Larry Engelmann, "Year in Review: Best Quotes of 2000," *Las Vegas Review-Journal,* December 31, 2000.

68. Claire Bickley, "Keaton 'Way Out There' as Nun She Stars in Festival-Bound Black Comedy," *Edmonton Sun,* December 27, 2000.

69. Nick Lachey, "Nobody Kisses and Tells Like Cybill Shepherd," *Oregonian,* March 16, 2000.

70. Sue Carroll, "Interview: Rachel Hunter on Life With—and Without—Rod," *Mirror,* February 28, 2001.

71. "Ventura Tries to Explain Views," United Press International, October 1, 1999.

72. Tom Brokaw, "Controversial *Playboy* Interview with Jesse Ventura," *NBC Nightly News,* September 30, 1999.

73. "You Can Say That Again," *Columbus Dispatch,* October 1, 1999.

74. Matt Bai, "Now He's the Man to See," *Newsweek,* October 11, 1999.

75. Nancy Gibbs, Reported by James Carney with Bush and John F. Dickerson and Priscilla Painton, "Fire and Brimstone; How McCain and Bush Waged a Holy War over the Power of the Religious Right,"

76. Richard Cohen, "Wrestler v. Religion," *Washington Post,* October 14, 1999.

77. ABC News, *20/20,* October 8, 1999.

78. Frank Rich, "Send in More Clowns," *New York Times,* October 23, 1999.

79. Howard Kurtz and Bernard Kalb, "Are Journalists Clueless About Christian Conservatives?" CNN's *Reliable Sources,* March 4, 2000.

80. Molly Ivins, "What Did He Say? Pure Ventura," *Fort Worth Star-Telegram,* October 5, 1999.

81. Jessie Milligan, "With Cancer Treatment Behind Her, Molly Ivins Is as Controversial as Ever," *Fort Worth Star-Telegram,* July 3, 2001.

82. Editorial, "The Body Holds Forth," *Washington Times,* October 2, 1999.

83. Robert Whereatt, "Ventura Hears Concerns of Nonreligious Community; Group Members Were Grateful That He Listened to Them and Acknowledged Their Beliefs," *Star Tribune* (Minneapolis), December 28, 2000.

84. Ibid.

85. Robyn E. Blumner, "In U.S., the Irreligious Bear the Greatest Intolerance," *St. Petersburg Times,* December 12, 1999.

86. Allison Jones, "The Ethnic News Watch: Jackson Says: Nazi, Slavery Forces on Rise," *Michigan Citizen,* December 24, 1994, p. A1.

87. Laurie Goodstein, "Jackson Offers No Apology for Blast at Christian Right," *Washington Post,* December 9, 1994.

88. Ibid.

89. George Orwell, *1984,* p. 154.

90. Ibid., p. 15.

91. Megan Rosenfeld, "The New Moral America and the War of the Religicos; Born Again Political Forces Not Singing the Same Hymn," *Washington Post,* August 24, 1980.

92. David S. Broder, "New Militants," *Washington Post,* April 5, 1981.

93. David M. Alpern with Howard Fineman in Washington, Stryker McGuire in Houston and bureau reports, "The New Right: Betrayed?" *Newsweek,* February 7, 1983, p. 21.

94. Charlotte Saikowski, "Religious Right Throws Its Weight Behind Reagan Reelection Effort," *Christian Science Monitor,* October 3, 1984.

95. James L. Franklin, "Falwell Will Disband the Moral Majority," *Boston Globe,* June 12, 1989.

96. Michael Fitzgerald, "Falwell Closes Moral Majority," *USA Today,* June 12, 1989.

97. Ibid.

98. Michael D'Antonio, "Fierce in the '80s, Fallen in the '90s, the Religious Right Forgets Politics," *Los Angeles Times,* February 4, 1990.

99. Ibid.

100. Michael Weisskopf, "Energized by Pulpit or Passion, the Public Is Calling; 'Gospel Grapevine' Displays Strength in Controversy over Military Gay Ban," *Washington Post,* February 1, 1993, p. A1.

101. Ibid.

102. David Frum, "Myth of Religious Right," *USA Today,* July 25, 1994, p. 11A.

103. David Von Drehle, "Coalition Reaching to the Middle," *Washington Post,* August 15, 1994, p. A1.

104. "Christian Coalition Gaining Strength," *ABC World News Tonight,* November 3, 1994, Transcript #4219-6. (ABC anchor: "Critics—and there are many—say they fear the Coalition wants to impose its view of truth on everyone and establish a Christian nation.")

105. Richard L. Berke, "Poll Finds G.O.P. Primary Voters Are Hardly Monolithic," *New York Times,* October 30, 1995, p. A11.

106. Cary McMullen, "Coalition's Political Power Ending; Beliefs," *The Ledger* (Lakeland, Fla.), November 14, 1998.

107. Michael Lind, "The Right Still Has Religion," *New York Times,* December 9, 2001, Sec. 4, p. 13.

108. Eric Lichtblau, "The Presidential Transition; As Attorney General, Ashcroft's Trial Would Be Abortion Issue; Rights: Some Fear the Nominee's Strong Beliefs Will Bring Curbs. But He Says His Job Would Be to Uphold Law," *Los Angeles Times,* January 10, 2001.

109. Tom Brokaw and Lisa Myers, "Groups Trying to Oust Ashcroft's Nomination," *NBC Nightly News,* January 9, 2001.

110. Brian Williams and David Gregory, "Bush Administration Beginning to Take Shape," *NBC Nightly News,* December 22, 2000.

111. *Inside Washington,* December 23, 2000.

112. CNN's *Capital Gang,* December 23, 2000.

113. Kate O'Beirne, Robert Novak, Margaret Carlson, Vic Fazio, Mark Shields, "Has George W. Bush Made the 'Right' Cabinet Picks?" CNN's *Capital Gang,* December 30, 2000, Transcript #00123000V40.

114. William Raspberry, *Washington Post,* December 29, 2000.

115. David Johnston and Neil A. Lewis, "Religious Right Made Big Push to Put Ashcroft in Justice Dept.," *New York Times,* January 7, 2001, sec. 1, p. 1.

116. See also Mary Jacoby, "His Faith Guides; His Duty Demands," *St. Petersburg Times,* January 16, 2001. ("If Ashcroft is confirmed, he will become the highest-ranking religious right figure ever in the federal government. What would his confirmation mean for church-state separation issues?")

117. Jeffrey Rosen, "Is Nothing Secular?" *New York Times Magazine,* January 30, 2000.

118. Maureen Dowd, "Liberties; Playing the Jesus Card," *New York Times,* December 15, 1999, p. 23.

119. Orwell, *1984,* p. 16.

Conclusion

1. Sam Tanenhaus, "Innocents Abroad," *Vanity Fair,* September 2001, pp. 286–88.

2. Editorial, "Newt Gingrich, Authoritarian," *New York Times,* November 13, 1994, p. 14.

3. "Capitol Hill Hearing of the Senate Judiciary Committee on the Supreme Court Confirmation for Judge Stephen G. Breyer, Chaired by Senator Joseph R. Biden, Jr. (D-Del.)," Federal News Service, July 12, 1994.

> SEN. KENNEDY: As you know, Senator Thurmond and I worked for many years with the chairman, Biden, to pass the Sentencing Reform Act of 1984, the law that abolished the federal parole and created a sentencing guideline system in the federal courts. And with all the talk about truth in sentencing, it's important to remember that we created truth in sentencing at the federal level 10 years ago. Before that time, the sentencing system was a matter of law without order. Judges in two different courtrooms sentencing two equally culpable defendants might hand down two completely different sentences. One defendant might get 10 years; another might get probation. And there was nothing the prosecutors could do about it. . . .

4. "The Candidates Respond," *ABA Journal,* October 1, 1988.

5. From the Ring Lardner short story "The Immigrants."

6. Blaine Harden, "2-Parent Families Rise After Change in Welfare Laws," *New York Times,* August 12, 2001, sec. 1, p. 1. (Quoting Wendell Primus, one of the three Democratic HHS officials who resigned to protest President Clinton's signing of the 1996 welfare reform.)

7. Clyde Haberman, "NYC; Racial Hype: Nasty Days Here Again," *New York Times,* March 23, 1999, p. B1.

8. Andrew Sullivan, "The Way We Live Now: 4-16-00: Counter Culture; Enemies, a Love Story," *New York Times,* April 16, 2000, sec. 6, p. 28.

9. Rick Bragg, "Racer's Death Leaves Hole in Heart of His Hometown," *New York Times,* February 21, 2001.

INDEX

ABOUT THE AUTHOR

ANN COULTER is an attorney
and legal affairs correspondent. Her first
book, *High Crimes and Misdemeanors:
The Case Against Bill Clinton,* was a
New York Times bestseller. She lives in
New York and Washington, D.C.